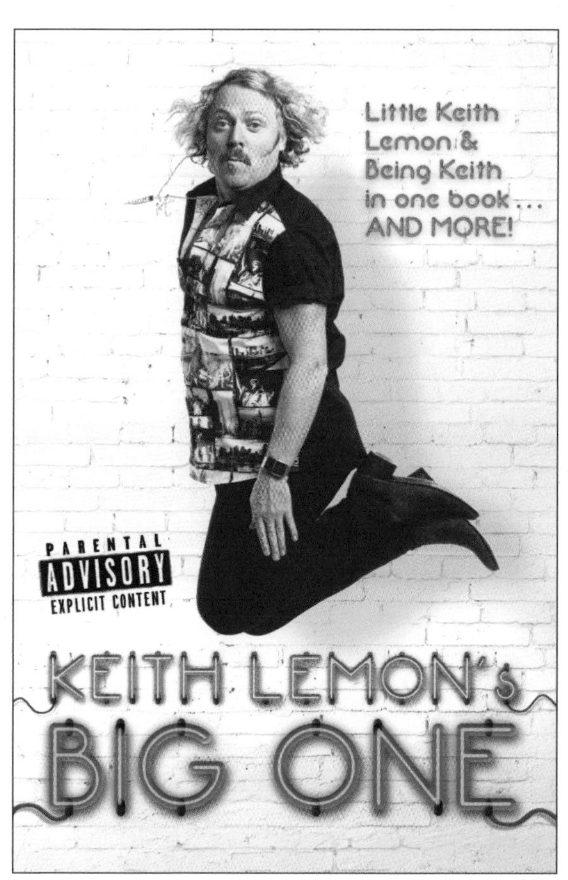
Little Keith
Lemon &
Being Keith
in one book . . .
AND MORE!
PARENTAL
ADVISORY
EXPLICIT CONTENT
KEITH LEMON'S
BIG ONE

Born and raised in Leeds, Keith Lemon is a northern sex symbol and national treasure. Along with *Little Keith Lemon* and *Being Keith*, he is the bestselling author of *The Rules: 69 Ways to be Successful* and a new series of children's stories, *The Beaver and the Elephant*. You may have seen him on TV shows such as *Celebrity Juice, Through the Keyhole, The Keith Lemon Sketch Show, Lemon La Vida Loca, Lemonaid, Sing if You Can, Bo! Selecta* and *Keith Lemon's Very Brilliant World Tour*. As you can see, he's a good-looking guy and quite a hit with the ladies – from Bang Tidy lasses to stinky mingers, he's had them all.

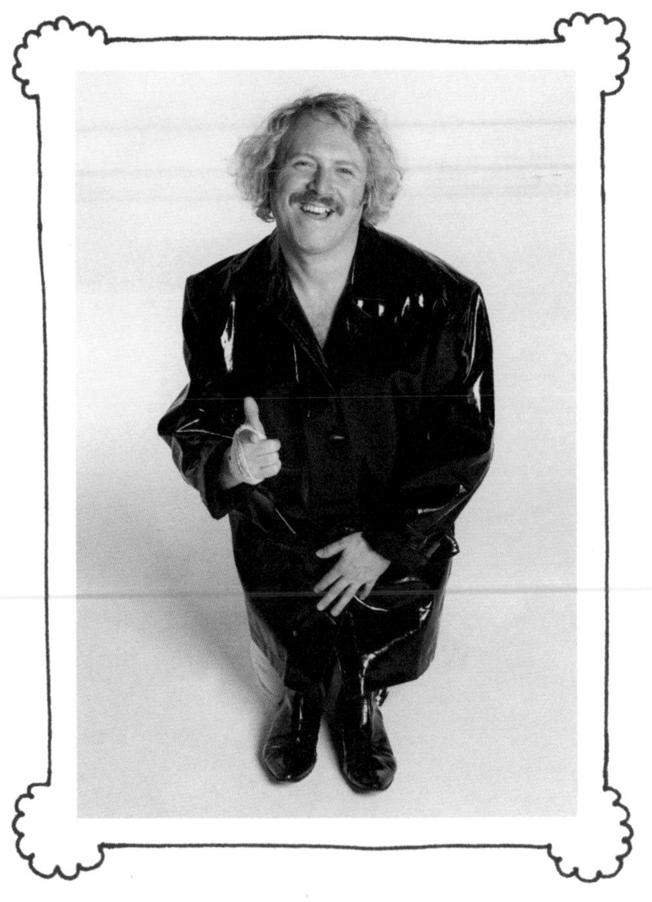

CONTENTS

little
KEITH
LEMON
memoirs of
me Childhood
PARENTAL
ADVISORY
EXPLICIT CONTENT

CONTENTS

This book is dedicated
to me mam, me brother,
and all the girls I've
mede love to. Oh, and
anyone who has bought me
a drink cos I'm on telly.
Love Keith x

Keith Lemon

A TWINKLE IN BILLY OCEAN'S EYE

If I'm honest, I can remember being a twinkle in me dad's eye. Just a twinkle. I'm not sure if he always had that twinkle in his eye but I knew he had his eye on me mam. I started out in life as a one-nightstand. Thirty years ago, me mam was at one of Billy Ocean's gigs. I fink she had won tickets for a Radio 1 roadshow where he were playing and that is how it all began. I fink it were in Leeds, near Yorkshire telly. Billy, me dad, were kind of like the Russell Brand of his day, except he were black, he din't have long hair and he din't wear girls' jeans. Not that there is anything wrong with wearing girls' jeans. I fink he looks right cool, Russell, I just don't have the gumption to wear girls' jeans. Every time I'd have to go for a wee and I have to do the buttons up the wrong way, I would get confused. Anywhere, Billy Ocean were like the Russell Brand of his day – a master of the art of seduction. Me mam has always said he were a right gentleman and very friendly. He spotted her in the crowd and asked her if she wanted to go backstage. He were so friendly that he let her play with his tallywhacker in his dressing room and you know the rest. I don't know if it is 100% true or not because I have never been on *Jeremy Kyle* and had a DMA test. But I have met him and we did have an

He were like the Russell Brand of his day...

instant bond. There was a real connection between us, like father like son. Both thick as a Coke can.

It's never really bothered me that I were the product of a one-nightstand. I fink me mam were worried about it but I got Billy Ocean as me dad! *Sha-ting!* Being a feminist, I've always thought it were unfair that if you were a man and you have a lot of one–nightstands, you get called a stud whereas if you ware a woman having one–nightstands, people fink you're a dirty slapper. But there's nowt wrong with being a dirty slapper. Dirty slappers have a lot more fun and as time goes on I'm sure that the stigma of being one is being eradicated around the world. Perhaps I should start a charity which brecks down the stigma around dirty slappers, it is somet I could really put me heart and soul into.

MEETING DAD – TWO HALVES OF ONE WHOLE

Anywhere, it were only two years ago when I met me dad properly. I din't see me dad when I were growing up. I only saw him on telly, on *Top of t' Pops*. That's why I used to love *Top of t' Pops* so much, it's the only time I would get to see me dad. When I were really young, I din't even know it were me dad but I just felt a real connection with him. Me mam confessed to me when I were about nine. She just came out and said it, 'I fink Billy Ocean could be your dad'. 'What? Me dad's black? How come I'm not black?' But she explained that sometimes it skips a generation. You know, like, ginger hair. Or in *Teen Wolf* where his dad's a wolf, and Teen Wolf is one – but he might not have been if it had skipped him. But it din't. Know what I'm saying? Good, I'll commence.

It were a strange experience coming face to face with me father. He were right nice and agreed to be in me film, which by the way did really well! £2.1 million to meck it and mede over £10.5 million. So, critics can go eat my arse! Oooosh! Anyway . . . He knew that I had

been going around revealing that he were me dad and I know to many people they thought it were a ludicrous idea, but he knew there were somet in it. Like I said, we had an instant connection and we both just knew. Even with his daughters. I knew we were related somehow as I didn't want to shag them I just wanted to hug 'em and say 'I love you, sister. I wish we could have been closer. You are the black sister I knew I had but never had but always wanted.' When we really discussed it, we just cried for two hours. He said that he din't really want to get with me mam because he doesn't really know her properly. In the 80s, he was a naughty lad, but everyone was back then. I wonder how many half brothers and sisters I have dotted around the world! He said, 'let's just continue how we are and we'll see each other every now and then.' He did a gig in the Epcot Centre in Disney recently and I went to see him. He did a shout out to me. Boy has he still got some moves. Must be where I got me rhythm from because it ain't from me mam! The fans were mental for him. It were nice to see he had so much love from people. I just kept finking, 'that's me dad up there!' Fucking 'ell!

THE HEAD OF THE HOUSEHOLD, ME MAM

Me mam is a wonderful woman. She has got two arms, two legs and strawberry blonde hair. Her's is out of a bottle because I remember her wearing one of those funny caps . . . I either have images of me mam looking beautiful or images of me mam with that rubber johnny with holes in with hair coming through. She's a Leeds girl through and through. She were brought up there and would never leave. As Billy was out and about touring, and I don't fink he even knew about me until recently, me mam brought me and our Greg up by herself. I remember when me mam and me found out for sure that our Greg was a willy smoker. We were both together at the time and we came home and caught Greg in the kitchen with another fella with a mouthful. So he got caught out rather than actually coming out. He said he weren't sure if he definitely were gay or not but I told him, 'Greg, cock in mouth, it means you are. You are hormone.' I fink it were quite a weight off his shoulders to have it out there, although it were a bit of a shock for me mam, especially walking in on them like that! I fink she did struggle with our Greg's sexuality at first. I fink she thought she could come up with a cure for it with the right mixture of Calpol and Lemsips. She'd not come across many gays because she's from a different time when people were less open about these things, but Greg and I have educated her about homosexuality, saying, just because he is a willy smoker, it doesn't make him a bad

person. Our Greg is the nicer one out of the two of us. If we're at a party he'll befriend everyone before I do. I'm more stubborn, you see. He'll go out of his way to be nice. But since that day we came home and found him smoking sausage, he has been happierer ever since, so that is all me mam ever wanted.

Everyfing me mam did was for us. I fink me mam is a bit like me, or I'm a bit like me mam. She does fings to make people laugh and start a conversation. It's like the bandage I wear on me hand. I've been wearing that ever since I were seventeen and me mate still says to me 'Your hand can't still be brocken.' But the dingbat is missing the point. It mekes me look like I'm a man about town. I look like I've had adventures. It is a good ice brecker and it starts conversations. I've said it before and I'll say it again, it's a minge magnet, let me tell you.

'Ooo look at that wounded soldier, he's probably been in the Navy.' 'What do you do in the Navy?' 'I do ship fings and stuff.' It depicts that you are an adventurous man, a thrillseeker. A real man's man, like David Hasselhoff.

Me mam is the same. She is really good at socialising and not afraid to elaborate on the facts to make a good story. Even though we can both be dingbats, other people seem to like us as we are fun and we have the banter. Me mam is getting on a bit now of course and she reminds me of the stupid one out of *Golden Girls*. But I mean that with all niceness. She is just a bit ditzy. She burns toast every time she cooks it. But she's always been a bit of a ropey cook. I once got food poisoning from a sausage roll and baked beans that she made me. I was shitting constantly for two days. I nearly fainted.

OUR GREG!

The final member of our family unit is our Greg who I've just mentioned. I remember when our Greg were born, I were seven years old and I were dead excited to have a little brother to play with. I've always been a little bit in a world of me own, so I didn't compete for attention too much and it were nice talking to someone else other than me mam. Up until that point, it had been just me and me mam so it did feel strange to have someone else, but there were enough of an age difference so it weren't like we were always wanting to get off with the same girl or anything. Turns out, I needn't have worried about that in any case as he is a hormonesexual. I've always thought it must have been hard for me mam. She had one really good-looking son, me, and one not so good-looking one as he were, you know, less physically blessed with aesthetics.

Gregory was always a lot quieterer than me, but he weren't shy. He just din't grab fings by the balls like I always did. I'll rephrase that, cos he did actually grab balls but not till he was older. But what I meant were that he din't put himself out there, if you know what I mean. He's different now. He chats to everyone, but he's not like me.

We never really looked alike as I was better looking and still am, but you could always tell we were related. We both had the same strawberry blond hair and cheeky smile. He never had as good a dress sense as me, he's a bit conservative. A bit preppy like. I looked out for him a lot when he was a kid. T' other kids cun't understand why he played with girls' toys. I cun't either really, but that din't mean there were owt wrong with him or he was a bad kid. Sometimes I envied him as he had a lot of girl mates. In fact, sometimes that was handy cos there were always girls hanging around the place. When we were a bit older, we had similar taste in birds. He always liked the fit ones like Kylie and Belinda Carlisle and stuff, but he wanted to be them, whilst I wanted to be in them!

I fink Greg used to look up to me as a kid cos I always knew how t' enjoy meself, whereas he was always quite sensible. It isn't till he's come out that he's really started enjoying himself and I'm right happy for him. I mean, don't get me wrong, I've walked in on him whilst he's been enjoying himself too much and I wasn't too happy about seeing that. Not pecifically cos he's a sausage smoker, it's nowt t' do with that. It's just embarrassing in't it? If he was a sister and I caught her with a mouthful of cock that'd be embarrassing too.

We don't talk about Greg's dad as he is in prison, but as neither of us had a dad around it din't really make much difference. We were a little band of three. I fink that is partly why I was quite mature. I had to be. I were the man about the house and me mam needed me to look after fings for her.

OUR HOUSE AND AUNTIE JEAN'S

Greg and I were both born in Leeds General Infirmary. But soon after I were born, me mam brought me back to our house – the same house that we lived in all the time me and Greg were growing up. It were in a little close with about ten other houses. In me head it was like an American sitcom with white picket fences and lots of beautiful children laughing in the streets. And there was a cool guy in a leather jacket that said 'Heeey' a lot. Oh no, that's the Fonze from *Happy Days*. In reality, it were a little bit different. Me Auntie, Jean, she lived in one of t' other houses at the end of the close and she were always popping round. There were a lad the same age as me who lived in one of the houses opposite, he were called Tommy Bell and he were me first friend. We spent a lot of time together when we were younger, we were proper best mates and we'd always be at one another's doing somet or other. Years later, it were Belly who used to write the rude words behind the door in the wardrobe that me mam

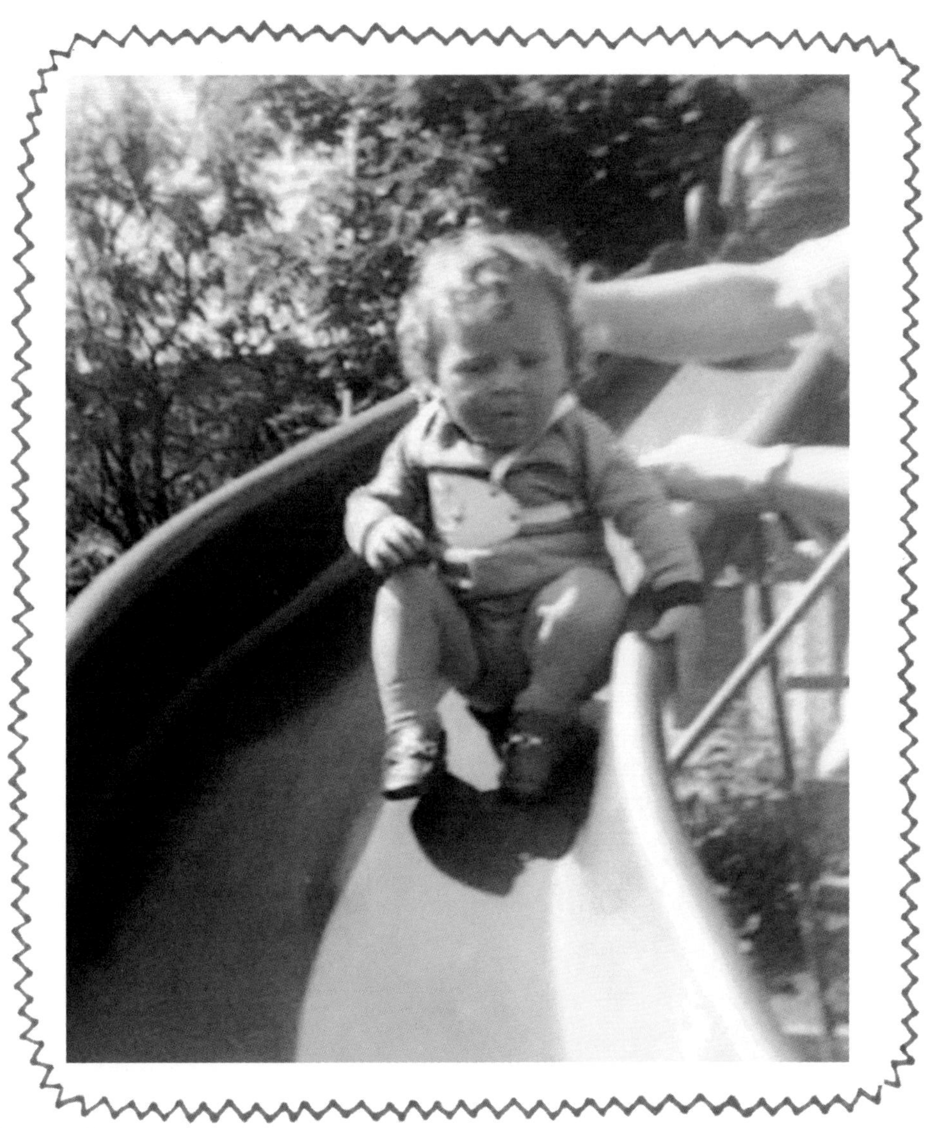

↖ KEITH
WOZ
ERE

got so angry about when she found them. He were clever and wrote my name so that me mam thought it were me. He were right cheeky but, like me, he had that ability to charm the ladies and me mam used to fink the sun shined out of his arse. She wouldn't have been so charmed if she'd known that he'd just drawn some bangers on the wardrobe with a compass. Proper round bangers!

Anywhere, looking back now, I can see it were a bit rough where we lived, but when ya know all't roughuns it don't feel that rough t' you. There was always a mattress outside on't road for some reason. You don't see that in American sitcoms, do ya? And it were always very exciting when a burnt-out car appeared in't street. It weren't a big house but it wasn't a small 'un either. Me and Greg always had separate bedrooms, so that was cool. I remember when we were kids we use t' get the mattress off t' bed and slide down t' steps on it. It sounds like I was obsessed with mattresses, don't it? Yeah, we'd have fights like any other brother and sister. Just play fights like that got outta hand. Once I kicked our Greg in't balls and he had t' go t' hospital cos it went up inside him. I felt really bad. Ya should never kick someone in't balls. The pain is incredible. Like a reverse orgasm.

Me mam and our Greg still live there in that same house. Our kid worships me mam, as do I, but he still hasn't left home. He still lives with me mam in that close! He's got a fella but I expect he'll move in to me mam's before our Greg moves out. It's good that mam is very liberal. When we were kids he stuck t' her like glue. Don't get me wrong, I worship me mam, but I just needed less guidance cos I've always been quite mature. I know what I wanna do and where I wanna go.

Our kid does too, he wants t' go in't arse – ha, ha, ha, ha. I'm kidding. He don't actually do that though, he's told me. Him and his fella just suck and toss. Not sure he'll appreciate me telling ya like. Anywhere, it's a nice comforting feeling knowing that our kid is there t' look after me mam whilst I'm down in't big smoke.

It were a nice place to grow up, that close. One of the best things was that our garden backed onto the local girls' school so when we were a bit older, Tommy and I used to sit in the garden encouraging the girls while they were running around doing cross country. In pants! They used to make them run around in pants! They wun't do that now, would they?

ME FIRST WORDS

Anywhere, other than being a twinkle in Billy's eye, I don't really remember much before I was about five. I don't fink your brain starts working until you're five, does it? Me mam always likes to remind me that me first words were biscuit and minge. I'm proud of that. Good to see I had me priorities straight from a young age.

But when I was a kid your minge wasn't a word you used to refer to a lady's love hole, yer minge was yer face. You'd say, 'Ooo, look at t' minge on him!' This would be the kind of conversation me and me mam would have:

Me mam: What's up with you?
Me: Nowt!
Me mam: Have you been fighting with him again?
Me: Yeah, our Greg's put a dress on me Action Man. There's summat wrong with our Greg!
Me mam: Cheer up! Look at t' minge on him! Look at t' minge on our Keith!

I remember the moment when minge turned, in my brain, to being a rude word. I couldn't believe me mam had been touting it around the kitchen saying 'look at me minge!' I don't suppose she knew but at the same, it's not right is it?! Yer minge was yer face. Yer mouth was part of yer minge. 'Mam, I want a biscuit for me minge'. That was the sentence I were working towards when I learnt me first two words.

I tell yer what term or word I never use to describe a ladyhole: Beaver. I hated it when me kids book,

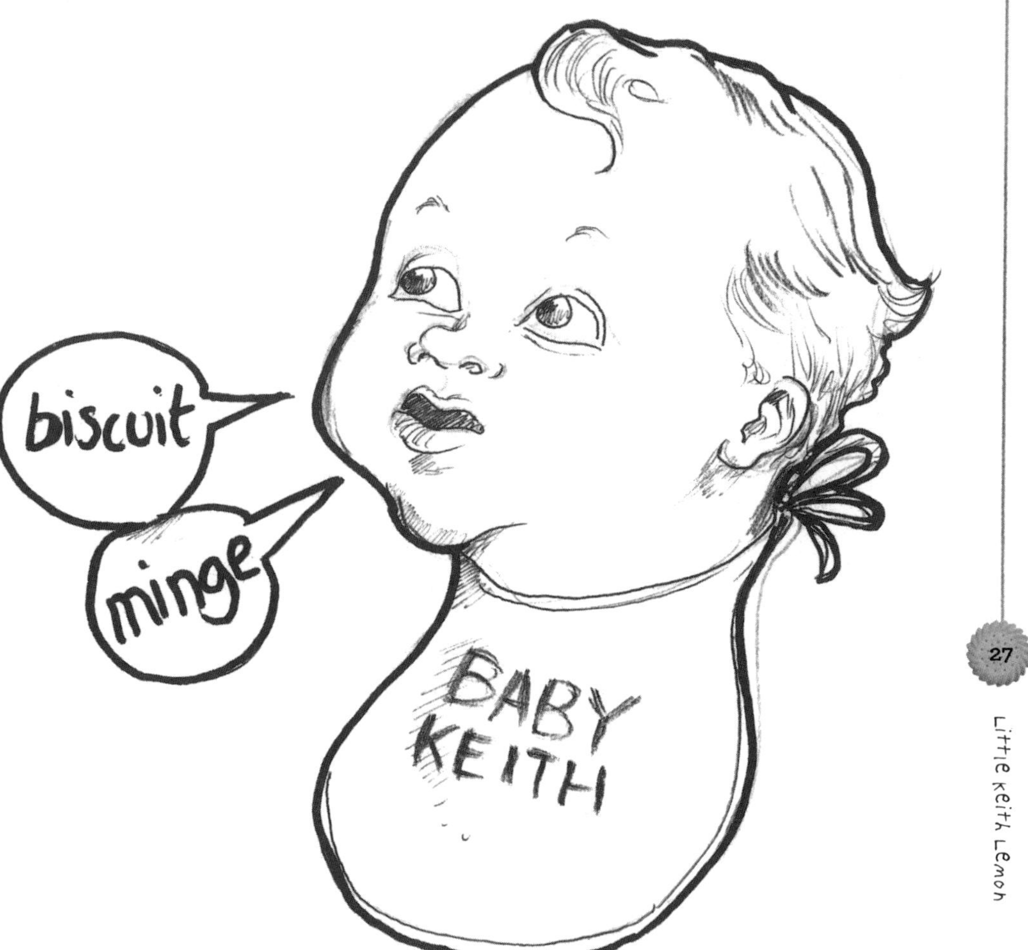

The Beaver and the Elephant, was announced and everyone thought I was referring to a lady's minge. It's a kid's book, why would I be chatting about minges? It's out now by the way. Get it for your kids, they'll love it! Cha-mone motha plugga!

I didn't start properly talking till I were about four. But I am making up for it now. I just pointed at stuff and would go 'ugh', 'biscuit', 'minge'. And then it just came one day, almost overnight, and I couldn't stop meself.

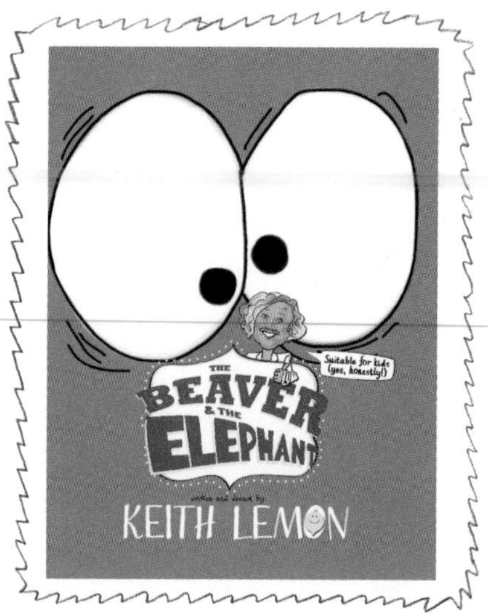

I were obsessed with Bourbon biscuits so I had to work out a way to get me hands on some of those. When I was a little bit older, I used to play out with me mates, and I can remember pretending to be Bob Geldof, saying 'do you all want some biscuits? I'm gonna get you some.' And then I'd go into our house, go t' biscuit tin and have a rummage in the bread bin, and I'd put loads of biscuits in between slices of thick white bread and make biscuit sandwiches. 'Just getting a piece of bread, Mam' because I weren't allowed to have biscuits, but I were allowed bread so if me mam caught me on the way out, she'd fink I were just having a piece of bread. And then I'd dish the biscuits out to me mates. I were a bit like the Milky Bar Kid but with biscuits. The biscuits are on me! I were a biscuit dealer and it made me feel like a hero like Robert De Niro. That's a line from a Finlay Quaye song. You don't hear owt from him any more do ya? I wonder what he is up to. You know Zammo from *Grange Hill* works as a key cutter? Well I'm not sure if he still does but I saw him at a key cutters in Soho a while back. Crazy times. I hope that don't happen to me. Not that key cutting is a bad fing. We need key cutters! But I don't fink it would be me cuppa tea. I'm not good with me hands – unless I'm with a lass, d'ya get me? Yeah boi!

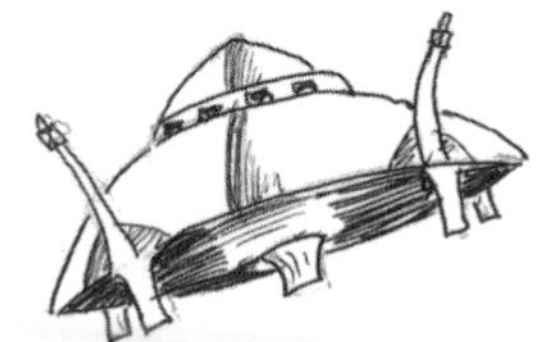

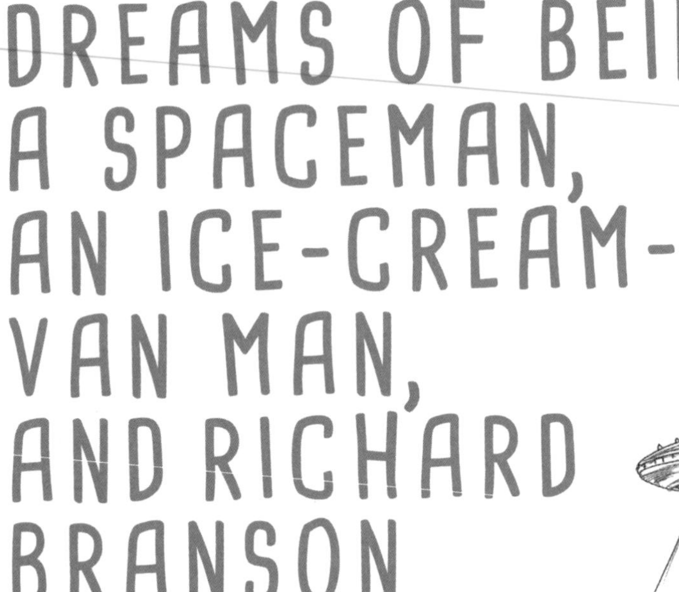

DREAMS OF BEING A SPACEMAN, AN ICE-CREAM-VAN MAN, AND RICHARD BRANSON

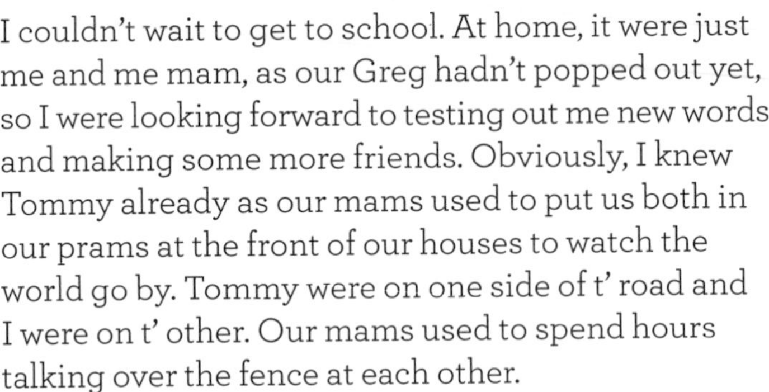

I couldn't wait to get to school. At home, it were just me and me mam, as our Greg hadn't popped out yet, so I were looking forward to testing out me new words and making some more friends. Obviously, I knew Tommy already as our mams used to put us both in our prams at the front of our houses to watch the world go by. Tommy were on one side of t' road and I were on t' other. Our mams used to spend hours talking over the fence at each other.

I remember me first day – running up to the gates of St Michael's like I were going to a theme park or summat. The first day at school weren't as intimidating as it might have been as I already knew Tommy, so that was cool. I fink it were a friendship of convenience at first but once I got used to having him around, he were like the brother I never had. Not that our Greg weren't a proper brother but he were more

Virgin

Barbie than Action Man and he weren't around for the first seven years anyway.

I can remember making friends with everyone straight away. I liked school and didn't have any of those days where you don't want to go and you're crying and clinging on to your mam's leg begging not to go in. When I got there I liked it cos I'd learnt to talk and I liked talking. It felt like school was miles away but it was just up t' road. Everything seems so far when you are a kid, don't it? In fact, I remember when we went camping with cubs, it felt like we were miles away and we were actually just on t' other side of the girls' school that I could see from me house.

But while I liked school, I don't fink I were one of the most academically gifted kids in me class. I din't need to be. I could talk me way in and out of most situations so it din't really matter whether a piece of paper said I were good at somet or not. When I were young I wanted to be a spaceman, an ice-cream-van man and Richard Branson. All at once. On his day off, the spaceman would sell ice cream at a lower cost to disadvantaged kids who can't afford to buy a 99 with a Flake. Even back then I understood that the ladies love it if they fink you go all soft over a few disadvantaged kids. The idea of being on telly din't properly enter me head until I were a fully grown adult. I had a trip to London and thought, yeah, I'd like to live there. It looks exciting. And when I came to London it *was* exciting. But it weren't a dream of mine when I was a kid, even though me mam said that I always wanted to be famous, but not a famous TV presenter, I just wanted to be known. I wanted to be known for somet, but I din't know it were telly. When I was thirteen, I just wanted to be known for having the biggest willy, but it

Little Keith Lemon

were right small... Was it fuck! It were massive! Like a straight cumberland sausage.

Come to fink of it, Richard Branson is another candidate for being me dad – I've been told I look like him. Can't fink why as I clearly look more like Billy Ocean than Richard Branson. Look:

But I guess it were his entrepreneurial spirit that I admired. I wanted to be an international businessman like Branson. I've met him more recently – I fink we admire each other's work. Me mam just wanted me to not be a thief or a drug-taker, really. The main fing that mattered to me mam was that our Greg and I were happy. I fink she's glad that I turned out to be the man that I am today.

TO OPEN, PULL HERE

My favourite subject at school was swimming. It weren't a posh school so we din't have a swimming pool at the school or owt, so we'd all get on a bus they'd hired instead. It were a bus bus, not like a school bus, a proper bus, like in London they're red, in Leeds they were green. They'd have one of them to pick us up to take us to the swimming baths and I don't know how many weeks we'd been going but one day I noticed there were a big red lever on the wall of the bus, near the window, and it said: TO OPEN, PULL HERE. I thought, 'right, I'll pull it then.' Whoo whoo whoo. It were like the whole bus were an alarm and it started going off. The bus stopped and we could all hear the driver huffin' and puffin'. And then the teacher, Ms Mumphries, came upstairs: 'Who opened the fire door?' Well I din't know it was for fire. It just said, TO OPEN, PULL HERE and then there were this big red lever. It were the back window all along the back of the bus. I just opened it. I fink she could tell by the look in me eye that it were me. So she made a big show of laying down the rules but I knew she were gonna let me off. She always had a bit of a soft spot for me.

Every time I was on a bus after that it came over me like a wave that I wanted to pull that red lever and open t' fire door but because I knew it was a fire door I din't. I couldn't go swimming for two weeks because I opened the fire door which meant two weeks of not looking at lasses in swimming costumes and also

meant everyone was gonna become more advanced. I had an image in me mind that they were all gonna be like *Man From Atlantis* by the time I went back and I was gonna be like some bellend that can't swim with fucking armbands! Armbands! Two weeks is a long time when you're a kid. Anyfing could happen!

I did get me bronze eventually but it took me a while to catch up. I had to swim 400m which took ages and I thought 'I'm gonna die here. Anything I have to do after this I'm gonna be too fucked to do.' And then I had to save a brick in me pyjamas. I can remember

finking, 'I don't understand this concept. So the brick represents a person that I'm saving that's drowning but I can only save them if I'm wearing pyjamas? So what if I'm walking past a river and someone is in there drowning but I don't have any pyjamas on me? Do I leave 'em? Do I run home and go get me pyjamas and go, 'right, now I'll save you because I've got me pyjamas on?'

Anywhere, I was really chuffed about having me sew-on bronze swimming badge. I'd sew the badges on me trunks but you got a little enamel badge in a red plastic case as well and you know what I thought when I got that? You can fuck all your other awards, all I wanted were that badge and I din't give a shit anymore. So the next year, when I had to do me silver, I cheated. I can remember t' bit where you're doing your metres, it looked like I were swimming but I were actually just walking along the bottom. You know when you get t' shallow end? Just walking. And every time I saw the teacher I'd lift me legs up. I got another badge but I din't care because I had me bronze. Forget silver, gold and lifesaving. But it was weird that kids the same age were doing their lifesaving whilst I were doing bronze. They were saving lives and I were saving some bricks in me pyjamas. Oh shit, that foam brick looks like it's in trouble! Better get me pyjamas on.

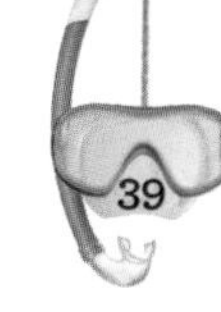

It set me up for the future though. When we were a bit older, me mate Talbot and I used to go to t' swimming baths on a Sunday. Oh it was disappointing if you forgot your goggles. We weren't actually there to swim. We just looked at girls. We din't even try and chat 'em up. We'd just jump in, get a right good look at t' girls under t' water and then come up out of the water like we were in *Apocalypse Now*. We'd just look at each other.

I don't even fink we said anything. We just smiled at each other, knowing. All that swimming gave me a few ideas for the future. A splash about in the swimming baths is one of my favourite first date ideas – I can show off my athletic ability and Olympic body whilst swimming to collect a brick. The only difference between then and now is that then I wore me pyjamas but now I just swim naked. It's like getting an advanced review in't it? You can have a good look and go, 'yeah, that'll do for me'. Otherwise you might fall head over heels for someone, get them back to your house, get naked and find out that she has a weird lump on her back that has a toenail on the end of it. From the front she's great but from behind I'm gonna see that toenail looking at me all the time. Do I ask, 'have you got a toenail growing on your back?'

Kylie is so fit it hurts. I would have liked to take her swimming and give her some TLC – Tender Lemon Cuddles

You learn a lot more about someone by treating her to a trip down t' baths than you would at the cinema. It's weird going to the cinema with someone, innit? A quintessential date, the cinema, but really you should go to the cinema with your mates or by yourself, not with a date. If you are going to go to the cinema on a date, make it a horror film. When she gets scared of the bogey man, you can slip your arm around her and play the gent. Then offer her some of your popcorn which you have previously put your tallywhacker in (you can cut a hole out the bottom) – she'll grab a right handful. Oooosh! Getting a handjob in't cinema . . . Living the dream!

Anywhere, Talbot and I also used to dare each other to dive off the diving board. I never did it. In fact, I only dived off top diving board when I was doing *Celebrity Juice* and it was Keith versus Jedward. Well, I didn't actually dive, I jumped, but I can remember finking, I'm not having those little bastards beat me at this. I didn't look down. I just walked straight off and then watched them go, 'oh, we can't do it, we can't do it, we can't do it.' The dingbats! Nice kids though.

LEMON FAMILY ALBUM

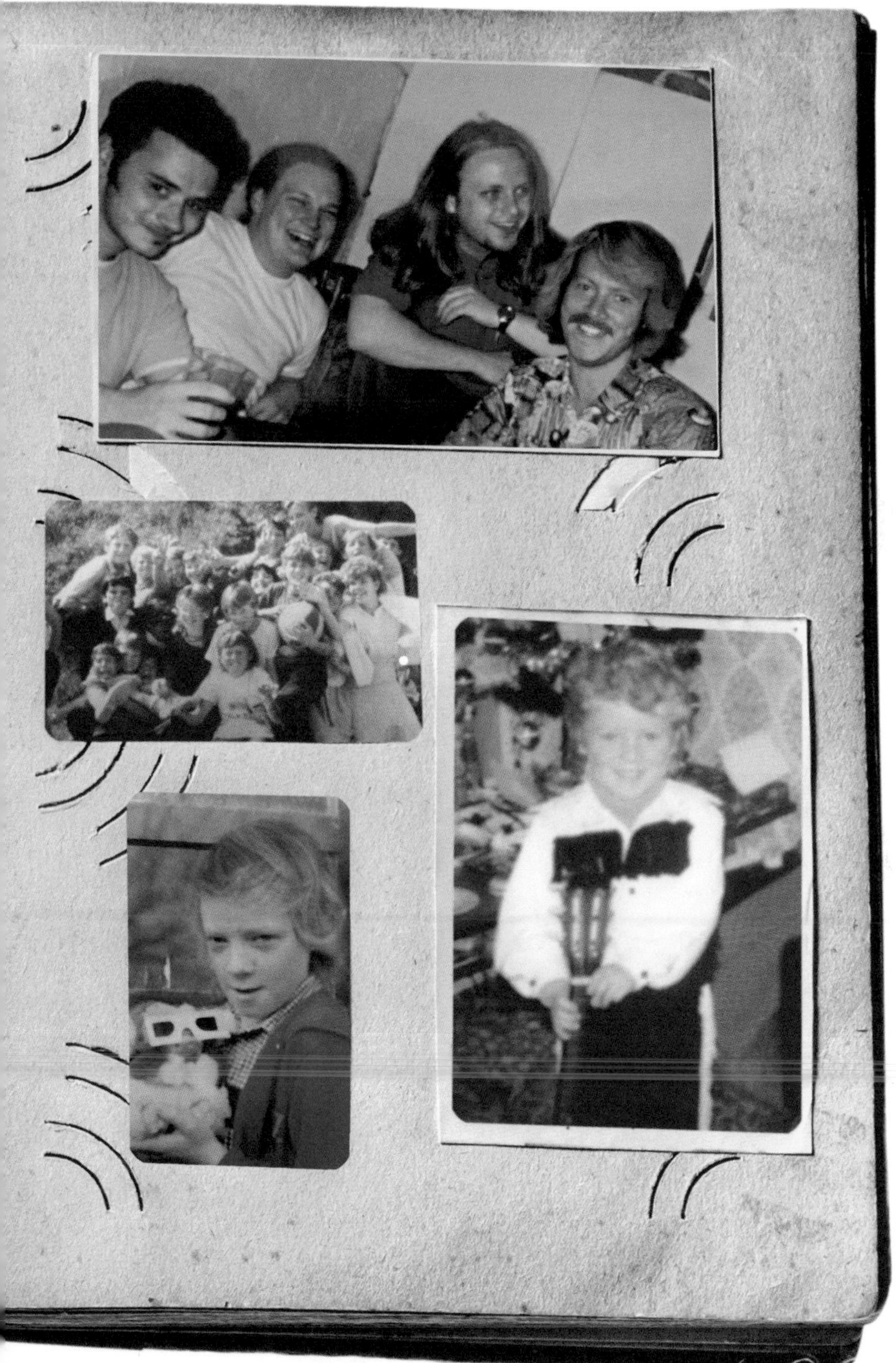

THE FAMOUS ~~FIVE~~ 4

Anywhere, back to St Michael's. Tommy and I met Dave Fletcher and Frank Pistle at school. We were like the Famous Five, only there were four of us and we weren't all gonna be famous. Obviously we din't know that back then but I were always a bit of a performer. Tommy became known as Belly as he had a bit of timber on him and his surname was Bell. Simple as peas. As I said, I'd known Belly all me life – even before we went to primary school – so we were like brothers really. Belly was a nice guy, bit strange, but a nice guy underneath it all. He still is! Nice but a bit strange. Because he lived over t' road from us, he would come over all the time. When we were older, I fink he were a bit intrigued by hormonesexuals so he came just to have a look at our Greg. He were completely bamboozled that he was playing with girls' toys as we played with Action Men and cars behind sofa. Once Belly and I both fell asleep behind the sofa and when me mam couldn't find us she thought that we'd been kidnapped or somet. She went out in t' street looking for us both. In't that weird, we were playing so hard with our cars we actually fell asleep? But because me mam thought we'd been nicked she called the police! I can remember just waking up behind t' sofa, both of us, rubbing our eyes and finking 'eh, what's going on? Why is me mam talking to a copper?' We knew that summat were going on. She weren't best pleased when we crept out from behind the sofa rubbing our sleepy eyes.

Frank Pistle's nickname were Pisshole. We used to tease him whenever he met a bird and say we gave him that name because he used to piss himself in class all the time, but it were really just because he had a daft name. Dave was just Dave. We were all in the same class and all sat on the back row of desks, apart from Belly who had to sit close to teacher cos he had a squiffy eye. We just used to mess around all t' time, passing notes to each other. We were never that naughty, just the right side of cheeky. If I ever started getting into trouble I would just tell the teacher how much I wanted to learn but how difficult I found it and how frustrating it were that I couldn't keep up with everyone else. It seemed to do the trick.

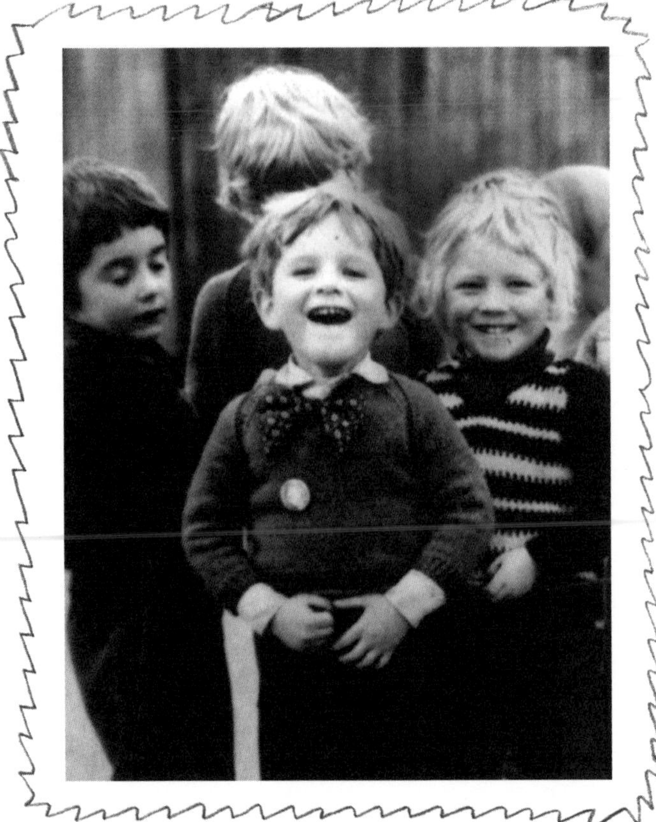

Hey Daz mate. Apparently you're got a scout walker for sale. I'll give you £1.50 for it..

Keith

Are you having a laugh? It was about £8 quid. £6?

Daz

Go stick nettles up ya arse, I'll give you £2.50

£5.50

I'll swap you it for skeletor?

Yeah nice one

Cool, I'll bring it in tomorrow.

Ha ha, what a dingbat! Skeletor cost less than a scout walker. I was always good at swapping shit. I once swapped a Panini sticker book for a BMX. It was a rubbish BMX, but still a bike for some stickers. I had business acumen at the age of seven!

MY FIRST CRUSH

I fancied girls before anyone started fancying girls in my class. When I first started primary school, I can remember fancying this girl called Penny and I were only about six. I'd fink about her all the time. I would chase her round the playground and then I would just ignore her when I actually got close enough to talk to her. When you're a kid you don't know what your emotions are and you can't deal with them, can you? I'd chase her, then ignore her, then chase her again. But I actually wanted to kiss her, but I didn't know what kissing was. I remember feeling very strange around her and then when she left school to go and live in America, I can remember being slightly sad but I couldn't tell anyone because I didn't know what I was feeling.

I soon got back on the horse as she had a couple of fit mates. I can't remember their names, mind. I tell you what though, finking about it, her sister was fit as well. Again, older. Her sister must have been about three years older and I remember finking, bloody hell, she's like a fitter version of her. Once some disabled children came to our school to prove that kids with disabilities can still play musical instruments, and one of the girls that were playing the harp looked almost exactly like Penny's sister. I can remember finking, right, this is my chance, I might be able to pull her. But I didn't because I thought it would be an awkward relationship. I tell you what, all credit to people who go out with people who have disabilities. They're good people them. Unless they're just using them for their disabled parking badge.

Anywhere, at that age we spent a lot of time trying to work out whether we disliked or if we liked girls. It were dead confusing. I remember Dave had a tree in his garden that we used to climb as he fancied his next-door neighbour and it gave us a right good view into her bedroom. It were a couple of years later that we found out that it were his cousin! Dirty bastard had been spying on his cousin all that time. I remember saying to him, 'you can't fancy your cousin!' And he'd go, 'yeah, but she ain't really me cousin.' But she were. Dirty Dave fancied his cousin. Dirty Bastard!

To be fair to him, she was right fit. She used to wave at us sometimes. Little tease. She were a nice girl, Emma Bunton girl-next-door kind of pretty. You know, with that little rabbit-nose thing going on. But we were getting to that age where boys become boys and girls become girls and we went through that stage where you hate girls, don't you? And girls hate boys. But you kind of love them at the same time. It's all a bit confusing. It might be overnight that you suddenly start liking them again and before you know it you've got your tongue in their mouth and you're cleaning the windows.

Dave's cousin had a little rabbit nose like that. Dead cute.

Michelle Keegan reminds me of Dave's sister Beth. F.A.F.

I could see why Dirty Dave fancied his cousin but I was more interested in his sister, Beth. She was Fit As Flip. If I had to compare her to anyone now it would be Michelle Keegan. She is one of me all-time favourites is Michelle. I would destroy her. We've had her on *Juice* a few times now and she drank a pint of lager that had some jizm in it. What a great lass. Good luck to her and Mark Wright. He's a good lad, too. But he wears his clobber too tight – it looks like it's hurting him.

DRESSING UP AND PLAYING THE HERO

Anywhere, I always wanted to hang out with Beth and hear what she and her friends were saying and stuff. I can actually remember when it was Beth's birthday and both me and Dave came down and ruined the birthday because we were both dressed as superheroes and stole her thunder. I was dressed as Spiderman and he was dressed as The Hulk and he ripped all his pyjamas up. He wasn't green, though, he just ripped his pyjamas and I fink all his sister's mates thought we were really cute and funny. We were jumping around finking we were superheroes and then he got done by his mam for ripping his pyjamas up and for stealing the attention away from Beth.

I remember that day very clearly as I remember it were the first time I thought that a girl was extraordinarily fit... but at the same time I knew I wasn't old enough to properly like girls. She made me tingle in areas that I din't know were supposed to tingle. She had this long super-straight brown hair and she used to flick it around like they do in't films. It has always been like that for me though. I've been advanced when it comes to women. I din't start writing poetry for girls until a little later but she did inspire me to put pen to paper. I was only eight at the time but with a few drawings I usually had 'em wrapped round my little finger.

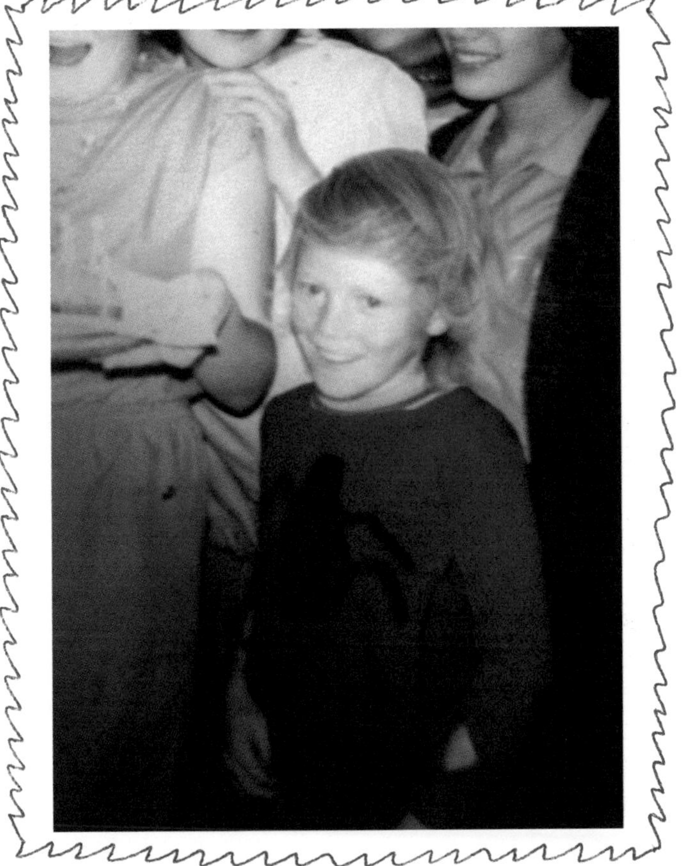

Beth, if you're out there, give us a call. Dave's got me number. We could go swimming together and I'll treat you to Nando's after.

I always knew I'd look cute when I dressed up. I was in t' cubs when I were younger as I knew I'd look cute in the uniform. I don't remember much about cubs except being in a tent in the wood round the corner from where we lived. Belly were there too. I had toothache so I put a Wine Gum in me tooth to act as a filling. I thought I were being really clever. That'll sort it out. That'd fill it. But the week after I had to have me whole tooth yanked out!

I did graduate to scouts but it were shit and I said to Belly, 'watch me, I'm gonna run out'. He said, 'no you're not.' I said, 'I am. I'm gonna grab me Michael Jackson Thriller jacket and I'm gonna run out.' And I did, I just ran for it. And that were the end of me scouting career.

In me mind she looks like this, like a little Pocahontas. I'd poke her hontas.

Me in modern day times.
I got this costume from a
Japanese website for $65.
I wore it at Comic-Con -
I looked ace amongst 300
other spidermen sweating
their tits off in the San Diego heat.

Date: No:

Beth asked me what me new years resolutions are. I had to make some up on t'spot to impress her. Going to try and stick to 'em.

1 STOP SWEARING. A few weeks ago, I watched a programme and it were called John's Not Mad. It were about something called tourettes and John used to say things he shouldn't say all the time. I almost wished I had tourettes because it would have given me an excuse but me mam is always banging on at me about swearing and she said she wouldn't buy us any more bourbons until I stop swearing.

Date: No:

(2) STOP CLIMBING OUT OF ME BEDROOM WINDOW WITH TOMMY AT 1 AM. Last time we did it, Tommy broke his arm and had a cast and all the fit girls signed it. But now he says it is starting to itch and it is really smelly so it weren't worth it.

(3) GET A SUPER FIT GIRLFRIEND and smooch for three minutes, no stopping.

DEE

I went out with a girl when I was nine; that was probably my first relationship. I mean it weren't a serious one – I was nine and she was nine. Her name was Dee and she was in my class at school. She was a pretty girl-next-door kind of girl with long blonde hair and she were a bit taller than me. She reminded me of a girl that used to be in *Baywatch*, I can't remember her name, but she was also in *ET* as a child. And I don't mean Drew Barrymore.

I went out with her for about six weeks. That's basically six years in grown-up terms. As we were both infants we didn't have any sexual exploits but there was a lot of kissing. Another friend would time us kissing to see how long we could last. I don't know why we were timed because we weren't gonna try and get in t' *Guinness Book of Records* or anything, but we could say to our

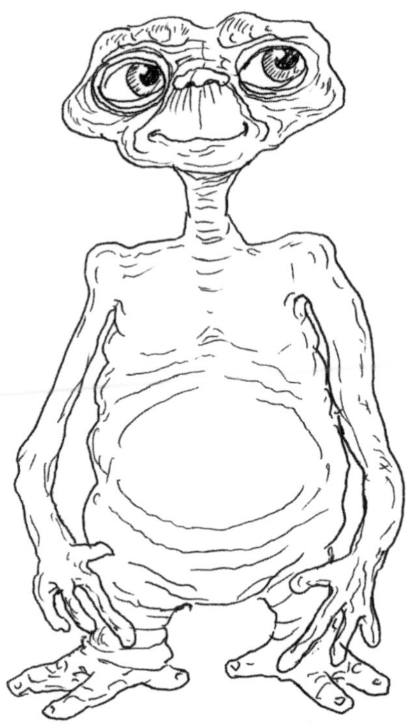

Keith 4 Dee

friends that we kissed for two minutes. Just smooching for two whole minutes! Can you imagine smooching that long now? Smooching and nothing else. There wasn't any tongue action. We din't really go on dates or owt, we just used to hang out after school. We went out for the school holidays and then six weeks after it all began, it ended. The summer of love. She went and did somet that only a right dingbat would ever do: she cut her long, super-straight hairs short and permed the whole lot. I said, 'it looks like you've got a wig on! What have you done to your barnet? We're over.' It were over. She looked like Kevin Webster from *Corrie* in 1989!

It were that same summer that we went on a family holiday to Rhyl – perhaps that put a strain on our relationship. She must have felt like I abandoned her so went and chopped all her hairs off. As a family we din't have enough money to go abroad but we did go on holidays by the sea. We went to Rhyl, Scarborough and Blackpool. Rhyl was me favourite – I even had a T-shirt saying, 'Keeping it Rhyl'. I've always been at the front edges of fashion.

The highlights of the holiday were always the same: fishing and eating hot doughnuts. I fink it used to cost a pound for about 136 doughnuts. You got such a huge bag of doughnuts for a quid. We'd be eating doughnuts all day. We'd go in t' sea back then because you didn't know it was full of shit. But you don't go in t' sea now in England, do you, because you just fink it's gonna be turds floating past you, don't you?

PICTURE

THE GRATTAN'S CATALOGUE'S ARRIVED. CHRISTMAS IS COMING!

When I were growing up, my favourite time of the year were Christmas. Not actually Christmas itself, but the build up to it. The first sign of Christmas for me weren't the Coca-Cola advert or the Christmas songs that would be playing in Woolworths from September, it was the Grattan's catalogue coming through t' door. We'd get a catalogue as thick as Yellow Pages through t' door and I were like, 'oooo it's Christmas soon, innit?' Me and Gregory would just sit there with the catalogue on our lap going, 'want that, want this . . . ' It was the way you would write down your Christmas list – 'want that, want that, want that, want that'. You din't circle them or anyfing, you weren't allowed to draw in it – you'd get into trouble with mam if you did that.
Once we were done with writing up our imaginary Christmas lists, I would turn to the underwear pages. Obviously Greg were less interested in the underwear section and always used to look at the curling tongs and such. I had some romantic nights with that Grattan's catalogue, I did. When me mam were out and our kid was in bed I'd wank over it on t' bra pages.

WARNERS French Collecti

1 Lightly padded underwired plunge Bra from the French Collection with wide set straps and stretch sides. Azure. NYLON 85%, ELASTANE 15%.

Order bust sizes:
34A 36A 34B 36B 38B 34C 36C

11W 298 Bra £6·85

2 Closely fitting shorter French Knickers in silky Trilobal Simplex. White and Azure. NYLON 100%.

White **10C 249** Azure **10B 225**

Order sizes: **S M L**
To fit waist: 23/24 25/26 27/28 ins.

French Knickers £5·50

3 Cami-Knickers in Trilobal Simplex with lace applique to neckline and legs. Soft stretchy satin straps. Press-stud fastening crotch section. Creme. NYLON 100%.

Order bust sizes: **34A 36A 34B 36B 38B**

10G 226 Cami-Knickers £10·95

4 Front fastening brief plunge Bra in Trilobal Simplex with applique lace. Stretchy satin straps for halter normal or cross-over wear. Azure. NYLON 100%.

Order bust sizes: **32A 34A 36A 34B 36B**

11H 297 Bra £4·75

5 Matching Suspender Belt to items (4) White and Azure. NYLON 100%.

White **10W 259** Azure **10T 224**

Order size: **M**
To fit waist: 23/28 ins.

Suspender Belt £4·75

6 Matching Brief to items (4) and (5). Wh Azure. NYLON 100%.

White **10W 222** Azure **10E 223**

Order size: **M**
To fit waist: 23/28 ins.

Brief £3·30

7 Beautiful plunge Bra from the French In Trilobal Simplex with applique lace stretch straps and sides of stretch sleeknit White and Azure. NYLON 88%, ELASTANE

White
Order bust sizes: **34A 36A 34B 36B 38**

11T 340 Bra £5·85

Azure
Order bust sizes: **34B 36B 38B 34C 36**

11E 299 Bra £5·85

SUPER BANG!

5

6

5
£4·99

6
£5·50

7
£14·99

8
£3·75

Aristoc
PACK OF THREE

9
£5·99

10
£7·99

Julie Anne

'Moonlighter' by Julie Anne. Underwired
...amour Bra with slightly padded
cup and stretch wing panels. Lingerie
stretch straps. Purple/Black or Red/Black.
... 83%, POLYESTER 12%,
...ANE 5%.

...Black **11C 296** Red/Black **11W 306**

...bust sizes:
...6A 34B 36B 38B 34C 36C 38C

...4·99

'Moonlighter' matching Brief and
Suspender Belt Pack. Purple/Black or
...ack. NYLON 100%.

...Black **10C 220** Red/Black **10H 221**

...sizes: **S M L**
...waist: 23/24 25/26 27/28 ins.

Suspender Belt Pack £5·50

7 'Moonlighter' Basque in satin and Lycra with hook and eye back fastening and adjustable front lacing. Detachable shoulder straps and suspenders. Gold. NYLON 84%, ELASTANE 10%, POLYESTER 6%.

Order bust sizes: **34A 36A 34B 36B 38B 34C 36C 38C**

10R 247
Basque/Brief Set £14·99

8 'Aristoc' Beauty Spot Stockings to fit foot sizes 8½–11 ins. Pack of three. Not sold separately. Black. NYLON 100%.

Order size: **M**

21W 528 Stockings £3·75

9 Short length lace trimmed Camisole Top Nightdress. Approx. length 36 ins. Black. NYLON 100%.

Order sizes: **SW W WX**

20G 332 Nightdress £5·99

10 Blouse top and brief Baby Doll Pyjamas in a striped fabric. Black. NYLON 100%.

Order sizes: **SW W WX**

20B 376 Pyjamas £7·99

Julie Anne

FASHION SHOW
GRATTAN 199

Anyway, a few weeks after the catalogue arrived in the post, some presents that me mam had ordered from the catalogue used to come through t' post and Greg and I made sure we were always there to greet the postman. I can remember a Scalextric coming one year and going, 'Is this for me?' And me mam said, 'no, it's for next-door neighbour, in't it. I'm saving it for 'em.' I remember finding the same box of Scalextric in a kitchen cupboard a couple of weeks later, next to the mop and bucket. So when me mam were out, we'd go downstairs, get the Scalextric out, me and Belly, and we'd play with it whilst keeping one eye on the clock. About ten minutes before the time she'd be home from work I'd say 'right, better put it back now. Did that piece go there or over there?' In the end we decided that she ain't gonna remember what piece goes where, as long as it's shut and the sellotape is back on it, then we'd put it back in t' cupboard. I remember that Scalextric so well. Even our Greg liked it. It were the only boys' toy he actually liked.

I can remember that build up to Christmas as clear as yesterday. As soon as mam went out: 'Right, let's hunt,' and we'd hunt like it were a mission our life depended on. Hunting. Belly would come round and join in. It was like a proper event, almost like Halloween, it should be in the calendar. Me mam never hid them in all different places, just all of them in one place and when we found them we almost felt scared to open them and we'd just end up shouting 'I've found 'em! Found 'em!'

Then on Monday, when you go to school, you'd ask yer mates:
'D'you know what you've got for Christmas?'
'No.'
'Eh? Ain't you been looking in t' house?'
'No.'
'Well look what I've got – Wurzel Gummidge with changeable heads.'

The best present I ever got were an Energized Batman. I can remember coming downstairs on me birthday and it was placed on the fire. We had a fire that had fake logs on it, and it were just placed on the mantelpiece above it. What a place to put it! It were practically melting! Anyway, me posh mate had an Energized Batman, so I didn't fink I would ever get one so when I did I were overjoyed. It's a Batman figure with a grappling hook. You just pressed a button, the

hook came out and you could hook it onto somet and Batman would actually climb up. That's it really, but it were exciting back then.

There was an Energized Spiderman too and I own that now, I bought it from a car boot once. I remember the same year I got the Energised Batman, Greg got a John Travolta annual and a *Girl's World* one 'cos he liked doing make-up. He liked to brush me hair and try to plait it. But I didn't want plaits, cos they'd give you a headache.

I remember one year, Greg and I got knock-off Action Men from me auntie where all the parts were just a bit off. I can remember finking 'I can't wait till she's gone so we can have a laugh about his weird hands. He cun't hold hand grenades but he could stroke his Chihuahua, like Ken. It were basically a Ken doll in an army suit. Our Greg wasn't bothered if he could hold a hand grenade, no. It was only if it could hold another man's willy, but it couldn't even do that. It could tap another man's willy cos his hands were stuck together like that. Fake Action Man cun't do anything. All he could do was give high fives. Well he couldn't really even do that because his arms didn't move that way. He could do his hair. Real Action Man weren't bothered about his hair, he shaved it all short like Dermot O'Leary. Action Man has Dermot O'Leary hair, I fink. Or Dermot O'Leary has Action Man's hair.

DOES YOURS DO THIS IF YOU "SQUEEZE" IT?

Everything were confusing back then. We had hormones raging around our bodies and we were still discovering our bodies so there was a lot to discuss:

'I've got one of these, have you?'

'Does yours do this if you squeeze it?'

'Have you ever tried this? It feels all'

'What does it taste like?'

All the usual stuff.

I remember when we were nine and we had the conversation about foreskins. I had just discovered that some of me mates had a fleshy sock over t' end of their willy. I went to school and we all start exploring our bodies and going, 'Let's have a look at your willy'. 'Eh? Mine ain't got like a sock on t' end of it.' A fleshy sock. I was surprised how many of my friends had foreskins – but at the time I din't even know that they were foreskins. One of me earliest memories is a horrific one. I can remember being circumcised – but I din't really know what that meant at the time. I remember being in a sink full of red water and seeing meself in the mirror and finking, 'I'm just a baby, what's just happened to me? Why is it really hot between my legs?' And I can remember panicking a little bit when I looked down at me prized possession. I was anatomically gifted from a young age and I din't like anyone messing with me bits. Why would I?! These were me crown jewels and even back then I knew they were gonna be dead important to me.

I was in hospicle and it were awful. There were little kids screaming everywhere. After the episode in the sink, I remember being on t' sofa, wrapped up in a blanket and me mam trying to 'coo coo' in me ear to make me feel better. It felt like I had been abused! More importantly, a few years later, when I saw *Roseanne* on telly, they had that same blanket on t' back of their sofa. Roseanne had me blanket! So I was wrapped up in a blanket, which became my blanky, and Roseanne had the same one on her sofa. It were the only good memory of that story. I didn't carry the blanky around like a hormonesexual, I din't do that. Greg did, but not me. I just had it to keep me warm. I recognised that blanket again when I saw the film *ET* and thought, 'now he's wrapped up in me

blanket'. Me, ET and Roseanne. Who'd have thought we'd all have the same taste?

I remember when Greg had to have his foreskin off like I did and it were good to be able to talk about it man to man, to sort of say, 'yeah, it hurts dunnit, when they cut your skin off.' I fink he looked up to me in that way. I mean, we did use to fall out all the time, but I used to protect him and teach him about the important stuff in life. I were there for him when people shouted rude stuff about him being a hormone and stuff like that. I remember when he first got a tape recorder and he taped *Fame* off television and played it over and over again. It would just be the sound, all crackly. I pulled all the tape out of the tape. 'I'm sick of hearing about paying for things in sweat, Greg.' And we started fighting. But it were a bit like hitting me sister because he couldn't actually fight. I punched him and I felt bad. We are right close now. He loves coming down to visit me in London as he can be as gay as he likes. It is a bit more open down here I fink. He loves it. But when we went out I felt a bit uncomfortable because more guys wanted to get off with me than with him – I felt bad for him.

Anywhere, when I saw Belly's willy had a fleshy sock on t' end, I were a bit panic stricken, like uh-oh, I ain't got one of them. Because I didn't link sitting in the sink full of blood with having no foreskin, I didn't put the two things together. I can remember finking, 'does your cock grow a foreskin? Will I grow one? Why haven't I grown one yet?' I din't know if you *grew* one. It looked right weird. And that's when I asked me other mates who else had one. 'Oh, I ain't.' 'He has.' Belly I already knew had a foreskin, obviously, but Pisshole had one too. Dave didn't have a foreskin though. There were one lad who weren't sure if he had a foreskin or not and he still doesn't know. He kind of had half a foreskin. I don't know why me and Dave din't have foreskins and, to this day, I don't know the pacific reason why our Greg din't have one either. Me mam can't have just had it cut off cos it were the done thing at that time – like a fashion statement! I mean, I always tried to follow trends but this felt like a step too far. I did play with me knob a lot so perhaps that were the main reason. I have always been a sensual and curious person. I used to like to get naked a lot when I were a kid and me mam tells me that I used to run around in t' street naked whenever I got the chance. I guess I've always been proud of me body. Back in t' day, when it was a lot safer and I were just a toddler, she used to just let me run about the close naked!

6 JUNE 1993

I learnt the word smegma today. Smeg. Smeggy willy. Dave said it and I din't know what he were talking about at first and he asked me whether I ever got a cheesy bell. Where the hell does this cheese come from? Where's it come *from*? Is that another thing I should have and I ain't got?

7 JUNE 1993

Date: No:

I've found out what smeg is. It's a fridge. I don't understand. Better find out before I get found out. I don't think I want it though.

ISN'T SMEG

When you're a little boy all these words – smeg, smegma – they just don't make sense. I din't properly know what smeg is and you daren't ask anyone at that age. Now I'm a bit older I can rightly say that I've never experienced having smeg and that is down to not having the fleshy sock I now know to be foreskin. Thank God for me mam. Obviously, as an adult who has had sex with lots of ladies, I'm glad that I've never had a foreskin. I always fink women prefer no foreskin because if you're with your boyfriend and it's that special time and you're finking, 'he's been good to me lately, I'm gonna give him a blozzer . . .' with a foreskin-less penis you're not gonna experience smegma.

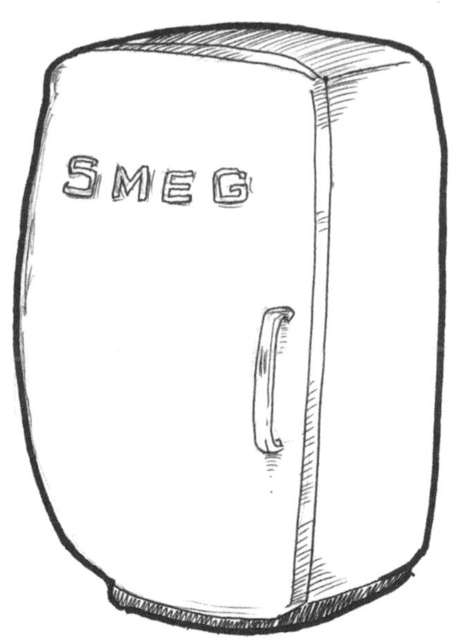

Do you think Ms Mumphnes would be fit if she let her hair down, took her glasses off and shaved her hairy mole?

yeah she's got ace tits.

I know she reminds me of Samantha Fox but fatter – look at cankles on it. She's got feet like pigs trotters. Something about her though.

yeah, I would.

You have to test things out when you're a kid, don't you? You need to find out if you're the only one, compare notes but without revealing that you don't know somet that everyone else knows. It is an art. I remember having the same chat with Dave and Frank the first time I had a double jetty, you know, the first time you don't have a single stream. I was pissing both ways. I din't know if that was just in me mind or I had made it up so I had to ask them if they had ever had it. Now, I'm older and wiser I know the science behind this phenomenon. For anyone who is a man reading this that does have a penis – that would make them a man – they'll know what I mean about a double jetty. If you don't know what I mean let me tell you what I mean: Let's imagine you've been pumping fist to *Babe Station* before you went to sleep. You wake up the next morning, you go t' toilet for a wee and you'll have a double jetty. The science behind this is that the jizm will have blocked up your hole creating a double jetty. To overcome this you have to push a bit harder until it goes to a singular stream. That's a double jetty.

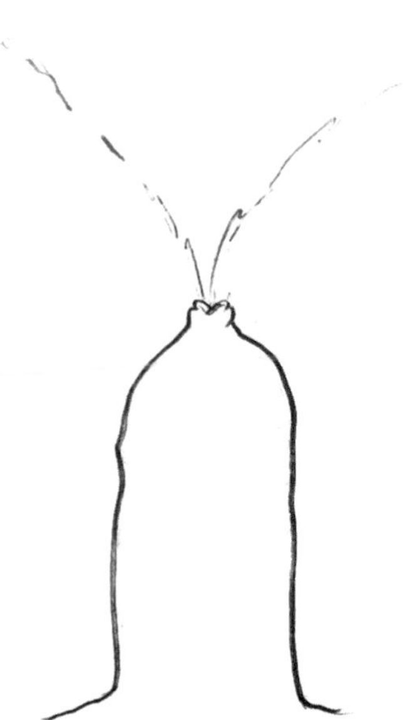

Any man who is reading this knows what I'm talking about. Girls, you're learning. The same fing happens if you've had sex as well. If you have sex and then go for a wee straight after, you won't have a double jetty because your jizm hasn't had a chance to set yet. It is like the jizm kind of glues your end up. If you have a wank into a tissue and then you clean your hole, you just wank into a tissue and throw t' tissue in t' toilet. But what many females don't know is that a lot of times, I'll say about 10 minutes after, you might get a little extra spit. There's a bit more for you. Same as when you have a wee. Dave were always panicking about having a crop circle, especially in the days when we all wore chinos. His knob always gave a bit of an extra spit at the end. I'm sure he won't mind me telling yer. He'd put it away, finking he'd finished and after a bit a little circular wet patch would appear on his chinos . . . I can remember him having a wee in a working men's club when we were sixteen, it was some Christmas do, and he were shaking it right thoroughly at t' end to make sure it din't dribble and an old man at the side of him said, 'Hey lad, don't shake it too much, you'll end up doing summat else!' What else did he fink he were gonna do with it? We took the piss out of him for months. 'Dave were having a wank in the loos! In the working men's club!' But we all learned a lesson: you can't shake your knob for too long after doing a piss otherwise it looks like you're having a wank, dunnit?

LESSONS YOU DON'T LEARN AT SCHOOL

I don't fink anyone knows the correct way of shaking your willy. Sometimes you shake it fully holding it and sometimes you just hold it a bit – like hold a bit of skin and shake it. No one teaches you that at school, do they? I fink they should make that part of a class at school. When I were younger, I should have just dabbed it with some tissue. I do that now sometimes – but no one is there to tell you these tricks, are they? It's a question I've often asked me mates – 'do you wipe your knob when you have a wee, know what I mean?' I tell you, you'd be surprised how many lads do but they don't suggest doing that when you're a kid.

But the first time I actually had a date with Madame Palm were after playing basketball in me garden and Frank said, 'have you ever pulled your dick loads of times and white stuff comes out and it feels ace?' I said, 'no. I'm just off t' toilet for a wee.' And then I didn't have a wee. I pulled me knob loads of times and white stuff came out and it felt ace and I went, 'yeah, it's ace innit!' Feels like you're gonna piss yourself but it's sexy. And then wanking was introduced. I had a new hobby! I can remember talking about it with Dave and he said he got so excited sometimes that he shoves his thumb up his arse. But to this day I've never shoved me thumb up me arse. When I had piles, after riding a camel, I went t' doctor, that's the first time a finger has been

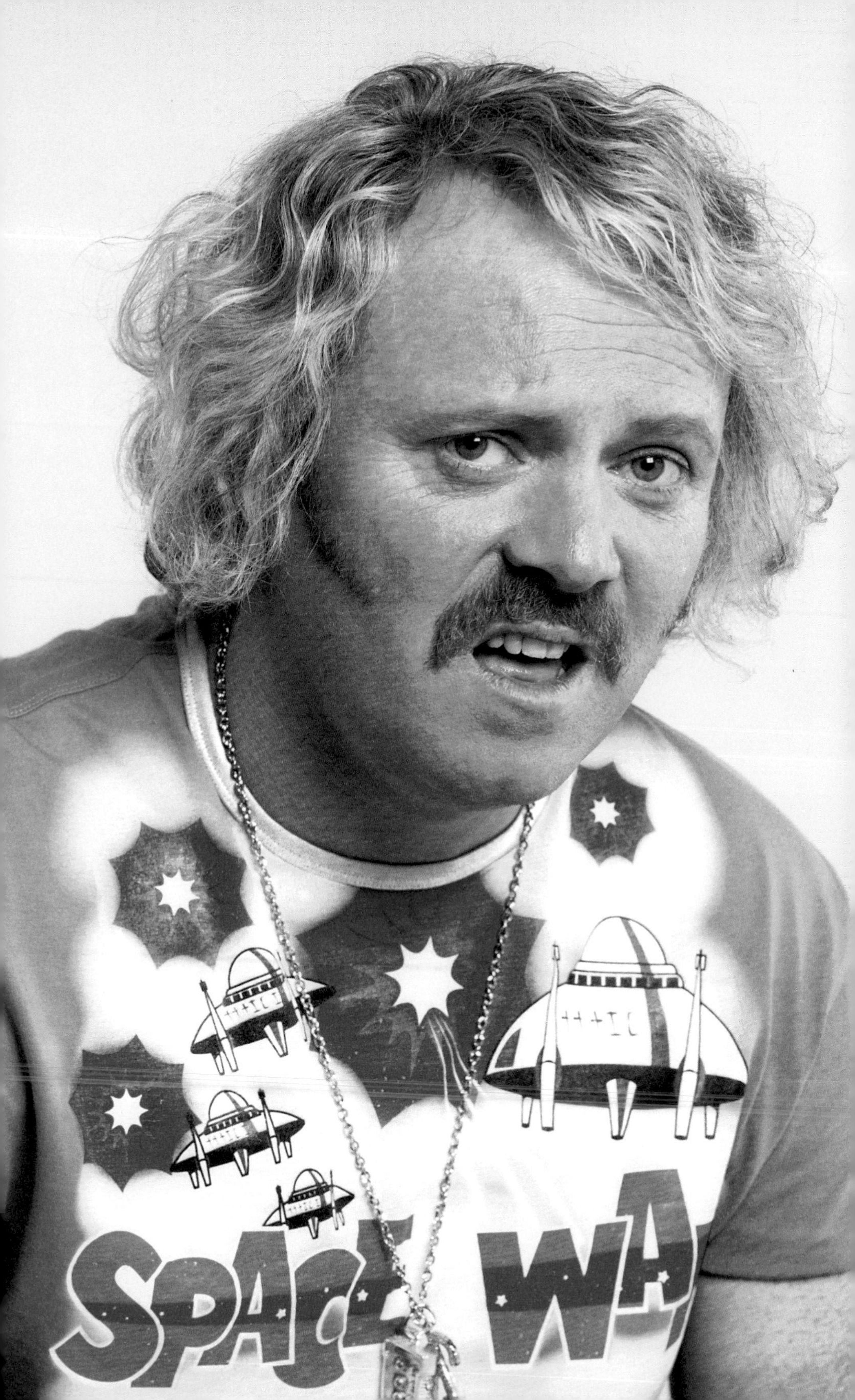

in my anus. When that doctor put their finger in my anus it felt like it was in me chest. I'm not joking. I remember she said, 'relax a little bit so I can get in'. And I said, 'this is as relaxed as it gets. I'm gonna probably snap your finger off. I can't relax. It hurts and it feels wrong.' And at that point, I thought Dave would have loved having piles then. He loved a bit of thumb up his arse. Every time we'd call for him and knock on his door after that we said 'Right, Dave, you put your thumb up your arse? You coming out?' Poor bastard probably wished he'd never said anything.

By the end of St Michael's we were beginning to understand what all our different bits did but we were now ready to learn how to use them properly. The bad news was that we were heading for an all boys high school. What was that about?! Me mam could already see that I were a bit of a hit with the ladies so she probably thought that it were a good idea to limit it a bit. It felt cruel at the time.

ALL BOYS SCHOOL

But even though there weren't any lasses at school, when we were eleven we were about to have some of the most fun years of our lives.

Belly and I both lived so close to our high school, Harlington High, so we could both go back to his house at lunchtime. He could literally just climb over the fence at the bottom of his garden and we'd be in. He used to like going home for lunch because he were a fussy eater. Strange for a big lad! But he used to hide the food he din't like down his pants! He were like Napolean Dynamite with Tater Tots in his pocket. What are Tater Tots anyway? Are they like potato croquettes? The only day he wouldn't miss school dinners was Friday. On Fridays, we had fish and chips. Fish and chips Friday, otherwise known as Food Fight Friday. It were a matter of how many chips you could throw, hit the bullseye – someone else right between the eyes – before the teacher turned round. We used to take it really seriously. I was always pretty good at it and finking back now I guess it were quite good training for Keith vs. Jedward.

I can't imagine what those two were like at school! I remember the first time I met Jedward. It were the weirdest day of me life. They just kept saying 'let's go to Tesco's, there's a Tesco's near here. Let's go to Tesco's, it would be so cool to go to Tesco's.' EH?

I asked them why it would be cool and they looked at each other and at the same time said 'I don't know but it would be really cool to go to Tesco's'. Weird.

Afterwards, I remember turning round to the Juice crew and saying 'were that weird or were it just me?' and I fink that I had a sixth sense as everyone seem to fink it were weird too. But now I understand those dingbats and I love 'em. I love 'em like they are me brothers. I remember a couple of Christmases ago, they called me five times on Christmas Day at about 5 o' clock in the morning. 'Hey Keith, Father Christmas is up! It's Christmas. There's a whole world out there! Let's go, Keith, let's do this.' Imagine you don't give a shite what anyone finks of you because your brother, who is just like you, loves you so much. I'd bum him I would, but is it a bad thing to bum yourself? I would anyway, just to see what I'm like. I fink I am a bit of a mentor to them now. They don't really drink or owt so I like to take them down t' Rhino and get them a lap dance. Who else is gonna teach them if it ain't their uncle Keith?

Anywhere, where were I? Oh yeah, me school dinners. I used to quite enjoy school dinners and not just because I were ace at food fights. I pacifically remember discovering coleslaw for the first time at school, not knowing it was called coleslaw but loving it. I'd have lashings of the stuff. I'd have a whole plate of it. You get shit coleslaw and then you get that nice stuff in a tub that's a bit more special. Well the school stuff was more like the special stuff out t' tub. I'd go up for fourths.

But I weren't too fussy. We'd all just bolt up for anyfing that were left over. When you got back to yer table, it were like you'd won. Like you'd been hunting and come back with a wild boar instead of some chocolate cake with some pink sauce. Pink sauce! I'd never seen that before and I've never seen it out of school. You'd get chocolate sponge and they had all different coloured custard: pink custard and green custard. But while everyone else were going back for t' chocolate, I were going back for coleslaw. I've never really had a sweet tooth, I've always liked Scotch eggs and crabsticks.

Apart from bread and butter pudding. I used to love that and remember I had it every day for three years. But I won't eat raisins now. I fink they're disgusting. I fink I must have overdosed on them at school. But I go through stages where I'll eat the same thing over and over. I'll eat it all the time until I hate it. I hate parsnips at the moment. When I go round to me mam's she'll want to make a Sunday dinner on a pancake and she'll still try and sneak a parsnip in there. I'll go, 'Mam, I know they're not chips. You try and palm them off as chips, but chips would never go with Sunday roast anyway, or a fucking pancake for that matter.' Me mam used to serve everything on a pancake – like an extra plate. Very modern.

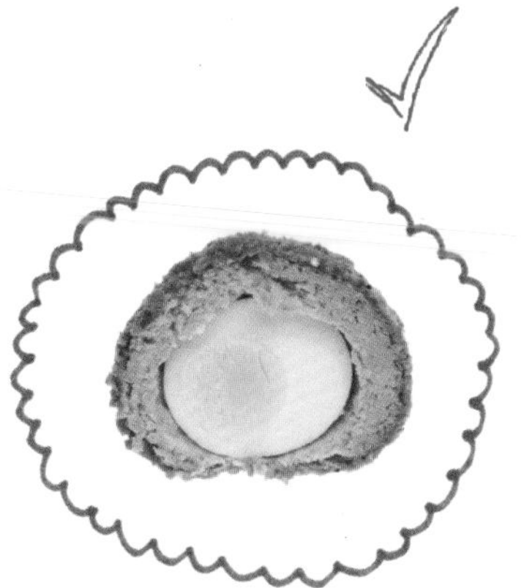

I'VE CAUGHT LONDON

I should say that whilst I am writing this book, I'm eating edamame. As a teenager I would never have known what an edamame was and probably would never have touched it. But I've caught London now and I'm eating edamame and sushi.

When I was growing up my favourite meal was shepherd's pie. We used to have it every Thursday. Thursdays, to me, were best day of t' week because it were shepherd's pie night but also *Kids From Fame* was on and I fancied Coco, who's bi-racial like me. But the black gene touched her more than it touched me. It were the best night of TV all week: *Grange Hill*, *Top of t' Pops* and *Kids from Fame*. I never really liked *Blue Peter*, I liked the people on the show, and I always remember Yvette Fielding doing the little item about *ET*. No, actually it was Sarah Greene.

I loved *ET*. It was the first film I ever cried at was *ET*. But I don't know how sad it actually was. I fink I worked meself up to being sad just because everyone said it's sad and you'll cry. So at that age, I thought I should cry. I remember I used to go to a cinema and it were 75p back then! 75p! I saw *Sinbad the Sailor* with me mam and our kid. A woman's foot turned into a pig's foot or a duck's foot and I shat my pants to bits so we walked out

of t' cinema and were confronted with this huge poster for *Jaws*. I can remember testing meself to see how close I could get to it without being scared. But I used to dream that he would crash through the bathroom wall while I were in the bath. I remember telling that to Paddy McGuiness once and he had a similar dream. Mad, in't it?! I also used to fink Freddy Krueger's hand was gonna come up between me legs like in the film. I saw a pirate copy of *Nightmare on Elm Street* and I watched it through so as not to be so scared. You've got to face your fears, haven't you?

I used to tape *Diff'rent Strokes* off the telly with a tape recorder. I didn't have video then so I would just tape the sound and listen to it. I couldn't believe I could tape the sound. Wow! So when videos came out I couldn't believe it at all. How come I can watch any film I want whenever I want? It's bizarre. It used to freak me out. I remember the first video we got. It were *Breakdance*. It inspired me.

OACH
12

Breakdancing

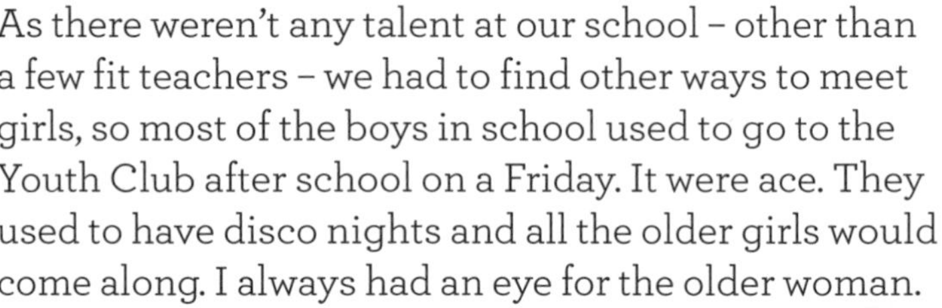
ME WAY INTO
GIRLS' HEARTS

As there weren't any talent at our school – other than a few fit teachers – we had to find other ways to meet girls, so most of the boys in school used to go to the Youth Club after school on a Friday. It were ace. They used to have disco nights and all the older girls would come along. I always had an eye for the older woman.

By the time we were eleven, I had started to breakdance. I started trying out a few of the spins and stuff at home after watching *Breakdance* the film and then when I found out that the Youth Club were having a talent competition, I thought I'd enter. It din't take long before the girls started to take notice. They were lapping it up! And so I learnt an important life lesson: all men should have a top five list of main primary skills. This is somet you should have prepared when a girl asks you 'what are your top five main primary skills?' Mine are:

1. Having it off
2. Dancing

3. drawing on t'ipad
4. doing the sound of a victorian bicycle horn
5. skateboarding

Our Greg were a good dancer too. He has still got aspirations of being a dancer, although I'm not sure if it will ever happen now. Maybe he needs to go on *Britain's Got Talent* or summat. All of the Lemons have got the moves! Yes, even you Mam. Gregory's a bit tall though, so when he goes for auditions, I fink he stands out but not for the right reasons.

TRYST WITH A TEACHER

Before too long I started looking to the older lasses – those with a bit more experience. One of me teachers, Miss Birdmuff (she weren't actually called Birdmuff, but it sounded like Birdmuff to me), I got it on with her. I knew she wanted to get on with me – it were obvious. She was like a friendly witch. She dressed like no one I'd seen before. She had right exotic clothes and she always wore the same long purple boots. Sexpot. She'd wear a patterned short skirt, bright coloured polonecks and neckscarves. She had black, greying hair and a lot of thick eye make-up on. She looked a bit like a lesbican version of Claudia Winkleman. Imagine a lesbican Claudia Winkleman going to a Halloween party – that's what she looked like.

But her personality was not of a lesbican witch. She always seemed to like me. She had nicknames for everyone and I was called Jelly Baby. I don't really know why. I hope it weren't anything to do with me looking like an orange jellybaby or a reference to the colour of me hair, cos as I say it's strawberry blond not strawberry or ginger. I remember she used to call Frank 'Old Man'. She used to say things like 'Come here Little Old Man.' I fink it was because he had the face of an old man on the body of a young boy. And she used to call Dave Lettuce. I don't know why.

Anyway, she taught me how to kiss properly. I remember when I was younger how wide I used to open me mouth when I was snogging. I din't know how wide to open me mouth as I was just graduating from the pecking style of kissing to full-on snogging. You don't know, do you? No one really tells you how wide to open your mouth when you're snogging. I can remember snogging some girl and we both had our mouths wide open, so wide I fink her lips might have been over the top of mine and I felt compelled just to blow in her mouth. Imagine if I'd have done that, like mouth to mouth resuscitation. Anyway, Miss Birdmuff taught me the art of proper kissing and she even taught me how to pass me chewing gum to her with my tongue mid-kiss. She was a right classy bird and that's a trick I still use to this day. The ladies love it.

She was me PE teacher so I used to get a bit of extra-curricular attention in the changing rooms. I didn't enjoy playing sports at school so I had to keep fit through out-of-hours methods – me breakdancing and playing specialist industrial hide and seek with me cousin Gary and some of me other mates that lived in the close. We'd play games that would last for weeks. It were like professional hide and seek. We were too old to be playing normal hide and seek but we thought if we played it industrial-style, it's alright. I often went up trees cos no one would go up to find you if you were in a big tree.

Anywhere, even though Miss Birdmuff had shown me how to appreciate a woman, it weren't quite the same when you were snogging someone your own age. There was a girl who I were seeing for a bit at school, I can't even remember her name so let's just call her Sweet Cheeks, and it were at that time when everyone else was doing the change over from mouth pecking to proper kissing. (It's a good tip that: have a pet name for someone if you can't remember what their name is. My favourite pet name now is butter tits. It is easier to remember one name than a string of different names.) Anywhere, as I said, I was advanced because I'd been there and Miss Birdmuff had shown me how it were done. I knew what to do but if I imposed that on another infant I fink they would have got scared and thought, 'he's too advanced for me'. I always had to be careful not to put girls off with my maturity. So I pulled it back and pretended to act like I din't know what I were doing either. I've always had an older head on me shoulders. I can remember finking, 'I've got to do it now. I've just got to do it now' – but before you stick your tongue in for the first time you can't imagine what you have to do with it, can you? It doesn't make sense

Looks like Miss Birdmuff must've taught me a thing or two about PE after all – I won this race against the horse.

to stick me tongue in now, eh? It was easier with Birdmuff because she would lead the way but when the other person is doing the pecking style it is hard to know how to change the style. I remember Sweet Cheek's sister would point and start laughing at us. We were standing really straight, not that close to each other, just our necks forward kissing and trying to work out what to do with our tongues. Her sister used to say:

'Can you come, Keith, can you come?'
And I'd say, 'Come where?' And they were all laughing.
They just kept saying it, 'Can you come?'
'If you tell me where you're going I'll tell you if I can come.'
And they'd go, 'No, but can you come?'

They meant 'cum'.

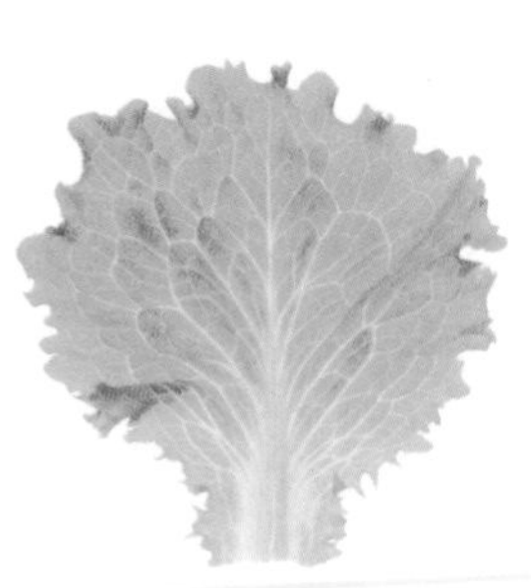

KEITH

Watched He-Man Masters of the Universe today. What a load of shite. All t'monsters sounded the same and Orco was a reet tit. Imagine if Skeletor was real though. That'd be funny. Funny how He-Man and Skeletor never actually have a punch up. They could sort it out once and for all. I wonder if He-Man could take him? I wonder who would win in a fight between Andi Peters and Jamie Theakston? I bet Andi Peters is surprisingly hard. Wonder if he has it off with Emma Forbes? I would! And that new lass Katy Hill. Got a lovely colour about her. Like a hotdog.

By the way, felt me mate's sister's tits last night. It were ace! Going round there again tonight. Ace times! I love tits. If I had a pair I'd just stay at home all day playing with 'em.

A NEW LANGUAGE

I din't know what they were talking about at the time. But it din't take me too long to find out. It were the same with blow jobs. When you first hear about blow jobs you fink that someone blows your willy, don't you? Still to this day I fink it's the wrong name. It's not a blow job. It's a suck off. The hardest thing about a blow job is trying to understand how to get one. How do you get a blow job? Do you ask for one? Do you push her head down? What do you do? I don't have to ask for them any more, they just happen, but back then you had to ask for it and it came down to persistence. 'Can I have a blow job?' 'No.' 'Why?' It would go round and round until I got one. But then, I remember the first time I actually got one, there were teeth scrapage. Obviously, she din't know what she was doing and I din't know what it was supposed to be like so I can just remember finking, 'that's it. Done it. Now I can tell me mates'. What else are they gonna do with their teeth? They're in there aren't they? They're gonna scrape. I can remember being a bit sore afterwards and she didn't finish it off. She just said, 'that's it'. And I went t' bathroom and had a wank.

Maybe she were scared about having jizm in her mouth or maybe she were scared of the projectile? She might have been scared that it might have made her throw up, like when you put a finger down your throat and it is an instant reaction. It is weird because sometimes it is just a dribble and sometimes it is

NEXTMAN

19 SEPTEMBER

I found another one! I wasn't sure at first but it ~~defin~~ definitely is one! Now I've got more pubes than Belly. Can't wait to tell him.

a burst and I don't know what it means. When I were a kid I would often be hitting the headboard. The panic was 'ooo shit, where's it gone? Oh no! Where's it gone!'. I remember coming downstairs once and chatting to my mam for a bit and then looking in the mirror and seeing this dirty mark on me face. It looked like hubba bubba had burst on your cheek and get stuck on your face.

I fink we all learnt at a similar sort of time what things meant. I felt more mature than a lot of the lads in me class but there were a few that were more mature if you took their pubes into account. It was very important to get pubes. I can remember the first people with pubes. They got mocked for having pubes. 'Ah, hairy willy!' And you'd always fink, 'when am I gonna get a brown willy like a dad willy?' Our teacher, Mr Sheep, he had a brown willy. He was a white man with a brown willy. So we used to fink in our minds, we're gonna get a brown willy when we grow up, like as you grow up, your willy gets a tan. But I never got a brown willy. And still, to this day, I don't know if he always had a brown willy or his willy went brown. Or perhaps he's just been having a lot of anal sex. We'd always compare our knobs, like when you'd go to your mate's house. 'Hey, look, I've got about nine pubes now.'

AND HER CHERRY-SMELLING HOUSE

Angela Chase were me first serious girlfriend, when I was twelve. Obviously the girls before that had meant somet to me but I weren't emotionally developed enough to really take it to the next level. I remember her birthday party and her house smelled of cherries, which got stuck in me head – a cherry-smelling house. She was quite posh, well, posher than me anywhere. She probably wanted a bit of rough. But I've never let little things like that stand in my way. I knew she were posh as she had one of those gaint Head bags. It were what all the posh kids had. I didn't have a Head bag. I've often thought, is that around the same time holdalls were invented? Cos it were basically a holdall that kids would use for school. Interesting that, in't it? Those bags were absolutely massive. I could have slept a night in it. Big school bags was a thing, a fashion. But by that age, I had already discovered me own unique style.

Anywhere, the fact that she had one of those giant Head bags and I didn't have one weren't gonna stand in my way. I could talk the hind legs of a horse and managed to win her over with me charm. She was in the same class as me at school and I knew she were making eyes at me across the maths classroom. After class, I just went straight up to her and kissed her. We kissed for five and a 'alf minutes! I nearly died. I used her as a snorkel. I could tell she were bedazzled by me. I fink she were the first person I said 'I would destroy you' to. She looked a bit like Sandy from *Grease* before she became rock chick Sandy. I liked the girl-next-door Sandy better than rock chick one, me. I've met Olivia Newton-John now, it's mad! She were really nice and gentle with a lovely soft voice, just like she were in me dreams. Anywhere, I told Angela that at the weekends me mam used to take me to a dog rescue place and I could see her eyes melt. Girls love animals, especially brocken ones. She pacifically liked dogs. And horses, even though they are horrible and too big for humans to ride. I know I've talked about Owen Wilson before and people say I look like him but that in't the only thing we have in common. He also used a love of dogs to his advantage. In *Marley & Me,* he shows his softer side by pretending he likes Guide Dogs. And he scored Jennifer Aniston because of it! You can't say fairer than that.

I right liked Angela. Me mam gave me a locket necklace and I gave it to her and I put two pictures of me in. I fink the idea was that you are supposed to have one picture of her and one of me but I knew she'd appreciate having two of me. And I didn't have a picture of her. We didn't have a camera to take a photo of her but I used to draw pictures of her instead. I though it were nice to draw a picture of your girlfriend. It were like, 'I like you, so I've drawn a picture of you.' It's like saying, 'do you want to wear me coat?' innit? When a girl wears your coat and you're a kid you fink, 'I'm in there. She's got me coat on. She's picked me coat up from goalpost. Yeah, I'm gonna kiss her for two minutes.' Anyway, a couple of weeks after giving her the locket, she came round to me house and dropped it off telling me we weren't boyfriend and girlfriend any more. It were like a bolt from the blue. I couldn't believe it. At least she'd brought the

locket back but I'd missed Frank's birthday so I could draw that picture of her. I was heartbroken and then I bought a plasticine Hulk kit and got over it. Some of me mates have told me that it's horrible when you get dumped. Your heart feels like it is broken into a million pieces – your pride shat on all over the floor. But I fink you've just got to pick yourself up and get over it. Don't fink too much about it. You can play it to your advantage if you are a bit clever about. Some girls like it if you are broken, they like to be able to help fix you. If you are lucky, she will want to try and help fix you physically. You'll soon forget about your problems. Anywhere, the best advice I can give to anyone who finds themselves being dumped is to go on t' rebound. Some people spend their whole life on the rebound and they are getting a lot of action. And if you're not looking for anything too serious, it can mean you can punch above your weight, getting some tidy totty that would normally be out of your league. And sometimes it can develop into somet bigger, if you play your cards right. I often fink that when I see famous couples. Jay-Z and Beyonce are a prime example. Surely Beyonce was on the rebound when she first got with Jay-Z? She is stupid fit. I'd let her kick the crap out of me.

This isn't the plasticine Hulk I got, this is another one me mam got me. I had two Hulks.

PLAYING TO ME STRENGTHS

I wasn't a star pupil educationally. I was always playing the joker and I talked a lot but I weren't naughty just cheeky. I would question a lot of things – always asking why:

Teacher: We're doing algebra.
Me: Why? What job will I need algebra for?
Me: When does a letter become a number?
Me: What? I'm not gonna need this in my job, I know I'm not.
Teacher: Comment t'apelle tu?
Me: Eh? I don't need French, sir.
Teacher: You might go to France . . .
Me: Well, if I do I'll ask someone there.
Teacher: Religious Education.
Me: Why?

But even if I weren't a straight-A student, I have always had many other skills. I have always thought the main purpose of going to school was to learn some social etiquette. I don't fink I would be the man I am today if it hadn't been for the lessons I learnt at school. For instance, I used to sit skinny Peter Wright, a boy from my class, on me knee and pretend he was a puppet that would talk back to me . . . Kind of like a ventriloquist fing. Everyone were laughing and we didn't prepare a fing. We just did it. He moved around and I threw him around a lot and asked him questions. We did the water trick and I'd say, 'do you wanna try some talking now and I'll give you some water?' That's what they do, ventriloquists, don't they? So he were spitting water out at everyone and I can remember finking, 'Wow, all you need to do is spit at the audience and they'll laugh at it, it's easy this in't it?!' I've used that trick a few times – once with some Weetabix. I won a competition at me mate's house, who could eat the most dry Weetabix – I started laughing and it sprayed everywhere. I fink that gave me my first taste of what it would be like to be an entertainer.

10 APRIL

I had an ace time at school today. Mick got a detention because he threw a brick at Mr. Price! It weren't on purpose. All the dingbats from the bottom set were throwing bricks over school but it were just a shame for him that he hit Price! He said it were funny though. He said he made a noise like a seagull being hit with a brick. 'Aaah'

At high school everyone got on. When you hear about bullying these days I find it hard to understand because we had no bullying. All the dickheads were dickheads and we loved 'em for being dickheads. It weren't like we were all the same either. There was a hierarchy, for instance, the posh kids shopped at Next because Next was a different world.

Anyone with a Next jumper, I just remember finking 'bloody hell, they're posh aren't they?' but you didn't have a go at them for it, and they don't care that you don't shop in Next.

Come to think of it, Mick were like the original Joey Essex.

It were the teachers that you had to look out for. If you were caught chatting in class or whatever, the teacher would turn round and throw chalk at you. I fink you could have physical contact when I was at school and they'd hit you. Pummel you, or flick your ear. I remember one teacher in particular, Mr Standish, used to pull your ear and flick it. And he was bald but he'd combed his hair from the back forward and when we went swimming his hair flowed behind him like a mermaid. 'He's got no hair . . . Standish's got no hair! Standish's a baldie!' But his hair went down his back because he'd grown it at the back, grown it there and combed it right up. I've heard of a comb-over but a comb-back?!

The only piece of advice I would give kids at school is if they are getting bullied, don't take it too seriously unless it turns into violence. If you have the balls, just say, 'fuck you' straight away and then they'll go, 'Oh, we can't bully him because it stops there.' If you have the balls, just say it. Straight away. Say 'fuck you and fuck off! Go fuck yourself you fucking fuckster'.

PEPE

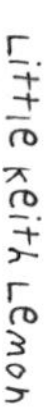

PERFECTING ME PLAYGROUND FLIRT

There were other lasses after that but I weren't really keen to tie meself down to one girl in particular. I don't fink anyone should when they are young. You're only young once! I was always just looking for a bit of fun.

I used to enjoy flirting with girls whether I got together with them or not. Often if I fancied someone, I would punch them in the face and set their hair on fire. 'Eh, your hair's on fire. I fancy you.' The method of flirtation was basically take the piss out of them and before you knew it, you've scored. You should try it! At school, one of the girls in my class Natalie, wrote me a letter asking me out and I wrote back and said, 'eff off, you dog' and showed me mates and sent it back. Then afterwards I thought, 'oh no, I fancy her loads, why was I such a dingbat?' so I said to her 'I just don't know how to be around girls, I don't want the other boys to see how much I like you cos I'm very sensitive.'

It din't work every time but it usually got their attention. This way of flirting I still use to this day. Take for instance on *Celebrity Juice* when I give Fearne a lot of grief about her massive nostrils. I do this as I properly fancy her so I try to belittle her so I can control my emotions towards her. She's an inspiration that woman. She does a lot of work for charity. I fink a lot of girls aspire to be her but with smaller nostrils. I have a lot of respect for that woman. I don't want to marry her or anyfing, but I do want

to have a go on her. I bet she's a right one in the bedroom. I've always said it: nice girl-next-door image but in the sack a proper dirtbag. I use the same technique on Stacey Solomon. I call her a sexy rodent – it sounds like abuse but I am actually paying her a compliment. Try it!

When I were doing the research for this book, I came across a shoebox full of the letters and poems I used to write to girls to win 'em over. I wrote this one to Melanie, a girl who were in me class.

Dear Melanie,
You sit only two seats away from me at school and I know sometimes I am silly in class and get me knob out but you are the prettiest girl I have ever seen. Even prettier than Wonder Woman. The next time I get my knob out, I would be really grateful if you let me put it in your shoulder. I don't really know what love is but I have strong feelings for you that I think are love. Its not pervy, me putting me knob on your shoulder, its love. I think I love you Melanie.

Keith x

Dear Keith,
You are a fucking dickhead. The next time you get your knob out in class I am going to smack it with a shatterproof ruler.
I have already told Mrs. Thompson about you getting your knob out, you should have a letter home to your parents.
Dont ever speak to me again.

Melanie

Dear Melanie
I am so upset that me getting me knob out has offended you in any way. It is very immature of me but at this difficult time in our lives where we are getting spotty skin and hairs in all sorts of areas, I feel I can't express meself unless I get my knob out. I would really like to take you for McDonalds. My mate works there and we will get free chips. Keith x

Even if I fancied you Keith I would never go to McDonalds because I am sure that McDonalds is responsible for half of our rainforests being destroyed. I saw it on John Craven's Newsround. It might just be propoganda but I don't like their chips anyway. I prefer chunky chips

What the fuck is propoganda? Do you want to go out or what?

Yeah ok.

Which obviously meant she fancied me.

So I took her swimming. It is a great way to get to know someone really quickly and see if you can take the relationship any further. Even though we were only fourteen, she had a body like a twenty-nine-year-old. She was Tick, tickety boo. I paid for everything like a gent, gave her a pound for her locker and bought her a hot chocolate and some mini cookies afterwards. She thought I were the don. I poked her and didn't wash me hand for a week. But it smelt more like swimming baths.

Every time I go to swimming baths now, it reminds me of Melanie.

Here are some of the other notes I found in the shoebox. I would tell you who they all are but I can't remember them so you'll just have to imagine what they all looked like. Imagine an even fitterer version of Martine McCutcheon.

Dear Molly
Everyone talks about your tits. I do too,
I love your tits to bits.
I love the shape, I'd like t'see them in
a Batman cape.
Nowt else, just that alone. You mek
me stiff I get a bone.
Meet me after school.
Keith.

Charlotte Needs, I bet you
have needs.
I bet I can satisfy your
needs.
I am a gifted man oh yes.
I am, my cock is fick
as a coke can.
Hope t'see you at the
youth club this Friday
xx

TINA

Lovely Tina I cun't be keener to flick your beaner, know what I meaner?

Wanna meet in the cantina

You have me desert, and me can of pop, on me list of fit birds you are top.

You have ACE tits.

Keith x

Dear Claire -

You have nice hair.
I wanna kiss your tits and flick your bits
I mean that in the nicest way.
So how about it, what d'ya say.
If ya give me a blow job
I won't tell me mates no matter how
long it takes..
I'd wait for 3 wks or if more,
I'll never fink you're a dirty whore.
You are so fit, how about it, can
I kiss your big juicy tit?
Left or right not bothered.

Keith x

CAN I BUY YOU A GOLD LABEL?

I wouldn' actually have ever said that. Buy your own own Gold Label – I've only got a few quid. But I like the idea that I were a gentleman, putting the ladies first, even back then. I fink we were about thirteen or fourteen when we started to discover alcopops and super-strength lagers. We realised that if we had a few bottles of that stuff before we went out, in our heads we became the best-looking boys at youth club. The first time I got drunk was in t' park, on alcopops: Mad Dog, Twenty Twenty, Breezers – all of it at once until our teeth dropped out. I can remember going home and walking through t' living room. I had mud on me jeans and on me hands as I'd fallen over a few times on t' way home. I were pretending not to be drunk in front of me mam. 'I'm off to bed, goodnight Mam.' I just walked straight in. No chat. She knew! I remember the next morning I were still puking me guts up on Mad Dog and saying 'I'm never drinking that stuff ever again.' And I din't. I fink me mam were a bit worried that I'd get in trouble if I were drunk, but at least I din't take drugs! That's cos I grew up in the era of Zammo singing *Just Say No*.

We used to go to park all the time and there were a little wooden gazebo type fing. It had seats in and it was all wood so you were under shelter. It would be filled with teenagers all just getting off with each other. Just feeling tits for hours. But it was weird how everyone just shared – the lads and the lasses. Because

it weren't your girlfriend and you'd try not to like 'em too much because you knew you'd go there next week and she'd be sat on someone else's lap and you'd fink, bastard. What am I supposed to do? Just let it go? Then you'd ask another girl to sit on your lap. And before too long you could ask: Do you want to go for a walk?

That wooden gazebo in t' park were also the site of many games of spin the bottle. They were good years, there weren't that much hassle about the whole thing – it weren't like you were girlfriend-boyfriend, were you? You just snogged, and occasionally you might clean the windows. A game not traditionally associated with snogging is Murder-word but it always worked for me. Basically, to play Murder-word, you needed two teams and each team would have a word. Then you had to get a letter out of the person to spell out their word. It were quite advanced and educational at the same time, weren't it? So you might tickle them to death to get their letter out of them or go, 'I wanna snog you'. If you're lucky you might get a girl who says, 'I don't care'. And then you snog. And you go, 'You know what? You can keep your fucking letter. Keep it. I don't want your letter. I wanna feel your bangers.' 'I don't care.' 'Right. Well, here's me letter, it's S.' When we got a bit older, you might get to finger-blast someone.

I fink it were around the same time that I started to fink about dressing to impress the ladies. I used to spend all me pocket money on *Star Wars* figures when I was at St Michael's, I used to have loads of them all lined up. And then I got to high school, started going to Youth Club and drinking alcopops and I thought, I am gonna sell me *Star Wars* figures cos I like clothes now, so I can get some fanny. Because I weren't gonna get any fanny with *Star Wars* figures, were I?

I had a paper round from the newsagent at the bottom of the hill, Bottom Shop as we called it, and that gave me a bit more spending money for clobber as well. We didn't have a corner shop because where I lived there were no corners. So it was just Bottom Shop and Top Shop. And top shop was one of those shops that sells everything. I still love those shops now. It would get right Christmassy over Christmas and you wonder where they'd stashed all the other stuff. I used to love going in. I never knew what I were gonna buy, just knowing there would be summat in there that I'd need. I go to B&Q now for the same reason. I wander round, I'm not after anything, but I'll see somet and go, that'll come in handy. 'Have you got any really strong double-sided sticky tape?' 'Yeah, I have actually. I don't know why I bought it but I knew it'd come in handy for somet.' 'Have you got any spray that'll go onto plastic garden chairs?' 'Yeah.'

But the newsagent in bottom shop was like Frank Carson. He didn't have catchphrases or anything like that but he really looked like him. Obviously, the temptation was to dump your bagful of papers and say someone stole your bag, but I learnt a good lesson about honesty doing that paper round. Rather than dumping the bag and lying about it, I used to set little challenges for meself. I'd time meself so I could do the quickest round possible and then go back to the shop quicker than I had the day before. I fink I am a good law-abiding citizen and it paid off as that kept me in decent clobber for a bit. I now shop in Zara, Top Man, River Island and asos. I like Selfridges a lot cos the sales assistants are fit. I had a go on one in the changing rooms once and she gave me a discount after, so that were nice!

LOOKING THE PART

I've said it before and I'll say it again, the rules of attraction are simple: you have to be attractive. And if you are not attractive, you've got to dress up as someone who is. Style is as important as the tiny arms on a T-rex. Without style you are not stylish. And if yer not fit, just dress up as someone who is. Easy. My look was inspired by different style icons fused with my own sense of fashion. Wearing the right clobber is a big part of that. It's what's on the outside that decides if you will get inside, if you know what I mean.

People knew who I were back in those days – and it is the same these days. Back then, when everyone else were wearing jeans or chinos, I wore a suit. I wore as much flamboyancy then as I do now. My favourite party outfit was a suit with one leg that was red, one leg that was black and it had red arms. It was a safari jacket with a belt and everything. I felt dead good in that outfit and if you feel good, you are confident and you are good. If I am not 100% happy with what I am wearing, I don't feel as good. If you feel stylish, you feel confident, I fink.

Once I found £15 in the street and I must have been about thirteen so £15 felt like £300 or more. I went into Leeds and Belly was with me, I gave him a fiver and I kept the tenner. We went into town to a shop called Class and I bought some bottle-green jumbo cords, some deck pumps with a palm tree pattern on and I bought a green roll neck with a zip. Head to toe in

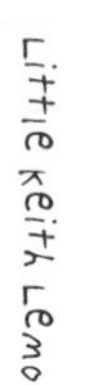

green. I always knew how to make a statement. It is back then that I learnt that a big part of being a style guru is knowing how to wear clothes, not just what to wear. If you can't carry off an outfit, you'll look like a right nonce. I strutted my way round Leeds market in that green concoction and if you don't know what strutting is let me tell yer what it is. It is walking with a swagger. Pick a song in your head and walk to that beat, stride with rhythm, it looks good.

I often used to pick a Duran Duran song as Simon Le Bon always held himself well. He looks like he has just walked out of River Island. He's got a good barnet, too, which helps. I was blessed with having strawberry blond hair which goes mainly with any colour. My hair was always thick and lustrous so I could carry off most dos. Gingers don't have the same luck – their ginger hair always clashes with everyfing and makes them look like geeks.

I remember going through a stage in me life where you would take labels off of fings and sew them onto other fings, like Le Coq Sportif. At around the same time there was a fad for nicking VW signs off of VW cars. We were inspired by the Beastie Boys. Frank and I used to go out and swipe them. I felt like the devil! But it was encouraged back then by pop culture. You had 'em round your neck as trophies. I collected three of them. A little one, a normal size one and a big fuck off massive one. And everyone was doing it and I'm not saying if everyone took drugs, I'd take 'em but to get yer hands on one of them fings was a pretty big deal. Anywhere, at school, the headmaster found out about it and the police came to talk to us to tell us we were stealing and vandalising people's property, and in our heads it didn't even register. We just thought, 'eh? No,

we're just looking cool like the Beastie Boys. Beastie Boys have done it. They've got proper jobs and they're doing it'. Anyway, they said they were setting up a box where you could bring in your VW signs – like an amnesty. I just buried mine in the back garden instead, I felt too guilty to admit that I'd stolen them in the first place.

It were the same time that bomber jackets were in fashion with badges all over. I fink I was a bit reminiscent of Tom Cruise in *Top Gun*. I used to hang around in Dortmund Square chatting up the birds and cos I came from a one-parent family, I had a cheaper version of a bomber jacket, it din't seem to have enough padding in. This girl I was trying to get off with, Melanie, I fink her name was, had a full, puffy one. There was a scale from t' budget ones right up the banging puffy ones. But again, it din't matter too much as it is more about how you wear it than how puffy your bomber jacket is. And when I teamed the bomber with a pair of PVC crocodile-skin jeans, all shiny, Melanie couldn't keep her hands off me. Sucked me t' hinge end in't toilets.

These days I'm trying to bring back some of the clothes that I got lucky in when I was kid – fings like Boy and Destroyer. And it's not just clothes, I've got a new Raleigh Burner recently. It's gold with all the competition tubing and me mam couldn't afford it when I were a kid, but now they have reissued it and I can relive me youth. It has become me chosen means of transportation. One of me Leeds mates came down and now I've got two BMXs so we went out for a ride just like we did when we were kids. I felt like I had arrived. That's what fame and fortune have bought me. Two BMXs.

I had a bit of a routine before I went out. The main part of that routine were that I sprayed on a lot of Lynx. It were the only thing I knew back then. I did graduate to Paco Rabane aftershave when me auntie bought it for me, but I were only ten . Ten! Aftershave when you are ten! I had a thick line of downy hair but I weren't gonna shave cos I wanted that to grow! I din't understand until I were a bit older that you had to start shaving to make it less fluffy. I din't need aftershave. I suppose I was mature for me age so they got confused.

SHAVING ME HAIRS

I was always that bit more advanced than me mates so I had to start shaving before most of them were even out of nappies. I din't use to make a big fuss about it or owt but other lads did. It were one of those things that people used as a sign of their manhood. 'Ave you started shaving? Ave you fingered a girl yet?'... that sort of thing.

I must have had about four hairs on me chest when I started shaving me face and I remember finking 'I'll shave them off as well. Don't need them, do I?'. And overnight, I sprouted this thick carpet of hair across me chest! I remember people saying that if you shave yer chest, it grows back thicker and it is true. Plus, as a teenager, you want to shave, don't yer? As an adult, you don't want to shave and you don't want any pubes, do you? You know what I mean? You don't want any pubes in summer time when it's hot. Ooof!

But I never used to trim me pubes, not until me mate Jade told me he trimmed his. 'Oh, you bender, you trim yer pubes? And then I can remember one day I was really hot and I just trimmed 'em. I was trimming me tache anyway so I thought I would just trim the rest while I were at it and it made a real difference. But first time you trim your pubes they go a bit spiky and sharp. But they don't now, especially if you use a bit of conditioner to keep them in good condition. It's like a Pantene advert down there!

We did have sex education classes at school where we learnt all about puberty, pubes and pregnancies. Everyone said that Ms Johnson got her tit out in it so we were well excited. Ms Johnson set a law: 'if you laugh or giggle I will ask you to leave the room' so I nearly just got up and walked out there and then saying 'Miss, I'm going to piss meself I can't help it' but then I'd miss Ms Johnson's bangers. I just remember finking, 'When's she gonna get her tit out, man? I thought she gets her tit out?' I can remember Frank got kicked out for giggling. I was finking, 'Please don't giggle, don't giggle. I haven't seen Mrs Johnson's tit.' Imagine ruining it by giggling and being sent out and then, 'did you see Mrs Thompson's tit?' 'No, I got kicked out for giggling.' Bastard!

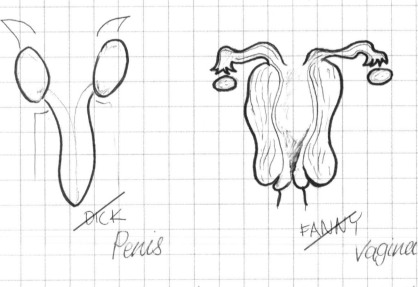

~~DICK~~

Penis

Keith, how many times do I have to tell you to use the scientific names?

A lot of people have a popular misconception of me that I am highly sexed. I'm not, I am just very honest. When I was youngerer before I became sexually active, I was embarrassed about it. I felt like if I became sexually active me mam wouldn't love me any more as she'd fink she had lost her little boy. So I remember rushing me sex education homework so I din't have to do it at home in front of me mam. They made us do these scientific drawings of vaginas and penises. The penis looked like an evil fox and my vagina looked like a tryphid. I fink they made you do sex education to scare you off sex. I remember looking at me scientific drawing of vagina and finking, I would never put me dick in that! It would bite it off, it looks like a sarlacc from *Return of the Jedi.*

ME TEACHERS

MR BILLDERCH

Billderch were a small fella and he had a tash. Almost all me teachers had a tash. As he were one of the PE teachers I very rarely saw him in anyfing else but a tracksuit. He wasn't as harsh as some of t' teachers but he did make us take our trunks off in t' showers which was a bit odd. I remember one of me mates who had no pubes drew his on with a pen. I pissed meself when they came off in t' shower.

MR ROXBRIDGE

Another PE teacher, but he also did Maths. I never understood that. Once he caught me cutting through t' park doing cross country. We were supposed t' go around t' park. But in my defence he never said you cun't go through t' middle. I thought I was beating t' system. But all I really was doing was inviting a detention. Which I talked me way out of.
Mr Roxbridge was a skinny fella who looked a bit like the weasel from *Wind in t' Willows*, and he stunk of fags. He would sometimes smoke whilst out doing cross country with us. He shouted at me a lot on t' football pitch but I din't care if we won or lost. Football isn't my cuppa tea. Neither is tea.

MISS PANTHORPE

Quite young for a teacher. She were the only female teacher at high school so we obviously thought she was fit. She looked like a rough Belinda Carlisle. She had a hairy mole as well unlike Belinda Carlisle. But, Belinda Carlisle was fit. I wonder how she earns her money now? It was rumoured that Panthorpe got her tit out in science but I never saw it.

MR MONNINGTON

Monnington taught Maths and English. He used to repeat everyfing he said under his breath. Really strange. Would head pummel ya if ya pissed about. He wore tweed head to toe. Bet he even wore tweed underpants. Must've been some reason he was pissed off. Imagine tweed under crackers . . . Fuckin 'ell that'd drive yer nuts!

MR LINCH

Foreign bloke who looked like a snake. He would throw chalk at ya if he caught you talking in class. I weren't mad on him. He always wore Slazenger jumpers.

MR LAWRENCE

He did woodwork. Looked like a garbage pail kid. It were like a baby's head on a man's body. He were a proper Yorkshire bloke. The good fing about his class though, were that he'd have t' radio on in class. I liked that. Right low like but ya could hear it. He dressed old-fashioned like most of t' teachers. Teachers were different back then, they proper looked and smelt like teachers. Coffee breath.

MR DARKWOOD (AKA BATMAN)

The headmaster. Old school. He actually wore a cape! In a good mood he was ok. Bad mood, I'd rather go t' prison than be sent t' his office. He looked like an American eagle. Grey hair. I say hair but it was like wool. He had a pointy, angry face. On t' wrong side of him and ya were fucked. Could well have been a murderer acting as a teacher.

MR GREENHILL

Obviously hadn't bought any new clothes since the seventies. He were balding but he had long hair at t' back. Really thick glasses. Could've easily been in Cheech and Chong. He looked like a stoner and was very easy going, just let you get on with it. He was more like a mate than a teacher. Smelt a bit off but ya just din't stand too close t' him.

POSTER GIRLS

Hey, I've found this photo of me bedroom. Me walls used to be covered with pictures of women. Kylie was up there! It was when she was singing 'I should be so lucky'. My mate said she looks like a goofy fashion bunny. But I was there from the start. When Michael Hutchence got hold of her, he turned her round. I can remember seeing her in some Levi 501s and finking she has got the best arse I have ever seen. You rarely saw that kind of arse in real life, how she wore those jeans back then. I fink it were because they were a bit high-waisted and it really accentuated a lady's curves. It were a bit different cut weren't it? But she always used to wear knackered 501s, and I remember her red leather jacket on t' front of *Smash Hits*. Seeing that photo, I thought, 'yeah, I'm nearly in love with you and I don't even know you so that's weird.' I thought I were never gonna meet her, but that's why you were allowed to be so obsessed with famous people – because you knew you were never gonna meet them, so you're allowed to like 'em more than a normal person. When you know someone, it's a bit different. I mean, Holly still sometimes looks at me and rips all me clothes off with her eyes. I can see it. She's got desire for me. I can see that but it is different when you see someone day in day out. I used to fink Fearne fancied me but I'm gonna have to work at that one. I fink I've lost that out me grasp now. She's all loved up. I don't want to go out with someone who's had a baby. She must look like a bin liner down there. Or even worse a bucket. Or a pint glass. I know I am as thick as a Coke can . . . but a Coke can that will fit in a pint glass and still have room for a couple of pens.

Patsy

I don't fink of them sexually but I feel really flattered that I hang around with such lovely looking ladies and I fink a lot of men are jealous that I do.

Patsy were another one that featured highly on me wall of course. That woman is so fit it cancels itself out. She were in a band called Eighth Wonder at the time. I were proper obsessed with Patsy. I know her now. She's a good mate of mine. If she ever wants to be more than just mates, it's her call.

CHEAP THRILLS

I remember the first time I got a bit excited by Jenny Agutter in the shower in *American Werewolf in London* and me mam asked me to make a cup of tea but I cun't get up. She would have seen I had happy pants. I wrote a letter of complaint t' BBC for showing such a sexually graphic film without warning.

Keith Lemon
36 Brudenell Close
Leeds

Hello Sir
I would like to make a complaint about the American Werewolf in London. There is no warning of the sexual content but when Jenny Agutter was in the shower it were extremely arousing. When me mam asked me to make her a cup of tea, I was unable unable to do so. I could have burnt me penis and blinded me mam with it all at once. Please put a warning in future.

Keith Lemon

Another film that got me tingling down below were one of the craziest films I've ever seen in me life, *Xanadu*. Olivia Newton-John is in it and she is so super bang in it that it shouldn't be allowed. I met her on Jonathan Ross and I told her. I thought the film was amazing and I still watch it. But I don't like the story. I just really like her. She was lovely. And Belinda Carlisle, obviously. I had a door poster of Belinda Carlisle. A long, thin door poster. I would go to HMV and Athena and spend an hour in there choosing posters. There was the classic tennis player shot, scratching her arse, which I've lampooned many times, or a man holding a baby. But whenever I fancied a famous person, I'd just fink I want to go out with someone who looks like her.

There were a film called *Perfect*, which starred John Travolta and Jamie Lee Curtis and a lot of high-leg leotards. That also used to send me blood rushing to me willy end. I remember at the time, Jamie Lee Curtis was rumoured to have both a tuppence and a tallywhacker. Anyway, I fink it is all the stuff of nonsense otherwise she wouldn't have known what to do when she went to the toilet – stand up, sit down, stand up, sit down. It's just like Lady Gaga. Some people say she is one of those marmafrodites. But she in't. I saw her at the BRITs and she got her bits out.

When I were youngerer, I were much more into film than I were into music but I do remember what the first record I ever bought were. They always ask you that in t' interviews, don't they? Not sure how interesting that is but anywhere. My first record was *Joshua Tree* and maybe I'm not as cool as I thought I was because I went back the next week and bought Terence Trent

D'Arby *According to the Hard Line*. That were probably me black roots kicking in. I felt a connection.

The first ever gig I went to were at Roundhay Park to see Michael Jackson. I couldn't afford a ticket, so I went with my scally mate who used to nick jeans off washing lines he knew someone who knew someone who could get us in. He didn't say it was through a sewage pipe though. And he got in stinking of shit! I said, 'I ain't going through a sewage pipe to get in,' so a couple of us climbed up a tree and we could see in anyway. We were just up a tree watching. He was inside but he stank.

It were a couple of years later that I went to a gig and actually had a ticket. There were a big group of us Leeds lads who went down to London on a coach to see INXS. It were one of the best days of me life and there weren't even any birds there! Just a load of blokes wondering round trying to look like Michael Hutchence.

If you ever see *Live Baby Live* or *Live Baby Live* . . . Live and live, same thing innit? It's spelt the same so I never knew what to call it. I'm on it. I got t' front. We went in and we just ran to the front, squashed against the barrier. It were only 10am! At about 11.30 I needed a piss and I looked back – and I'd never seen so many people in me life. I thought there's no way I'm gonna go back there for a piss. I'll never get back here so I just sucked it back in. Back then I had a bumbag on and every time I jumped up, the bumbag stuck in me pissbag, in me pisswomb and made it worse. I know what yer finking – you wore a bumbag? What a dingbat! But it were the fashion to wear a bumbag back then – or I made it a fashion.

Anyway, I din't go for a piss ALL DAY! It would have been a better day if I'd have just laid down on t' floor and dug a hole and done a piss into that. But I needed a piss all t' way through. I can remember when it had finished we got on the coach to go back to Leeds and I was pissing in a Coke can and I said, 'give me that bin liner' – there were a bin liner for rubbish – 'give me that bin liner because I'm gonna fill it' and then I kind of just put the bin liner onto me penal area and just pissed in the bin bag. And yeah, it were the longest piss I've had in me life. I remember finking I could have got one of those Guinness World Records for the longest piss into a bin bag ever.

THE BAKERY IS NOT THE BEST PICK-UP JOINT - UNLESS YOU FANCY GRANNYS

Our school made us do work experience and we all had to troop off and do two week's work experience in the summer. I never understood it because they sent me to a bakery. Shouldn't it be somet that I actually wanted to do when I grew up? I don't want to be a baker! No offence to any bakers out there, but I weren't going to waste this face on being a baker. I were making sandwiches with women that were old enough to be me Auntie Jean. Am I fucking making sandwiches with me Auntie for a job?!

They were all old women. I thought it might be a good opportunity to pull birds but they were all old women. There were one other girl who were the same age as me who were there to do work experience too but she had a wob eye. If you talked to her for too long her eye would go off t' other way. I couldn't do that, I just din't know where to look at her. I just looked at the floor in embarrassment. She were right nice though, I wonder what she's up to now. I would definitely bang her now. I wouldn't let that eye stand in me way.

All the others were me mam's age. I often thought, 'when will I fancy mams?' And now I'm in me late twenties (ok, I'm in me thirties), I fink I am starting to fancy mams. Unless mams have got fitter. I wouldn't have fancied the ladies in the bakery now so perhaps it is just that mams have got fitter. I have been on the facespace and checked a few of them out and they are not as aesthetically pleasing as you might like. You'd have to be really drunk. And definitely one of them would scrape your dick when she's sucking you off. It's a real problem that. I don't know if there's a technique which you learn about where they don't scrape your dick but it should be talked about. I don't fink you should suffer in silence. I don't fink you should sit there and take the pain. You should go, 'Oi, you dingbat, it's hurting!'

Pupil: Keith Lemon
Dates: 14 July – 25 July
Workplace: Bradbury Bakery

Keith's baking skills were nothing to shout about. He managed basic sandwich making. He wasn't happy about wearing a hairnet which is required. All in all, Keith is pleasant and I'm sure if it's something he is interested in then he will excel. Not sure working at a bakery is for him though. If Keith has any interest in doing more work experience here in the future we'd be happy to take him back but not just on his charm alone. He'd have to be more committed. The girl from t'other school doing work experience at the same time as Keith was a perfect example of what we'd expect if Keith was to return. She was also wanted to ask if she could have Keith's telephone number. I said I would ask.

Yours sincerely

Lynne Patrick

Wispa, Brad Pitt, Johnny Depp and Terry

For my fourteenth birthday, me mam bought me a rabbit. We called it Wispa – named after the chocolate bar. I had transfer stickers on the outside of the hutch and I used to change its name every week. I changed it to Brad Pitt once and it were also Johnny Depp the following week. And then we settled on Terry. And then a fox got hold of it and wrecked it's back legs. It were a traumatic time and I learnt about the fragility of life. I had to hit it on the back of the head with a spade to put it out of its misery. It were terrible. I remember crying. It were like a man test, I felt like I were in a live version of the film *Watership Down*. It did used to bite me though. And it did shit loads which I had to clean out so I weren't sad to see the back of that. I fink me mam were trying to teach us the responsibility of looking after somet.

After that, she arranged for me to go and look after an old man called Tony. At the time I thought he were about 200 years old but he were probably about 75. Me mam said that after his wife had died he got lonely so he could do with a young visitor to cheer him up. I used to take me gran's betamax and we'd watch stuff, but one day he started having a wank so I had to leave.

That were too much even if he were lonely. I fink he were a bit mad. I tried going to see old ladies instead and this one old lady, Florence, she got a bit friendly too. I don't know what it was about them! 'Oooo in't your hair all shiny. What do you put on it?' she used to say. I used to put Brylcreem on it but, I don't fink that were the point. I knew she wanted somet more from me and I remember finking 'I don't even fancy mam's, so when am I gonna fancy grandmas? What age do I have to be before I fancy a grandma?' I fink the age difference was just a bit too much.

WHO NEEDS PORN WHEN YOU'VE GOT LADS' MAGS?

I was very clever with porn. I didn't really look at proper porn mags, I just bought lads' mags, so if me mam busted me I could just pretend I were reading one of the articles about what were on at t' cinema that weekend. Those lads mags were basically soft porn weren't they? You could have a wank and see what's on telly. Sha-ting!

I remember *Loaded* used to feature Liz Hurley a lot and she were right fit so I used to pump fist to that one all the time.

Another reason why I din't need any pornos of me own were that Pisshole used to have an old suitcase under his bed which were rammed full of pornos. We used to both have a torch in our hands so we could see the ladies and then we'd just bash off in the dark. If the batteries ran out, you'd have to wait until your eyes adjusted to the dark so you could see the breasts. Pisshole were on one side of the room and I were on t' other side of the room. It were like we were having a three-way affair with the suitcase. I guess looking back at it now it were a bit weird that we were both in the same room, knowing the other one was bashing one out, but at the time that were pretty normal. It were a bonding experience.

It were the same with watching porn on telly – it weren't somet you necessarily did by yerself. It wasn't a singular thing, we all used to watch it together. We used to go over to Mick's house and all watch it together. It would be like this:
'Has yer dad got any pornos?'
'Yeah.'
'Right, we're coming over'.

And that was their reputation made, someone would always be famous for being the one with the pornos and in our little group it were Mick. Mick's dad had loads of videos so we used to hang out there quite

a lot and watch 'em. We'd wait until the parents went out and we'd all sit there with pillows over our laps hiding our stiffies.

But porn were different back then. We didn't have Brazilians back then so everyone had a hairier bush. In the porn mags when I were growing up, the women had as much hair on their minge as they have on their head, din't they? You could place a table tennis ball on it, couldn't you? It would just sit there. It was literally like a pyramid of pubes.

Porn were basically the next step up from Wonder Woman. You started with Wonder Woman and then a year or so later, you were watching porn in Mick's sitting room. Wonder Woman looked ace though, din't she? I remember finking 'I wonder what she looks like in between the change where she is taking her normal clothes off and changing into her Wonder Woman clothes because those bumps on front look magnificent!' and that were the signal. You're ready for porn, son. She's got a wonderful chest Belinda Carter. She were one of me early crushes.

I have never had a wet dream but if I did I bet it would have been about Wonder Woman. I don't understand wet dreams though. Like every other man, I used to wake up in the morning with a hard on but I never had a wet dream. I remember waking up on the number 42 bus and having a hard on and not being able to get off the bus. I had to walk all the way back from top of hill to get back to me house while I waited for it to subside. Again, I used to fink about algebra to take my mind off it and turn me stiffy into a flop-on. Takes the pressure out of it. When you are a teenager you are basically walking coathangers.

5 NOVEMBER

OH MY GOD.

Me mam just walked in on me having a wank.

OH MY GOD

I am never going to wank again.

We both just pretended it didn't happen But it did.

Oh my god.

I've got to go downstairs now cos me tea's ready

ME MATES FROM SHEFFIELD

I were about fourteen when I first met Gino, that's why I don't understand why he denies his Sheffield roots. Sheffield's not far from Leeds and we used to go Meadowhall shopping centre and hang out there. One time when we were there, we were messing around on our BMXs and Gino was there and was pulling a few tricks so we adopted him into our gang for a bit. He had a beard, which were a bit weird as he were only fifteen. He looked a bit like he was from *Withnail & I*, you know, like he stunk with a long coat on. When ITV got his hands on him they definitely did a makeover because he looked a bit like a tramp when I met him. He was very good at doing an Italian accent, it were like his party tricky. I'm not sure why he was called Gino. Perhaps it wasn't his real name? It sounds exotic though, don't it? But it is has worked out for him. He stays in character longer than anyone I have ever known. He is a lovely fella. He is very open sexually. He was a bit of a wild child. His Italian accent was a bit like me bandage. It were his fing. I fink that is how he got ladies actually.

He were, and still is, a right charmer. You had to keep him away from me mam. Me mam liked all me friends. She knew some of them were a bit cheeky and naughty but there were no malice there. They were a right nice bunch. They weren't drug dealers or owt, just cheeky buggers, but Gino always knew how to smooth talk his way into her heart. He even said he liked her pancakes. Gino's been on *Juice* loads of times now. Everyone loves him on it. With his Italian impersonation he can get away with saying things that normal people can't say as it would be too rude. The funniest time was when he was referring to Fearne's humungous nostrils and he said 'I bet she can suck like fuck'. I pissed meself laughing.

Dermot O'Leary was in our gang when we were at school, too. He was always very stylish. Not to the extreme, though. I fink he's subtle with it. I'm more showbiz with it, more flamboyancy. Dermot lets his bulge do the talking these days. Good old Dermot. It is funny because he had a small penis at school. He's a top bloke. Good on him! At school, one of me mates said that the more you wank, the bigger your tallywhacker gets. I remember he said, 'Fink about it. If you're just pulling it all t' time, it's gonna grow, innit?' Makes sense. Science.

THE SEVEN-A-DAY WALL

There were a rumour going round school that you'd go blind if you wank too much. Once I started wanking I wanked religiously all day and night, all t' time. Especially in school holidays. You'd wank like a lunatic. I developed a clever way of getting round the blindness though. There were a parade of shops at the bottom of our road and we used to climb up the lamppost to get a cheapy. Fun, and I could still have the use of me eyes! Before I knew it was a sex thing, I thought it was because I'm higher up and it was summat to do with the atmosphere that's giving me willy a tingle! You'd climb up and you'd see who can climb up and not do a piss. Ya know, spunk up!

But by the time we were fifteen we had our fake IDs ready to go and we started to work out which pubs would let us in so there were less time locked in our bedroom or up the lamppost. It weren't much of an issue for me as my moustache gave me an air of maturity beyond me years but for some of me mates, it were a bit more tricky. But with pubs came a whole new breeding ground. I met a girl who worked behind the bar in a pub once and she were an animal. I can remember saying to her, 'can I have two pints of lager and your phone number please?' And she said, 'yeah.' Ooosh! Simple as peas.

28TH MAY

Been at home all day. Mam's at work. Fink our Greg is out making daisy chains or somet. Always doing girly fings. I've had 6 wanks already today. One over Kylie Minogue, one over Betty Boo - not the cartoon, the singer. Can't wank over cartoons not even Jessica Rabbit. If she was real yeah, but I ain't wanking over a drawing. Oddly enough I had a wank over Anthea Turner. One over me next door neighbour, then I did Patsy Kensit in't back doors. I'm now gonna have a frankenstein wank. All those women merged into one super woman. That'll be number seven! I'll probably hit the wank wall and faint. Wish me luck. Speaking of superwoman, I'm gonna put her in there too! Helen Slater she is fit. OOoosh!

First time at me house, she just took me hand and took me up to me bedroom and then she just ripped me trousers off. I thought, 'eh? No, don't I do the moves?' And then on the weekend she came over again and we had a full day session and of course because you're a teenager you just never know when you're gonna get some sex again, do you, so you just spend all day having sex. Couldn't do that now. I couldn't be bothered. All day? I fink me knob would hurt. But when you're a kid, you might never get sex for a year so you have to take all you can get when you can get it.

Anywhere, it din't last too long as her brothers din't like me. It were like a modern-day, gritty Romeo and Juliet. The hassle of it wasn't worth it. I thought she was pretty and that but I weren't besotted by her so when her brothers started getting lairy I just thought, I can't be bothered getting chased.

There was another girl I was seeing at the same time anywhere so it were getting a bit complex trying to balance the two. I met her in t' hospital as she was in the hospital bed next to me mam when me mam was having her knee looked at. She looked like Patsy Kensit – super bang. I remember I asked her whether she liked sharks and she was perplexed enough to want to find out more. I have always been good at asking people questions and it keeps the conversation flowing which is what ladies like. To talk. A lot.

Do you like sharks?
Can you body pop?
What is your favourite type of dinosaur?
I like your shoes, are they la bootins?
What is your name?

That sort of thing. But it's a great place to chat up birds – the hospital. People are often emotional wrecks when they're in there and are looking for guidance. They're like little Bambis on ice. Again, persistence is key. And if they are hooked up to a drip there ain't nowhere for them to go so they'll say they'll go on a date with yer just to shut you up for a bit. Plus, if they look fit when they're in hospital – no make-up or tan – then they are gonna look super bang when they get out of the place.

ME BIRD BECKY

But even though I were riding a lady wave, me main significant major relationship of me teenage years was with Becky Ramsey, when I were fifteen. I met her at the local youth club. We went out for about six months, which is a long time, in't it? Six months is a long time when you're fifteen. She wanked me off in t' back of car, it was so romantic. She had sort of dirty blonde hair. Not like as blonde as me but maybe as blonde as Mel Blatt from All Saints. She was a pretty girl, a bit taller than me and not much in the way of bangers.

She were at the bus stop on the way home from the local youth club. I said, 'Will you go out with me?'. She said 'No'. 'Will you go out with me?' 'No.' I knew she were gonna give in if I kept asking, so I kept at it. I got the 83 bus home with her and we sat on t' back seats obviously, still making her laugh and whatever else. And then, just before I got to the door to get off at my stop she said, 'yeah, alright then', and I snogged her there and then. I came away with her phone number in me hand.

Sometimes I used chat-up lines but you don't always need 'em. In this pacific case, it just took a bit of persistence and charm. But when that doesn't work, see over the page for some of me favourite lines:

I know milk does a body good, but DAMN . . . how much have you been drinking? I'd love to see you gargle it. I hope you know CPR cos you take me breath away. You can give me t' kiss of life if you like and stick yer tongue in.

Do you eat Frosties because you're bringing out the tiger in me? You look greeeaaaat! I'd love to have it off with yer.

I used to write her poems. Girls go mad for that sort of stuff. I can remember seeing some programme about poetry and it said that poems didn't have to rhyme. But it came straight from the heart! I wrote love letters too. I was big on love letters, I was, always writing love letters to Miss Birdmuff, to Angela, and to Becky. And cos I was good at drawing I would always draw a little picture of them in a different scenario. I'd often turn them into sort of fantasy characters and give 'em big shotguns. Imagine a beautiful girl holding Rambo's gun. How ace is that!

Becky, you are
stupid fit.
I'd let you kick
the crap out of me.

ROSES ARE RED
VIOLETS ARE BLUE
WHAT'S THE DILIO?
WANNA GO SWIMMING?

THE ART OF SEDUCTION

I remember the first time I buffed her. It were amazing. We had been watching *Basic Instinct* and had a nice bottle of Bianco that I bought from Wilkinson to get us in t' mood. I started to shove me fingers in Becky's mouth just like Michael Douglas does to Sharon Stone and I could tell she were getting turned on. I'd cleaned me hands especially as I'd had a doner kebab on the way over. I started to whisper sweet nothings in her ear. I can't remember exactly what I said but it would of being somet like: 'I'm as stiff as a brick for you. I want to sex you up, down, around and all over your god damn sexy body' or 'Would you like me to kiss your bangers on t' end? Not near the end but right on bloody end!' or as me mate Paddy might say, 'Let the tash see the gash.' She were going wild for it. I could see she were undressing me with her eyes.

As we were at her mam's house, we needed to find somewhere that her mam weren't going to come in offering us a cup of tea so we went to the car, which were parked in the garage. We put the back seats down to make it comfortable and we found an old sleeping bag that her brother had taken to scout camp the week before. She said it were perfect. I am a very giving lover and I always fink about the woman. Miss Birdmuff taught me that. I made sure that Becky had her fun before I blew me beans. What I normally do is fink about trivial things while me lady is having a great time and when she's had that great time and she's been up the hill and back down again, then I can start finking about what I'm doing. But I'll always try to give her one first. I normally fink about algebra. How can numbers equal letters? Eh? That doesn't make any sense! It keeps you going for another minute or two. It got right steamy in that car, it were like that scene from *Titanic*.

I remember bringing Becky home and introducing her to me mam for the first time. Me mam's inherently very nice and always very nice to every girl that I brought back. Sometimes she liked them more than I did and were quite saddened if I split up with them. I got over it quicker than she did! But she always liked Becky so when things had run their natural course, me mam was right sad. I don't fink I ever cried about it. I were too much of a man to cry. I still don't cry very easily these days. I remember when Rylan came on to *Celebrity Juice* and we played Keith vs Rylan to see who could push out a tear first. We looked at all this sad stuff, like a picture of Gary the dog RIP and I still couldn't push out a tear. Rylan won that one hands down. Rylan lost it after that. He were crying out for Gary and Nicole.

1 JANUARY Date: No:

Me new ~~resaltion~~ resolution for this year is to stop wanking so much. Seven a day is insane. When you hit the wall - the seven wall - and it is just smoke coming out of t'end, you've got to stop. Will aim for five a day

See, I were ahead of me time on the five a day thing - everyone talks about it now. Perhaps I should be prime minisher?

Most of me relationships had the same cycle. You stand around with yer mates on a street corner drinking warm beer out of a can wishing you had a bird. You eventually persuade one to go out with you. It gets all intense and you don't see your mates for a bit. Then you see your mates and you fink, 'oh fuck, I miss me mates. I don't want a girlfriend. I want to stand on t' street corner with me mates praying that I had a girlfriend.' So you go all boring until they split up with you. Then you see 'em somewhere, you might see 'em with another guy or whatever, and you go, 'fuck, I liked her.' Then you'd try going back out with her and she did the 'no, no, no,' thing and then said 'ok'. Me and Becky went round like that for years.

It were normally Becky that would start fancying me again. One time she actually created someone that I was supposed to be jealous of and a mate told me. Girls are clever, aren't they? A mate told me that she weren't seeing anyone. I confronted her about it and said 'I know you're not seeing anyone, you're just making it up to make me jealous, but I'm not jealous. You fucking wanker!' I fink she were a bit surprised by me language but I thought she were a fucking loon! As an adult I fink these things happen all the time but back then I thought she were mad.

But a couple of months later we were at it again, this time in the loos of a nightclub. 'Oh hi . . . Yeah, oh, nice to see you . . . who are you with?' 'Oh, me mates'. And then she was feeling me leg under t' table. I had baggy chinos on so I had to stay sitting down for a while until all me happiness had gone. And then she said, 'do you wanna go for a bit in t' toilets?' We went to girls' toilets and I remember her saying, 'harder, harder, faster' and I thought I can't go any harder or faster, this is as fast as I go. How fast are you supposed to go? In the girls' loos! I didn't know how fast I was supposed to go. I thought if I go any faster I'm gonna look silly. Nowadays, I take it nice and slow. Whisper sweet nothings in her ear, right breathy like 'you make me wobbly like jelly, oooosh'. It does the trick. Anywhere, I didn't blow me beans because someone came in t' toilet. It's a bit like having a poo. I weren't finking 'Oh, this is a beautiful moment.' It was all practicalities. Do this, get over with this and then tell me mates. And I remember me balls killing me afterwards.

But then, a few months later someone said, 'did you shag Becky?' When I said that I had indeed shagged Becky, they said I didn't. Now, I don't know the Laws of Shagging but I reckon if penis is in vagina, it counts. Otherwise it would be like saying when a lady fakes an organism, they haven't actually done it.

I wasn't worried about getting her pregnant as I used to pull out just in time. Finking about it perhaps that should be one of my top five main primary skills – pulling out on time. I've got good willpower. No one's ever come forward saying, 'Keith this is your baby.' Well, a few have but I can't remember. Me and Becky had sex many times at school but she went out with a lot of people and so did I.

You're confused, aren't you, when you're a kid. Mates or muff? Muff or mates? You all want muff but you don't want to leave your little gang. If you've got a girlfriend, all yer mates will call you a poof. You puff! It doesn't make sense really. How can I be a puff if I've got a girlfriend?

But despite all of the activity I were getting, I've never actually fallen in love. I thought I did, but I wouldn't be able to get over it so easy if she really were the one. I've seen *The Notebook* and other films and it takes 'em ages and their soul's all broken up and they can't operate, can they? But when I've broken up I go, 'stupid witch. Fuck it!' And then I get on with life, so I can't have been in love.

MUFF
OR
MATES ?

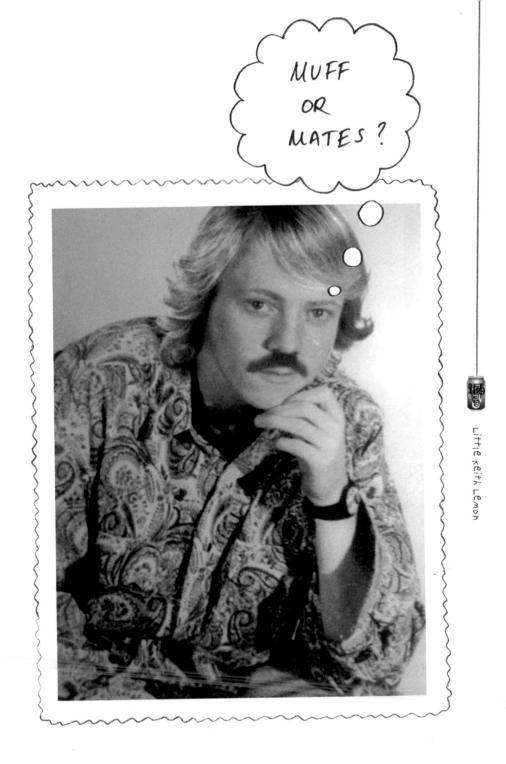

VALENTINE'S DAY

I always used to make an effort on Valentine's Day – girls love it. This is one of the Valentine's Day cards I sent to Becky.

But even if I weren't seeing one bird in particular at the time, I would make sure I sparkled a little bit of the Lemon love out there. Just to cheer a few girls up. It's only fair. Sometimes I would send a special mysterious message and other times I thought it were best just to cut to the chase: 'I fucking fancy you, it's Keith, by the way. Will you go out with me?'

Those were the words. I must have said that sentence a million times to different women over the years. 'Will you go out with me?' 'No.' 'Go on.' 'No.' 'Go on.' 'No.' 'Go on.' 'Alright.' 'Ace.'

That was me strategy. Be persistent. Even today if I talk to someone who finks that they're out of my league or whatever, I'll say to them:
'I could pull you if I wanted to.'
And they'd say, 'no you can't cos I wouldn't go out with you.'
'Yeah, you would.'
'No, I wouldn't.'
'Look, if I wanted to I would.'

Persistence. Until you get the police phoning you asking you to leave her alone, just keep asking the question. That's never happened to me as I would have

Valentine

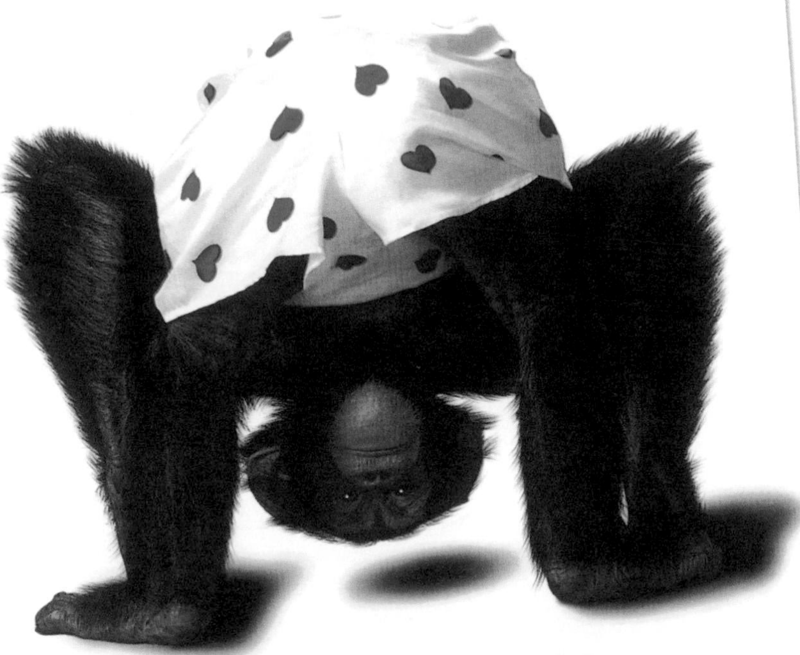

I'm head over heels...

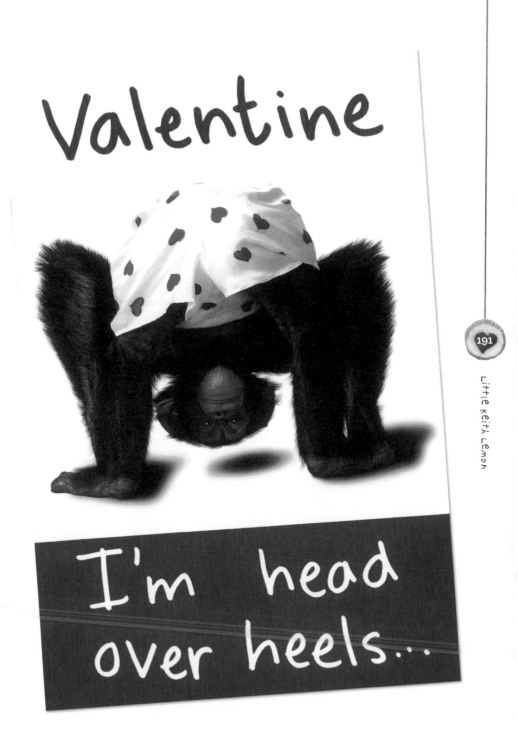

hooked them in by then. But I always fink guys are too quick just to give up. But if there is one thing I have learnt it is that the ladies like the chase. Especially when they're a bit older. They don't really care what you look like, you can just go at it until they say yeah. They'll be bored one day, won't have anything to do on a weekend and just say 'oh fuck it, how bad is it gonna be?' and then that's when you do your work. When you take her out, that's when the work kicks in. You use every trick. Every trick. And if you don't know what the tricks are let me tell you what the tricks are. Actually, I'm not gonna tell yer, you have to get me other book – *The Rules: 69 Rules for Being a Success*. Go and buy that yer cheapskate. Did yer fink I were just going to repeat the same stuff over and over? Dingbat.

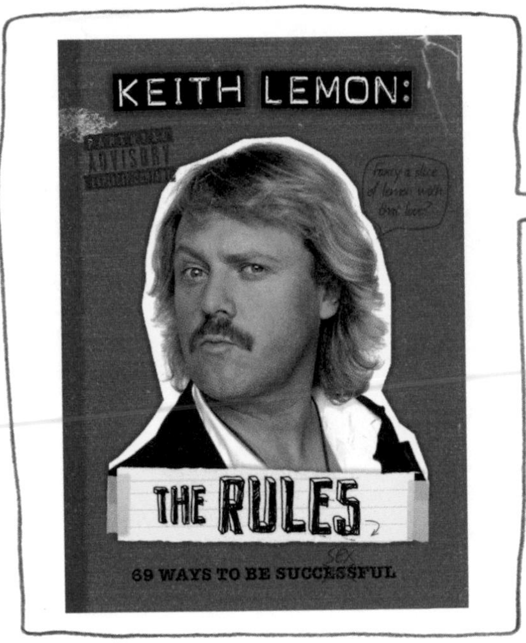

In my case, the hardest fing weren't actually getting someone to go out with yer, it were the splitting up with someone. I'm hard on t' outside and soft on t' inside you see. I always felt really guilty about it so what I would do when I was a kid was I'd just pretend to be fucking boring. Boring. And stop laying on all the compliments. Stop all that being nice stuff, go a bit quiet. Eventually, they will ask 'Is there summat wrong?' 'No.' It won't take long before they come back to you saying 'I don't fink it's gonna work out.' Job done. And you have done your bit for empowering women. All round winner.

One of me mates, Gay Simon, now he actually were a puff. He din't tell us at the time but he were always the one saying you were a puff if you had a girlfriend. I remember when he first told us, we were at a house party in Beeston. We were only going to the party because Frank fancied this girl and she were gonna be there. It was in a house that looked a bit like a squat. I din't know anyone there but I were feeling pretty merry as I'd had a few jars by this point. Frank had come round to ours and we'd drunk four cans of Gold Label barley wine. The first mouthful tastes like the devil having a piss in your mouth, but then you have another one and then another one and then you can't taste anyfing.

We'd have four of them because we had no money and then we'd go out and spend about a fiver. Anyway, at the party, I can remember impressing some of the girls when I drew pictures of them with these coloured soaps I found in t' bathroom. I were like Neil Buchanan on *Art Attack*. Frank were getting it on with the bird he fancied so I ended up chatting to her mate who was less aesthetically pleasing, and Gay Simon came over, a few cans down and just came out with it. Everyone kept having these backflashes to times we had spent together and finking 'was he looking at me then?' 'Did he fancy me?' 'Was he trying to get his end away after football?' and all that. He did ask me how I felt about him being gay. I wasn't fucking bothered. I said to him, 'I live with a gay, don't I, so it don't bother me if you suck dicks or get your arsehole poked or bum men or jizz in the face.' I like all kinds . . . black, white, pink, yellow, lesbicans, pillow-biters. I don't get irate about it.

RHINO JEANS

Other than a few Saturday jobs and me paper round from Bottom Shop, me first step on the entrepreneurial ladder were selling Rhino jeans on Leeds Market. I were saving up to get me mam a new pair of teeth. She needed 'em. Her teeth looked like a dirty picket fence in her mouth so I thought after all the years that she had been looking after me and Greg, it would be nice to give her a little somet back. The jeans were a bit dodgy though. I don't know where they came from. A lad that I knew, he had a whole pile of these jeans and they were rejects, factory seconds, so they'd all have a belt loop missing or they wouldn't have any pockets. The most common problem were that one leg would be fatter than t' other. We basically bought them, got a few labels printed saying RHINO JEANS, stuck 'em on and sold 'em on.

I saw a gap in the market – Branson, see? – and thought I could fill it. I knew from experience that jeans got a lot of wear and tear around the crown jewels area and the material can get worn out. I'm not sure if it were just because I had a big cock and balls but it were always worn out down there for me. So Rhino jeans were made out of much tougher material – like a rhino's skin – so that those who are well-endowed could wear them without fear of their tallywhacker flopping out.

People would bring them back and say 'oi, Keith, one leg is bigger than t' other' but I used to say, 'yeah, but you are encapsulating both ragamuffin and emo style in one go so everyone will like you in those jeans, won't they?' I have always been a good salesman me. I don't

fink the emo look had even been invented back then and now it's caught on. I invented that. The other solution I had was that you could get a skateboard to make one leg more muscly than t' other and then it would pad out the wider leg. Sorted. I've still got a couple of boxes of them for old times sake.

I got good banter from working on the market. You have to shout stuff and make people want to come and look at your stall rather than anyone else's.

'COME AND GET YOUR JEANS, £11.60 FOR YOUR JEANS. RIGHT GOODUNS. LIKE LEVI'S BUT NOT AS GOOD AS LEVI'S.'

We sold them on Leeds Market, next to the stall that sold chickens. I fancied the girl on the next stall, Donna, and I had a little dabble with her as well. She used to give me a bit of breast for free.

Harlington High

Careers Assessment
Student: Keith Lemon
Class: 5B

Keith Lemon seems to either have a very positive attitude of his own future or is living in a fantasy world. Has no interest in further education which is a shame as I don't feel academically he is at the same level as his fellow students.

He is convinced he has work lined up straight from school in the form of his own business? Apparently he has a stall on Leeds Market selling denim jeans. Not sure if this is true and I very much doubt this will lead to anything with any kind of longevity. But he seems very confident that he knows what he is doing. We did discuss other options in case things don't go to plan but again, he seems determined and already has his mind set.

He is very different to the rest of the students, whatever the future holds I'm sure his flamboyant dress sense and interesting use of the English language will get him noticed somewhere and thus dictate his path.

Dains

Mr Dains
Careers Officer

Harlington High
Form teacher's report
Student's name: Keith Lemon
Class: 5B

Student's strengths

Keith is very good at communicating with the class even though sometimes he doesn't seem to understand exactly what it is he's trying to communicate. He does need to concentrate more in class. It's good that he enjoys school but sometimes he enjoys it too much. If he put as much effort into his actual schoolwork as he does with the highly detailed sexy drawings he does in the back of his exercise books, he'll pass his GCSEs with flying colours. A lot of the time when our students struggle academically they excel in other areas. Unfortunately Keith doesn't. He is good at talking and drawing sexy pictures. I'm not really sure what the future holds for him.

What can the student do to improve?

As above, if he could pay more attention in class, I think he has the potential to be a satisfactory student. It would also help if he attended class a bit more.

Harlington High
Form teacher's report
Student's name: Keith Lemon
Class: 5B

Overall

Keith is a kind-hearted young man with a mind of his own. He doesn't like to listen and although he's not completely disruptive to class, he doesn't make it easy for any of our tutors either. Our female tutors, in particular, report that he seems to show off in their presence and is unable to concentrate. Saying that, if Keith knuckled down and didn't bask in the glory of being the class clown, he could do better. The one area where he really excels is art, especially when it comes to the female form.

LAST DAYS AT SCHOOL

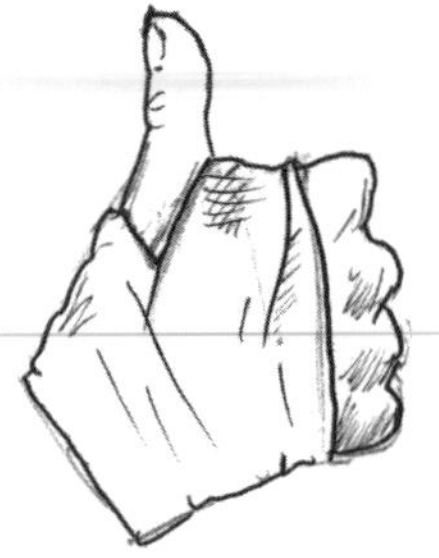

Our last week at school was really fun. We had all finished our exams and hadn't yet had our results so we could just mess about. I was excited cos as much as I enjoyed school whilst I was there, it seemed like the start of adulthood. Our Greg went on t' further education. He's got a lot of qualifications. I don't know what for. It's like he just likes collecting degrees. I'm sure he'll do somet really good one day. He's got a good job now I fink but I don't know what he does. Somet with t' ozone layer I fink. I din't know we still had one. Nobody talks about it anymore do they? They always use to go on about it on John Craven's *Newsround* don't they, saying we're gonna fuck it up if we use hairspray. It must've healed.

I remember the day we got our exam results. I'm not gonna embarrass meself and tell ya what I came out with but the brainiest kid in't school only came out with four GSCEs. And he was brainy as fuck. He were like a scientist, he could've built a time machine that bastard. I fink the marking system must've been defunked back then. Fink it was only the second yeah or so that they'd being doing GSCEs. It don't matter, I've never needed 'em anyway. That's not to say anyone young that's reading these should just fuck about at school and come out with nowt though. Anywhere, I cun't wait t' get a proper job and have some proper money. I wan't sad that I wasn't gonna see me mates again cos I never thought that were gonna be t' case.

It's only now that I miss 'em. Cos I don't see 'em as much now. But we're all still in touch.

When I left school they din't have one of those Yearbook fings like they have in American teen movies, but I always liked the idea of one. So over the page is me virtual Yearbook – what might've been if they had've been.

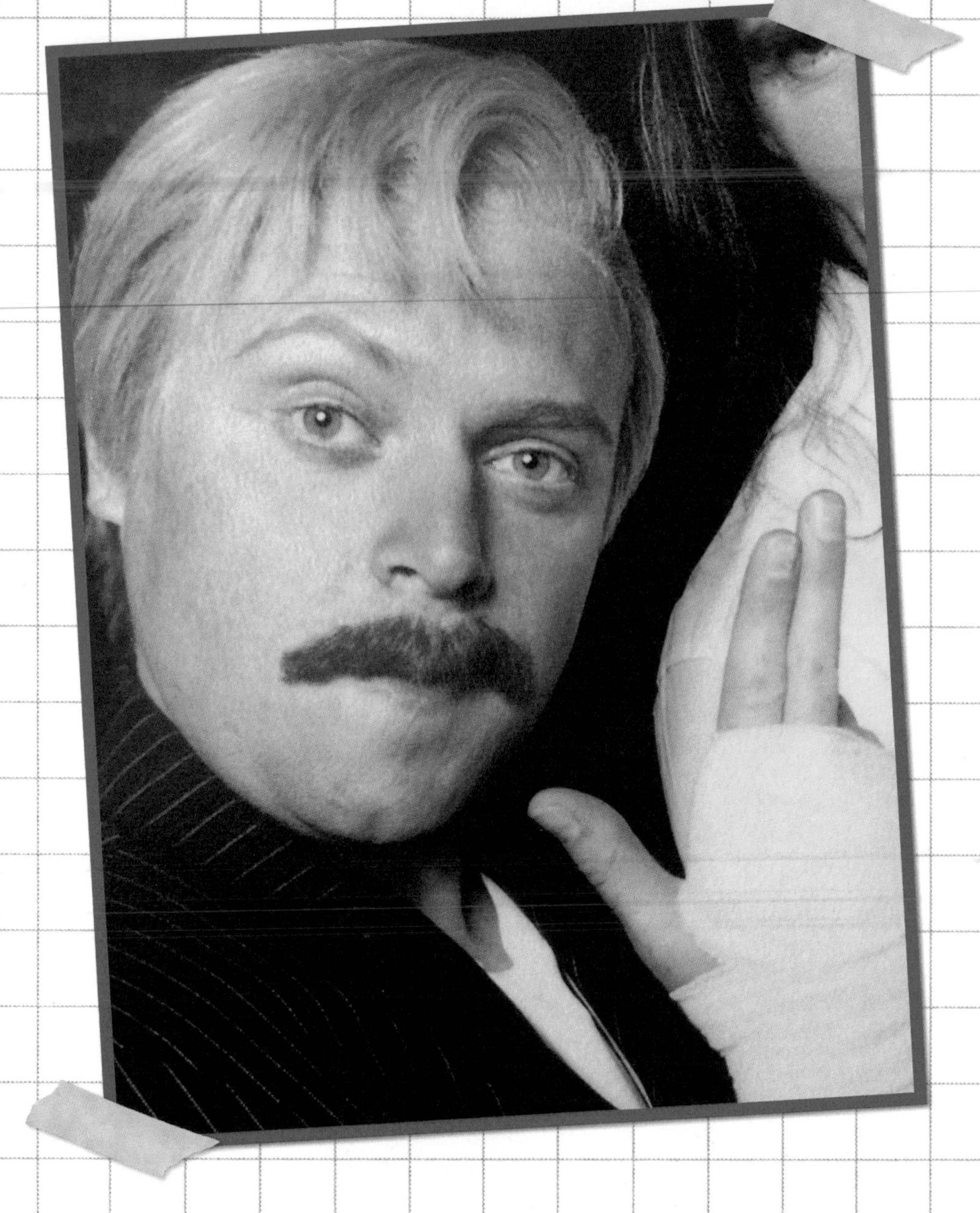

KEITH LEMON YEAR BOOK 1992

Well, what a great time we had! We din't learn too much. But we had fun and copped a feel of some of the birds from the school opposite. Sometimes, whilst learning nowt and looking at the girls playing netball in t' other school outta the window, I wished that our school was mixed. But I'm sure I'd be a dad by now if that were the case so maybe it was a blessing. Maybe I am a dad. I've had a few experience where me welly has ripped while I've been paddling but always prideded meself on having the ability to pull out at the right time.

Most of us will probably go on to have boring jobs but one day I'm probably gonna have me own company and you'll go on Facebook and tell people ya went to school with me. I'll message ya back and I'll say 'yeah I went t' school with ya and din't we have a great time', whilst all along I'll be finking 'cor, you've put some timber on.' By now I'm probably the boss of Securipole which is gonna revolutionise urban car protection in a way than equals what Playstation did to the games console or what the crab stick did to the fish food industry. Good luck t' all I went t' school with, I hope ya wife is fit and you've got a good job. Remember if ya can dream it, ya can lie about.

PS. *Facebook doesn't exist yet but if ya don't know what it is, let me tell you what it is, is a social network fing where ya can look up ya old birds and see if they're still fit or turned fat.*

Cheers!
Keith Lemon

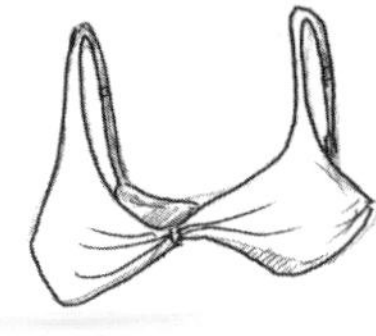

THE LEEDS BOYS GO TO KAVOS!

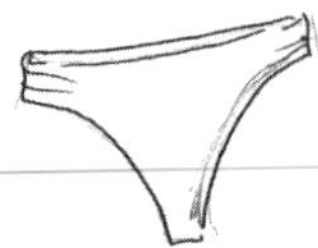

After me GCSEs, I were keen to get out into t' world and start making a name for meself. But first things first, we were gonna go on our first proper lads' holiday. To Kavos. Ay up Kavos! The Leeds boys are in town! We were staying in this mint hotel by the beach. Belly just kept going round getting photographs of him with random lasses in bikinis. But the only people he were showing these photographs to were us and we knew that he hadn't shagged any of 'em. You can't go, 'look, shagged her on holiday . . . shagged her on holiday. . .' We were with you! You can't just get a picture. I fink it were for his wankboard at home.

I went on holiday with Belly again recently and he's still doing the same thing! Taking photographs of fings. We got kicked out of a nightclub for him taking photographs of girls cos it was a bit more upmarket nightclub and they got a beef on about it. They kicked us out. We din't know we were getting kicked out at the time. They just said, 'gentleman, would you like to come over here.' We thought we were getting VIP treatment and then we looked back, and we're outside.

Anywhere, it were a wicked holiday. It were ace. It was sunny all the time. And all the women are pissed. It were incredible. We went on one of those paragliding things that hurts your middle bits.

I didn't go on a banana boat and that's one of me biggest regrets in life that I didn't go on a banana boat that holiday. I don't know what I were finking. You get to straddle girls in their bikinis and act the hero when they get thrown in. I was made for it! I remember we went on a boat trip to some other part of the island with the old town and it was shit. 'I fink we should go to old town . . .' 'Really?' 'Yeah,' 'Ok.' But it's old. It's shit.

I can remember when we first got there, we went out too early. We went out at about six o'clock, cos we were so excited. Nobody was out! We realised on about the third night that no one goes out till about 10, by which point we were already a bottle of Malibu down. We were like, 'hey, it's a bit dead, innit?' And by the time it got busy we were all so drunk and couldn't even walk. It were hard because we were used to drinking before you go out so it's a cheaper night, innit?

The only problem for me were that I were going out with Becky at the time. Now you don't want to go on a holiday like that and have a girlfriend. The two things just don't go together. I mean, I did all the right stuff. I even sent her a postcard:

I'll have to tell you what it said because you can't see what it said now that I've stuck it in:

Dear Becky
Having a shit time in Kavos. Got asked to partake in a 3some with Frank. But said no. These two other girls wanted me to have a 3some and I said no. The idea of a threesome makes me sick unless it were two of you. Can't wait to see you. I hope you understand I only came here to make Dave feel better because his dad died. And now I am going to have to stay an extra week to make him feel better. Sorry, this is the only postcard I could find.
Love you.
Love Keith.

I was having such a great time, I stayed an extra week. Dave's dad isn't dead. He were off work and slipped a disc. It would've broke her heart if I had told her though and I were too young for this type of commitment. And at least I had sent her a postcard. To be honest, I were excited to see if the postcard even got to her. Whenever I have posted somet from abroad, I always fink, 'it's never gonna get there' and when it does you can't believe it can you! I get lost in the airport so how does it get there?

YOU'VE GOT TO HAVE A THREESOME

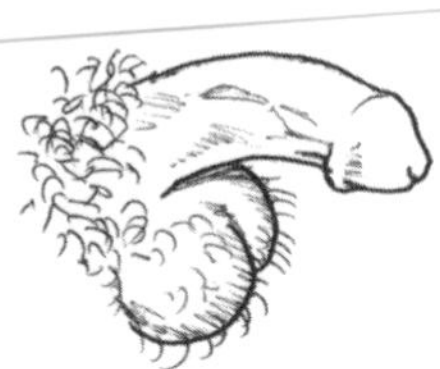

Anywhere, back to Kavos. You've got to have had a threesome in life, haven't yer? It's one of those boxes you've just got to tick. I mean, only just to tell your mates. Obviously, if you were mature enough you wouldn't do it because you wouldn't rush into somet you didn't necessarily want to do, but you *are* rushing because you don't want to be left behind. If someone else has done summat you don't want to be left behind, so you all want to fuck and suck and lick and whatever else just so you can say you've done it and know what people are talking about when they give it all the chat at school.

It did feel a bit weird having sex with Frank there, especially when your knob touches his. More recently, I've done it with two girls, which is better. But when your knob touches another man's knob by accident, it is like you are in a Willliam Shatner nightmare, it is like the whole world goes wonky and wobbly. You can get an instant flop on. Like two swords moving around and then there is an instant reaction when another man's knob touches yours and it goes flaccid and it is over. It is very similar to using a public toilet. You don't really enjoy the woman as much as you are looking at the ceiling most of the time as you don't want to be looking into the other guy's eyes. But I were glad to have ticked the box.

One box I have never ticked is having me arsehole licked. I have never had my arsehole licked and I have never licked anyone else's arsehole. I am a bit scared. What if she has a smelly bum? What if she is super fit and she has a smelly bum, you'd go off her wouldn't you? I remember when Becky tried to stick her finger up me arse. It were the time when you heard rumours of sexual exploits and you'd try everything out just to say you'd done it but she tried to stick her finger up there and I could have snapped her finger off. 'Eh? What are you doing? That is a deposit box only. I don't need to go up there, so you don't need to either. It is a drop-off zone, you can't put money into it, you just get money out of it.'

I find quite a few of me fans want to stick their fingers up me arse. The older the fans, the dirtier they are. They are always trying to get their fingers up there, it's weird. I don't know what it is this obsession with arseholes. I know that an arse looks right nice from a distance but when you get up close, all you can see is this star, a tight little star. Further back, an arse is nice but close up it is like a brown space door.

SECURIPOLE

After I got back from Kavos, I knew I had to find meself a job. Me experience on the market had taught me that my skills would be best utilised as a businessman. I had a couple of other options at the time. Because of me breakdancing skills, I had got meself noticed on dance floors across Leeds. Me moves were basically a mating call. I sometimes used to mix it up a bit and do a bit of Russian Cossack dancing. I fink the girls were impressed by my athletic ability. You have to be careful though because your legs ache like bastards the next day. The other option is to just do a body shake. The closer you get to the girl, the sexier it is. I've copped off with many girls like this.

Anywhere, as I were saying, me dancing was getting me noticed across Leeds and further afield and I was asked to take part in an audition for a new pop group. When I got there, I was standing in front of Steps. They were looking for an extra member and they thought I were the man for the part. I wowed them with me dancing and I could sing right good too. They were desperate for me to be a part of the group but I didn't want to wear that yellow outfit – I'd look like a fisherman. So I turned it down.

The only thing that made me fink twice were that Claire. She were a right one. She has that same bunny rabbit nose that Emma Bunton has. Dead cute.

But as I say, I discovered I wanted to be a businessman so I set up Securipole. I found a load of poles in a skip. I don't fink that is stealing, I just thought 'I will have

Be a robbing bastards bone of contention with a 'Securipole' right now!

Our prices range from high to low. So don't worry. Call us now for a FREE! Quotation on

0113 777 777 8900000

There is almost no obligation and before you know your car could be being protected with a pole.

Choose from a variety of styles and prices from just a few of our recommended models below. Spoil yourself it's my treat!

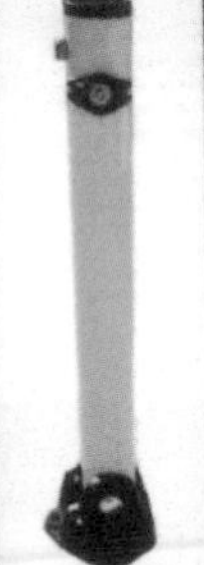

Securipole Bruce Lee PPFWL - Orders 10 to 25 off (Reference #198)

Fold down parking post in yellow finish. Height 63cm.

Built-in top locking tubular key cylinder. Right tough and light on it's feet.

Special discount for orders of 10 to 25 off.

Price : £85.00 £99.88 Including VAT at 17.5%

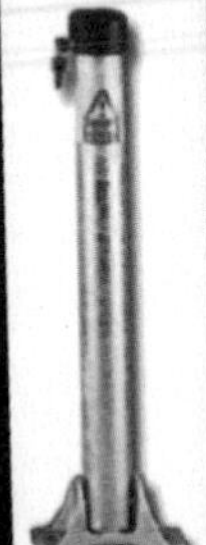

Securipole 'Predator' (Reference #215)

Secured by fitting a suitable padlock through the locking pin which is engaged at the base of the post. This pole will kick the crap out of any unwanted visitors. Galvanised finish is to B5729. Supplied c/w black polypropylene weather cap.

Price : £136.83 £160.78 Including VAT at 17.5%

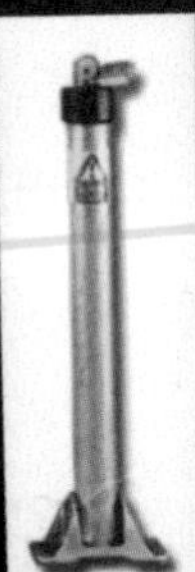

Securipole 'Terminator' (Reference #216)

Galvanised finish is to B5729. Supplied c/w black polypropylene wea cap. Socket flap closes flush to the ground. This mean mother has m aggression than a house brick in the hands drunken naughty man!

Price : £136.83 £160.78 Including VAT at 17.5

Securipole

for every man!

**ello my name is
eith Lemon, owner of
ecuripole'.**
ot deputy head, but full wner of the whole mpany. That's right I was impressed with ecuripole' I bought the mpany just like that man th the Remington thing. o why was I so pressed I hear you ask? ell, let me tell you if isn't vious for you to see just looking at the picture ljacent to this text. Many eople don't like it when stards thief their car,. at's right bastards! The ly word that can be used to describe these low lives. To a man his car is his castle on wheel's, a house that can be moved from A to B. So he wants to protect that house. With a 'Securipole'! What 'Securipole is a two-foot reinforced aluminium shaft installed in the driveway. It's so easy to use even a woman or a disabled person can use it. You'll be able to sleep at night knowing your car is safe like an hamster or indeed a budgie in a cage, or any other family pet, because it might sound daft, but a car is also like a family pet. I believe in this product so much I have two erections. One in my back passage and one up my front. It doesn't take a genius or a clever scientist to know that your car is going to be safer with a pole in front of it.

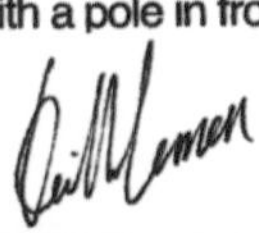

PECIFICATION:

ubular posts with top caps. All products strong welded steel construction with a eatherproof galvanised finish.

inged posts: mounted on base plate. Hinged with facility for padlock to lock in ither raised or lowered position. (Padlock not included) Either predrilled base plate ith 4 holes for bolting to the ground (surface fixing) or base plate with extension iece for concreting into the ground (submerged fixing). Post height 900mm. Overall eight 920mm, base plate size 150mm x 110mm. Also available in key lock versions etails on request.

emovable posts: socket for concreting into the ground with removable post. Socket as hinged top cap to cover when post not in position, also provides facility for padlock

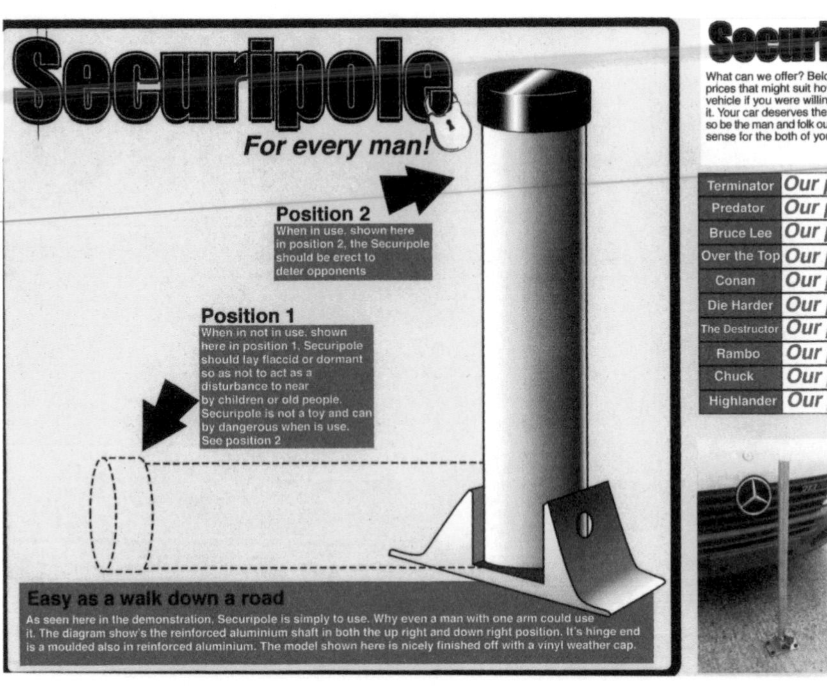
Securipole
For every man!
Position 2
When in use, shown here in position 2, the Securipole should be erect to deter opponents
Position 1
When in not in use, shown here in position 1, Securipole should lay flaccid or dormant so as not to act as a disturbance to near by children or old people. Securipole is not a toy and can by dangerous when is use. See position 2
Easy as a walk down a road
As seen here in the demonstration, Securipole is simply to use. Why even a man with one arm could use it. The diagram show's the reinforced aluminium shaft in both the up right and down right position. It's hinge end is a moulded also in reinforced aluminium. The model shown here is nicely finished off with a vinyl weather cap.
Securipole
What can we offer? Below are range of prices that might suit how you care for your vehicle if you were willing to put a price on it. Your car deserves the best a man can get so be the man and folk out! You know it makes sense for the both of you.
Terminator Our price $287.00
Predator Our price $185.00
Bruce Lee Our price $268.00
Over the Top Our price $185.00
Conan Our price $355.00
Die Harder Our price $345.00
The Destructor Our price $98.00
Rambo Our price $298.00
Chuck Our price $498.00
Highlander Our price $104.00

Mr Jones got a thing going on with...
Securipole
-Tom Jones 'My, my, my'
-Tamzin Outhwaite 'It's just what the east end needs'
-Will Young 'magnificent erection!'

them, I will be able to sell them.' If you don't know what a Securipole is, let me tell you what it is. It is a two-foot reinforced aluminium shaft you can have installed in your driveway to prevent evil scum buggers from stealing your car, or your auto moto vehicle as scientists call them.

The skills I learnt on the market came in useful as selling anything on a market is quite similar to door-to-door selling, which is how I first started selling the Securipoles. Obviously, I didn't shout when I knocked on someone's door:

'Would you like to buy a Securipole? The finest Securipoles are here.'

You say it, but it is similar communication skills. I connect with people. The phone number was on the parking posts so that whenever people saw them and thought 'I need to get me one of those reinforced aluminium parking posts to protect my auto moto vehicle from being nicked by evil scum buggers' they could call us up and order one. That is marketing. I came up with the name Securipole which I thought were genius. They were poles that kept your car secure. Securipoles. I remember getting done by some sort of trading standards thing because my slogan was 'It is scientifically proven that gyppos like your car more than you do. Get a Securipole'. It doesn't rhyme, but that is why it made you fink more: 'You know what, I should watch out'. We take fings for granted, and we shouldn't.

SPLASHING THE CASH

It was nice to have some proper money and say to girls, 'I've got me own business.' I fink the ladies were always quite impressed when I handed them me business card with a wink. Better than writing your phone number on a cigarette paper, in't it? My card was one of the first cards to be made out of sperspex. I don't know if you remember that trend? Instead of a paper business card, for Securipole we had nice clear sperspex ones.

I didn't actually drive meself when I first started the business. I was selling security for your car but I didn't have a car meself. It din't take me long to save up enough cash to buy one though. Me first car was a red Escort. It was really eyecatching and a bit of a minge magnet.

Anyway, for me services to Securipole, I was awarded the Northern Business Man of the Year and that is when me business life as an entrepreneur all got a bit more interesting. I suppose winning Business Man of the Year at such a young age kind of confirmed I was special and having the initiative to sort meself out. I'm not working for someone. I'll set up me own shit and sell parking posts. You had to be nominated to enter the competition so I nominated meself. I don't fink people do that enough. Why not? All you have to do is enter yourself under a different name. So the Northern Business Man of the Year panel had a letter from Denzel Murgatroyd saying 'Keith Lemon's the best. His reinforced parking posts are beyond compare. He has grown his business one post at a time and he looks set to be the Richard Branson of the Leeds parking world.'

Then I had to go for an interview at Leeds Town Hall with a board of judges. I used half a bottle of the Paco Rabanne before that and put on me best linen suit. It did the trick and I cun't believe it when I won. I entered as a bit of a laugh. And I won! I won! I was on t' *Calendar* as well, which is the Leeds TV news. It were basically like going on *This Morning* with Holly and Phil, though not quite as good as there were no Holly and there were no Phil, who are two of me favourite people. Holly and her massive bangers. She's a lovely bird. Drinks like a tramp. Uncle Phil has still got it. His hair is silver but his pubes are as black as a raven's wing. I love it when he comes on *Juice*. The second time he were on it were one of our most-watched episodes of all time. He told us a story about one guest who came on to *This Morning* who showed him and Holly her minge all the way through t' interview. Ooooosh!

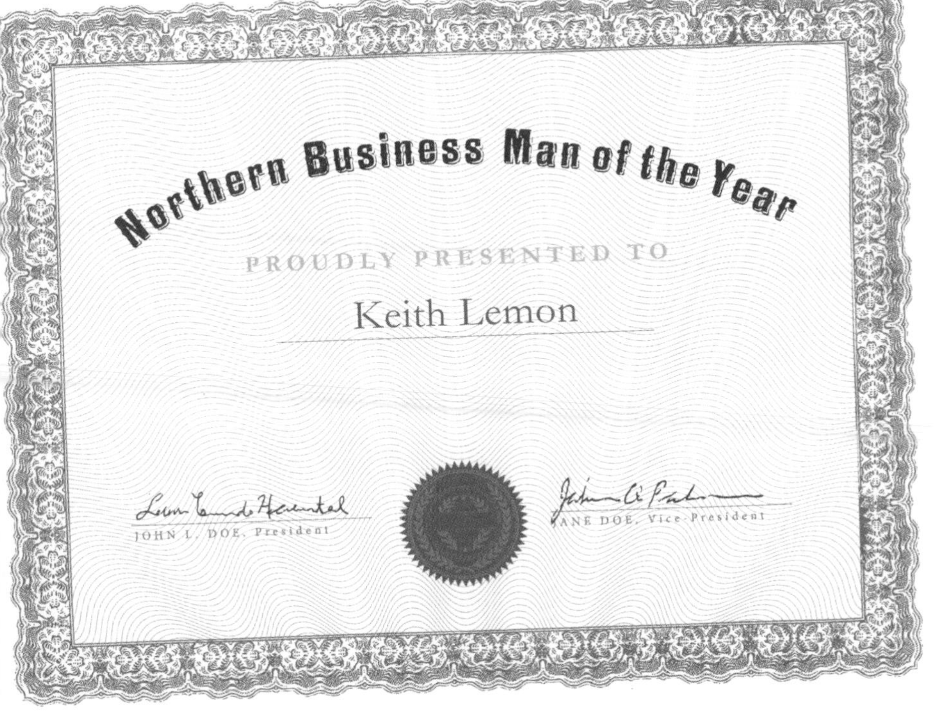

Northern Business Man of the Year
PROUDLY PRESENTED TO
Keith Lemon
JOHN L. DOE, President
JANE DOE, Vice-President

I weren't doing anything like that on *Calendar* but I guess they wanted a bit of totty in front of the camera so that must've helped. I even crossed paths with the late, great Richard Whiteley. What a hero! I were really excited because I thought I might get to meet Carol Vorderman as well. I like Carol Vorderman. She's saucy. She is bang tidy. After she saw me in me pants on *Loose Women* I sent her a text every day with me in me pants. Not me face, just my panted area. I stopped after seven days as you can have too much of a good thing, I fink. It's like blowjobs. They should only be granted as a treat.

What I find mad about Carol Vordeman is that she likes numbers. That woman likes maths. There's somet not right there. The only thing I remember about me maths lessons was the teacher saying, 'now bring down an extra nought.' I couldn't understand that concept of bringing a number down. 'What you on about? An extra nought? Where do I get that from?' And why is it cheating to use a calculator? It's like saying 'Did you write all that by hand with a pen?' 'No, I did it on the computer.' 'Well, you need to do it with a pen.' It's all bollocks. Sorry Carol.

To celebrate me being crowned Northern Business Man of the Year, me and a group of me mates went to Amsterdam. It's a right funny old place. Belly were in his element, walking up and down the red light district, looking at the ladies and taking photos. He couldn't afford to actually go in. He were a virgin so he were desperate to get laid. So we all put our hands in our pockets and bought him a treat. As we'd never been to Amsterdam before and none of us knew how long you're supposed to be with a prostitute or what

happens even, other than the obvious, we were waiting for ages and thought, effing hell, there's somet going on, there's somet wrong with him, what's going on? And then the lady came out and said 'your friend wants more time.' Cheeky bastard! I actually got so sick to death of sex. It cancelled itself out. In the end we just went to the pub. But you couldn't even get away from it in the pub! Right behind the bar, there were a huge telly showing a big tallywhacker coming out of a hole it shouldn't be coming out of and when I blinked all I could see was that wide-open hole. It were like when you have a photograph taken and you get a green dot in your eye every time you blink … all I could see was a wide open hole. I fink we were all ready to go home after that. We din't even have any space cakes!

TWENTY-ONE AT LAST

I never thought I would make it to twenty-one. I always thought I would get run over. I was too carefree. I remember when I did make it to twenty-one and I thought 'ace, now I can have arse sex.' But now that I have had arse sex, I'm not sure it is that big a deal. I know on *Celebrity Juice* I talk about smashing a lady's back doors in but that's all bravado. I'm quite a sensitive guy really. I just haven't found love yet, but I'd like to. I'm not the dickhead I was when I was younger, only when I'm pissed up. I'm probably a good catch. I have many TVs and a soda stream!

When we were growing up, you had to do everything and then tell your mates about it. It were like a tick box thing. And I'm not talking about doing any number ones or number twos on anyone, that's just gross and dirty. 'I like you, can I do me toilet on you?' What's that about? It's mental! Belly went out with a bird who was in to that stuff but only in the bath so she could wash it off afterwards! He weren't so sure about it but out of manners he returned the favour. That's right weird that.

Anywhere, now that I'm here and I've passed the twenty-one mark, I have started to get a bit philosophical about life. I fink me mates are proud of what I've done. At school, they were obviously really jealous of me as I was right good looking. But you can't help it if you were born that way. It is like that woman on *I'm a Celebrity Get Me Out of Here*, Amy Willington. They all hated her because she was

F.A.F but I met her and she was right nice. I'd let her kick the crap out of me.

Looking back I don't fink I'd have done anyfing differently. Maybe I'd have timed it so that when I met Fearne Cotton I'd have been single, and who knows, instead of marrying Jesse Wood she may have got lucky and married me. He's a lovely bloke though. I'm so happy for her. I even cried at her wedding – I've obviously been hanging out with our Greg too much. Of course, there's been a few ladies out there that now looking back I've thought maybe there was somefing special there but I just din't realise it at the time. For an example, I should have at least had a go on Kelly Brook's bangers. She's another one that's gonna be married soon, or she might already be by t' time this comes out. Sometimes I worry I am just gonna be left on't shelves. Ha, ha, ha do I fuck. I'm a right fanny magnet at the moment!

Anyway if you can't be bothered to read the whole book, here's a little summary of what I got up to. Then you can just look at the pictures.

BIRTH TO TWO YEARS OLD

Once me neck muscles had developed so I din't have a floppy head, I became more interesting. I crapped and pissed meself a lot cos I din't know what I was doing cos I was a baby. Imagine if Holly Willoughbooby was yer mam. Feeding time would've been a totally different experience!

tv choice
Daz

TWO TO FIVE YEARS OLD

I was a little shite. I was naughty cos I din't know right from wrong. I was frustrated cos I cun't talk properly until I was four. My first words were minge and biscuit. But minge weren't a word for a lady's love hole back then, it meant yer face. Anywhere once I started talking I couldn't stop. And that's not all I couldn't stop, I were constantly tugging at me willy. It was me best friend. I fink that's why it's so big today. Yer know like how you talk to plants and they're supposed to grow? Well I din't talk to it but I nurtured it with me hands a lot. And I mean a lot!

FIVE TO TEN YEARS OLD

I grew up pretty fast. Between five and ten, I'd gone through t' playing with toys stage to having a sexually active brain. I was fascinated with women. Loved 'em. I had no control of me willy. It kept going straight. Not fully up, but straight out like it was pointing at girls. I often sat with a cushion on me lap.

TEN TO SIXTEEN YEARS OLD

I'd had many sexual experiences by this stage, including with me teacher Miss Birdmuff who taught me a thing or two about how to pleasure a female. I grew a full complete set of pubes – armpits and knob hairs, and a moustache. I had a constant erection, which I tamed with my seven a day. I was like a walking coat hanger.

I were a breakdancing champion and am still pulling those moves to impress the birds to this day. Must have got the dancing jeans from me dad Billy Ocean.

SIXTEEN TO TWENTY YEARS OLD

By the time I were sixteen, I could totally control me penis. I owned it, it din't own me, and I liked using it. I thought I knew everything about t' world. I was a proper man's end! Had me first holiday with the lads to Kavos, which led to me first threesome. Me girlfriend Becky weren't too pleased when she found out about it but she were getting too clingy. And I sent her a postcard, what more did she want!

After selling jeans on Leeds market (they were right good ones – Rhino jeans – really strong in the happy area), I set up me own business selling Securipoles: two-foot aluminium shafts to install on your driveway. They were right tough and protected cars all across Leeds, and so easy to use that even a woman could use it. I was crowned Northern Business Man of the Year as a result and I got to go on Calendar and meet the bang tidy Carol Vordeman. Shaaaa-ting!

And that is where this book ends, and the first book *Being Keith* begins. So go and read that one. If you don't know what it looks like, here's what it looks like . . .

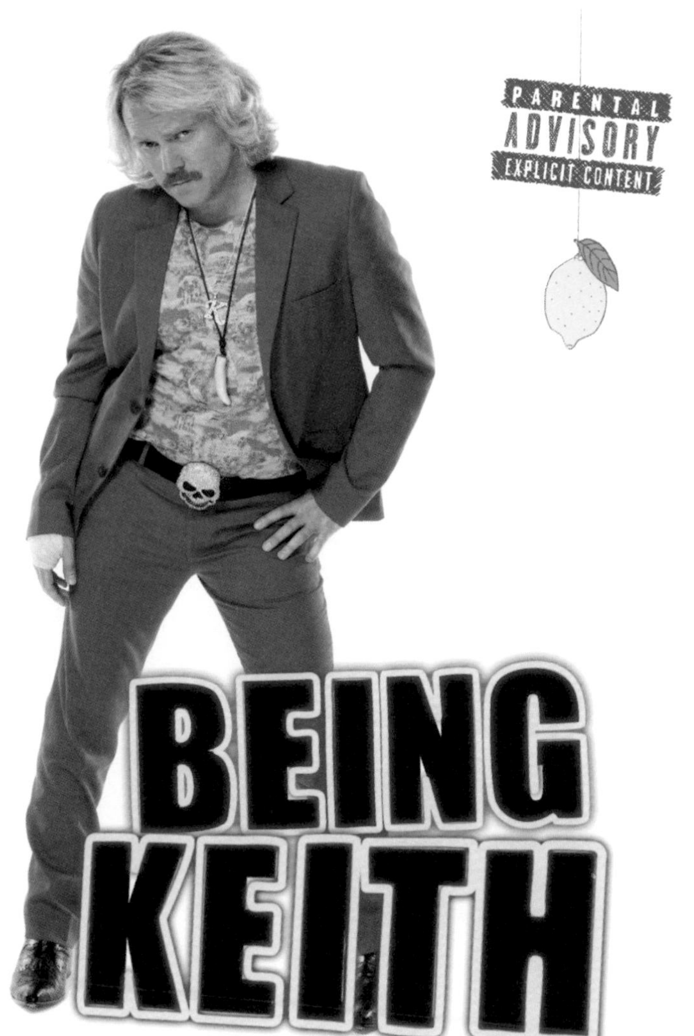

How I Got 'Ere
If you Dont Know How
I Got 'Ere

LOOKING BACK

As a rule I don't have any regrets. Shit happens, and shit hits the fan, and shit comes out of yer bum and what do I do with it? I flush it away! Oooosh!

I often get asked if I have any advice for the younger generations and if there is one fing me mam taught me that will stay with me forever it is this: Always wear yer wellies if you go paddling – and obviously by wellies she meant rubber jonnies. I've only ever had unprotected sex about twenty-two times but I've been lucky, touch wood. I ain't got wood, I'm sat at a computer writing this! But I've been lucky that anyfing that has touched me wood hasn't given me any STD fings. There may be a few mini Keiths out there but if they come forward I'll go on Jeremy Kylie and do a DMA test and if I am the father I'll do the right fing and send 'em twenty quid a week.

I do wish I had all the knowledge I had now as a kid. But I would've been even more of a cheeky little bastard. Not cocky, just cheeky. It's always strange peoples' perceptions of 'celebrity' (it's getting a bit deep this in't it) people always fink yer minted, but I was doing ok before telly with the Securipoles. I had me own business. But being rich in't about having wedges of coin. It's about happiness I fink. I've always been happy. I fink that's why I look so young cos I've got a positive outlook. Negativity just ages yer. I have a very young and playful nature. Of course I wake up in a bad mood sometimes, just like everyone else, but I'll pump fist, have a shit and a shower, put some mousse in me barnet and scrunch it so it looks like Michael Hutchence, put some stylish clobber on and

I'll fink about what I've got on that day work-wise and I feel overwhelmed with happiness. I never wake up and fink I'm not funny anymore. I don't really set out t' be funny. I set out t' have fun!

T' quote Ferris Bueller: 'Life moves pretty fast. If you don't stop and look around once in a while you could miss it'. I remember the first time I heard that and it stuck with me. That's why I always try and enjoy meself and live in the moment of that enjoyment. Like when yer having it off or copping a feel of some fit bird's boobs. I cherish these moments.

I try to just live in that moment. For everything whether it is a recording *Celebrity Juice*, or *Through t' Keyhole* or what have yer. I always remember Dan the producer of *Juice* (and Holly's husband) asking me before I went on stage, do I ever worry that I'm not gonna be funny … And I told him, no, cos I don't try be funny. I just do t' job and proper enjoy meself and I fink that's why *Juice* has been a success, cos people enjoy watching us enjoy ourselves.

Sorry I've lost me train of thought. I just popped t' bog t' scrape me hand bag out. I won't eat that again. Oooft! I ate some prawns last night and I fink I got food poisoning from it. Look at me eating prawns! You see, that shows how far I've come! I never thought the day would come when I'd be putting a prawn in me gob, a little pink thing with legs and a pair of black eyes. I must've caught posh. I even buy me bread from M&S. I haven't changed though. And Belly, Pisshole or any of the lads will tell yer that. I still tell fibs about me age, take too long looking in t' mirror, get a bit drunk and cry at girlie films. I love me mum and our Gregory and try t' give back t' people less fortunate than meself,

I'm nice like that. I'm still little Keith Lemon, but I've said it before and I 'll say it again, I'm thick as a Coke can.

It could've been a big gamble throwing away what I already had t' come down t' big smoke. But t' quote George McFly, Marty McFly's dad, 'if yer put yer mind to it yer can achieve anything' and I fink that's true.

I was a big fish in a small pond, then a small fish in a big pond, and now I'm riding this telly wave until I fall off. Cos I could do. I could fall of and land right on me bollox.

Right I'll send this t' me publisher, who by the way has the hots for me. Unfortunately for her I'm seeing some fit French bird at the moment. Can't tell what she's talking about but she looks good on all fours.

If I don't see ya through t' week. I'll see ya in me next book.

To be continued . . . maybe, we'll see.

All t' best,
Big Keith Lemon

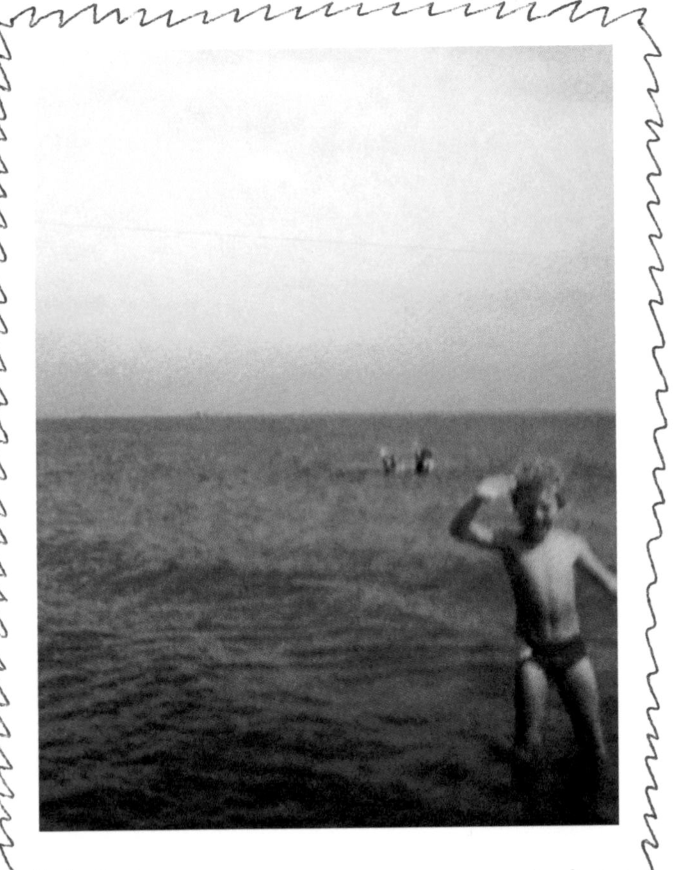

FANKS!

Fanks to all the people that have been nice to me.

Fanks to all me school mates that took part in me life. You know ya names, well ya don't as the names have been changed to protect the innocent.

Fanks t' me mam and dad, and our Greg.

Fanks t' me agent who's fit and me publisher who's also fit. Fanks to everyone at Orion for helping produce this book.

Fanks t' me stylist Heather and me make-up lady Emma. There's a few Emmas I wanna fank actually so fanks to all of them.

Fanks t' all t' people that helped me meck the telly programs I meck. Dan and Leon, Dan and Jamie, Chappers, Arron, both of them! Meriel, erm ... Joe, Pete, Roy, Paul, James, Ben, Spenny.

Big ups t' Mrs F and the kids! Yeah boi. Fanks for all ya support.

Big ups t' twitter kids, pacifically Ann!

Shout out to everyone at me school, Leeds Market, and Leeds – the whole of Leeds generally.

Fanks t' Keith who's also called Keith and the other Keith (sound man).

Fanks t' all me mates that I hang out with now – the celeb ones and the real ones.

Big ups t' ITV and ITV2 and the other channels that I've been on.

Shout out t' Hooch, adidas and Nandos.

Fanks to everyone who's inspired me but mostly A BIG FANKS TO YOU for buying this book. Ya din't have to but ya did, and I fank you from the bottom of me heart.

If I don't see you though t' week, I'll see you through t' window!

Cheers!

THE IN-BETWEEN CHAPTER

How do!

Well here I am again. It's that all important crossover from one book t' next. I don't know whose idea it was to put both me books together with extra chapters, but it was a goodun! Like 'the selfie stick' fing.

I was doing a book signing of *Little Keith Lemon* in Manchester I fink it was, and someone kindly gave me one, not 'one' as in 'gave me one' but one as in a 'selfie stick' fing. I thought it was incredible! I'd never seen one before. I must've been lost in work when they first came out cos usually I'm all over that shit boi! But, yeah, they're a great idea – like combining both *Little Keith Lemon* and *Being Keith*, with extra stuff! Even though this is an extra chapter I'm not really counting it as a chapter. Like I say, this is just a crossover fing before we go in't next book. So let me start by saying I hope you enjoyed the first part of me 'big one' (I fink that's what we're calling this). As I'm writing this there isn't a definite title for it yet but I fink its gonna be called *Keith Lemon's Big One*. If it is called that then all this chat is a waste of time and I'll just get on with it. I like to write in real time. Same with telly, I don't really sit down and write much. I have a view beers and just get on stage. Especially with *Juice*. *The Keith Lemon Sketch Show* is all proper written scripted stuff. It's a bit like doing homework, but laughing whilst ya do it.

So yeah, anyway, I had a childhood. As ya can see I was a pretty normal kid despite people's popular misconceptions of me. I suppose telly has had an effect on me. Not in the sense that I've become a diva and gone up me arse as I'm far from that. I mean that it's given me a licence to be as flamboyant as I want and as daft as I want. It's like it's me job to do so. People often say, 'I saw you on *Juice* t' other week, I don't know how ya get away with it.' I guess I get away with some of the shit I say or do because I don't really mean it with any malice and I'm in a domain I can do what I like really. I wun't say half the shit I say t' Fearne on telly in real life, I'm just joking. I love her really. As a mother she's really grown into a woman. I use to fink she had a dick. But she can't have cos she's got baby Rex now. Right happy for her. And Holly has three now. Crazy! She's very gifted at bearing children. Her bangers go massive too! Lovely woman.

Just gonna stop there for a bit and have a fink. Cos I don't really know where I'm going with this 'in-between chapter'. Let me have a look where I left off in t' first book and started on't second, even though the second book comes first in this 'big one'. Confusing in't it? Well it in't really, the second book was obviously a prequel t' first. We din't know how well the first one would do till it started selling enough to meck a second, d'ya get me?

It's like those *Star Wars* films in't it. Wasn't the first original *Star Wars* episode 6? Jeff Lucas din't know it were gonna be massive so that's why he brought those newer ones out that weren't as good. But they were never gonna be as good. When t' first ones came out I had no pubes and thought Chewbacca was real. As an adult I wanna watch deeper fings that I'm gonna get

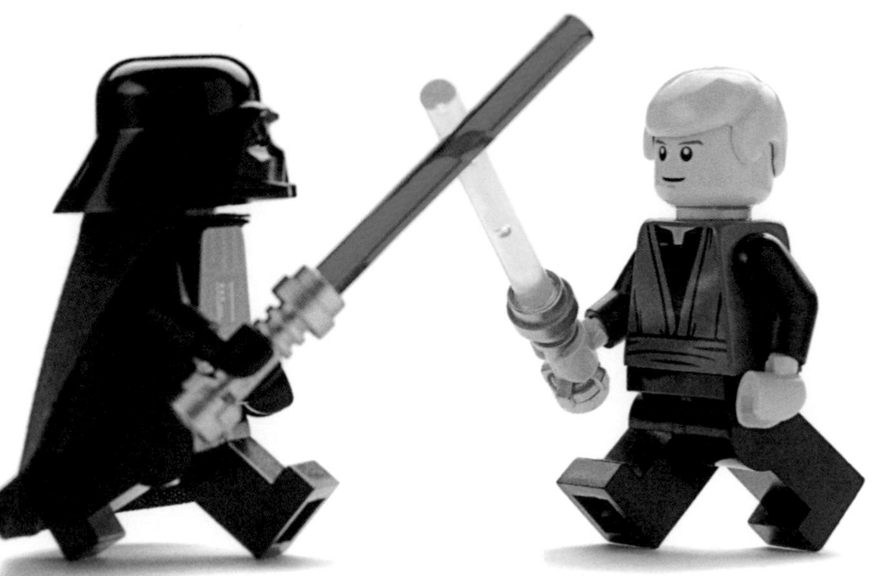

inspired by. Do I fuck! Give me *First Blood* any day. Love them *Star Wars* films! I tell ya what I've just seen – *Birdman*. By it were weird, and the sound track all t' way through was just drums. Did me tits in by t' end. Emma Stone's in it though! Not very gifted in the chest area but she's very fit. But I'm not just about tits me. I have honestly grown up a bit. I don't care about the size of a lady's tits. It's what's inside that counts, and as long as it's me that's inside then I'm happy! Oooooosh! Kidding.

No, but seriously I could go out with a munter if the conversation was insightful and I felt a connection. Saying that the lass I'm seeing at the mo, the conversation is very one-sided. She's French and can't tell a word I'm saying and I don't understand her either. But we do have a connection somehow. And she's fit as fuck! Brunette, like a cross between Kelly Brook and Michelle Keegan. Keegan and Mark Wright should be married by t' time this book is out. Massive congrats to 'em both! They meck a great couple. Both right down t' earth. Nice and very good-looking like me. See good-looking people can be nice! That given, you'll always get better chat from the less better-looking of a pair of twins or brothers or sisters, cos they've had to work harder at getting noticed, living in't shadow of the better-looking sibling.

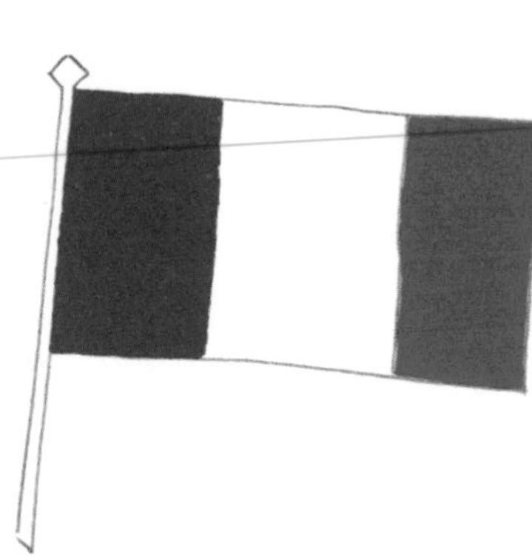

Let's have an example:

Nicole Kidman is fitter than her sister Antonia, but I bet Antonia is a better night out.

Victoria Beckham has got a sister. Louise. I bet she's dirtier in bed though! Ya can see it in her eyes. Naughty.

Penelope Cruz and her sister Monica. Both fit as fuck and would let 'em do a shit on me neck.

Beyoncé and her sister Solange literally had t' fight for the limelight. See it when she had a fracas with Jay Z. Christ on a bike. Gotta be careful what ya say around her. Allegedly Jay Z had just joked with Solange saying somet along the lines of 'Don't abuse the Nando's card, it's a privilege to have one.' She took it t' wrong way and thought he was insinuating she'd put a bit of timber on. That's what me mate Mad Paul told me anyway.

Just gonna turn t' light on. I'm sat in't dark here like a loon.

That's better. Right where were we? The crossover from little Keith to big Keith. Hold on . . . Right me dinner's ready. No doubt she'll have cooked up some 'French food'. Posh stuff!

We shall commence with this another day. What time is it? Ok signing out on Thursday January 8th 2015 (can't believe its 2015, will talk about that later), 4.25 p.m.

All t' best x

Ey up! I'm back. It's now Saturday January 24th 2015, 12.15 p.m. So it's been a little while since I wrote owt. Been busy winning at the National Television Awards, in't edit finishing me forthcoming sketch show which hopefully you will have seen by now and we maybe working on't second series, fingers crossed!

Funnily enough, the next part of the book starts two years ago when *Juice* won its first NTA. Was a great night, but not as great as our 2015 win. I'll pick up on that after *Being Keith*. By this is a smooth link, I'm like a Jamie Theakston of bookery. He does some smooth links on't radio does Jamie. Nice bloke and obviously works with a good mate of mine 'The Bunton' as in Emma as in 'Baby' Spice. Was her birthday party t' other night. What a night! Was wrecked the next morning though and had t' go t' me mate's young 'un's birthday party. By it was tough. So odd when I get recognised by kids. Especially when they say, 'Keith will ya smash me back doors in.' They obviously don't know what they're saying. I fink it's their mums talking via their kids asking me to smash their back doors in. I'm quite a hit with 'the mums'. And can I just say mums don't look like they use to when I was a kid. Just look at Kim Marsh! She is a mum! Fit as fuck! Proper silk! Definitely would let her do fings I've not let other women do to me. Like finger me bumhole. Well I've tried it but it din't feel right. Maybe you have t' be with the right person.

So let's commence to the second part of me 'big one'! See ya on t' otherside . . .

x

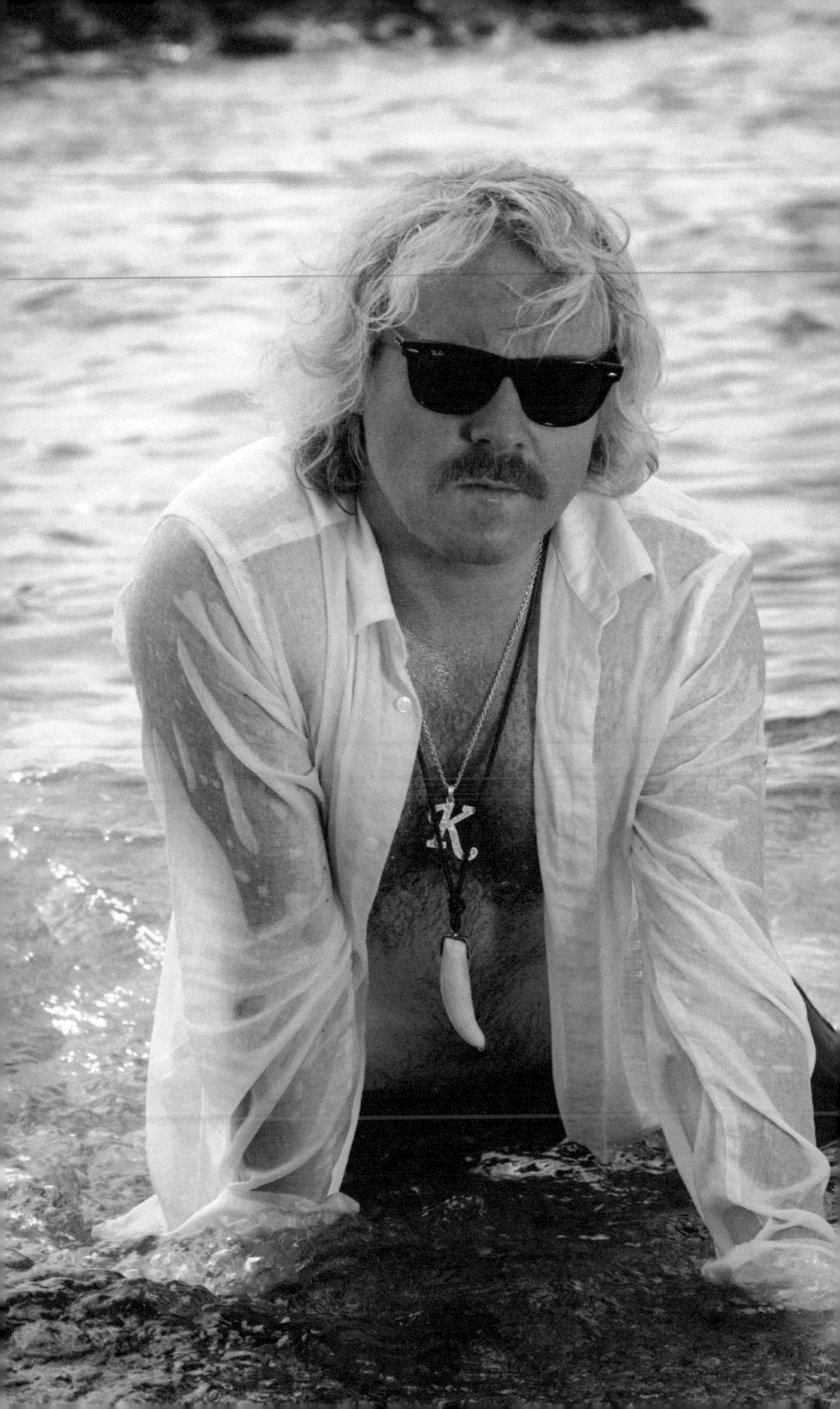

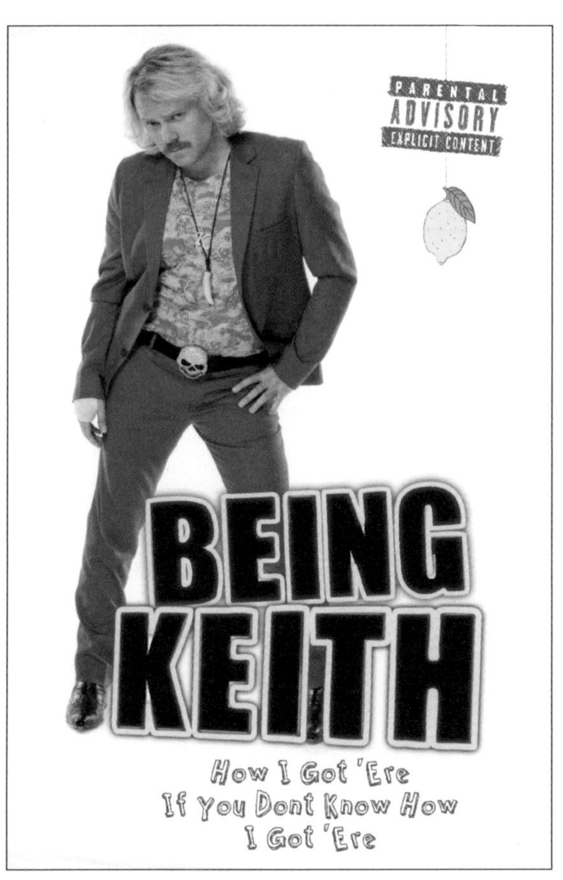
PARENTAL
ADVISORY
EXPLICIT CONTENT
BEING
KEITH
How I Got 'Ere
If you Dont Know How
I Got 'Ere

Contents

This book is
dedicated to the
Francis Household

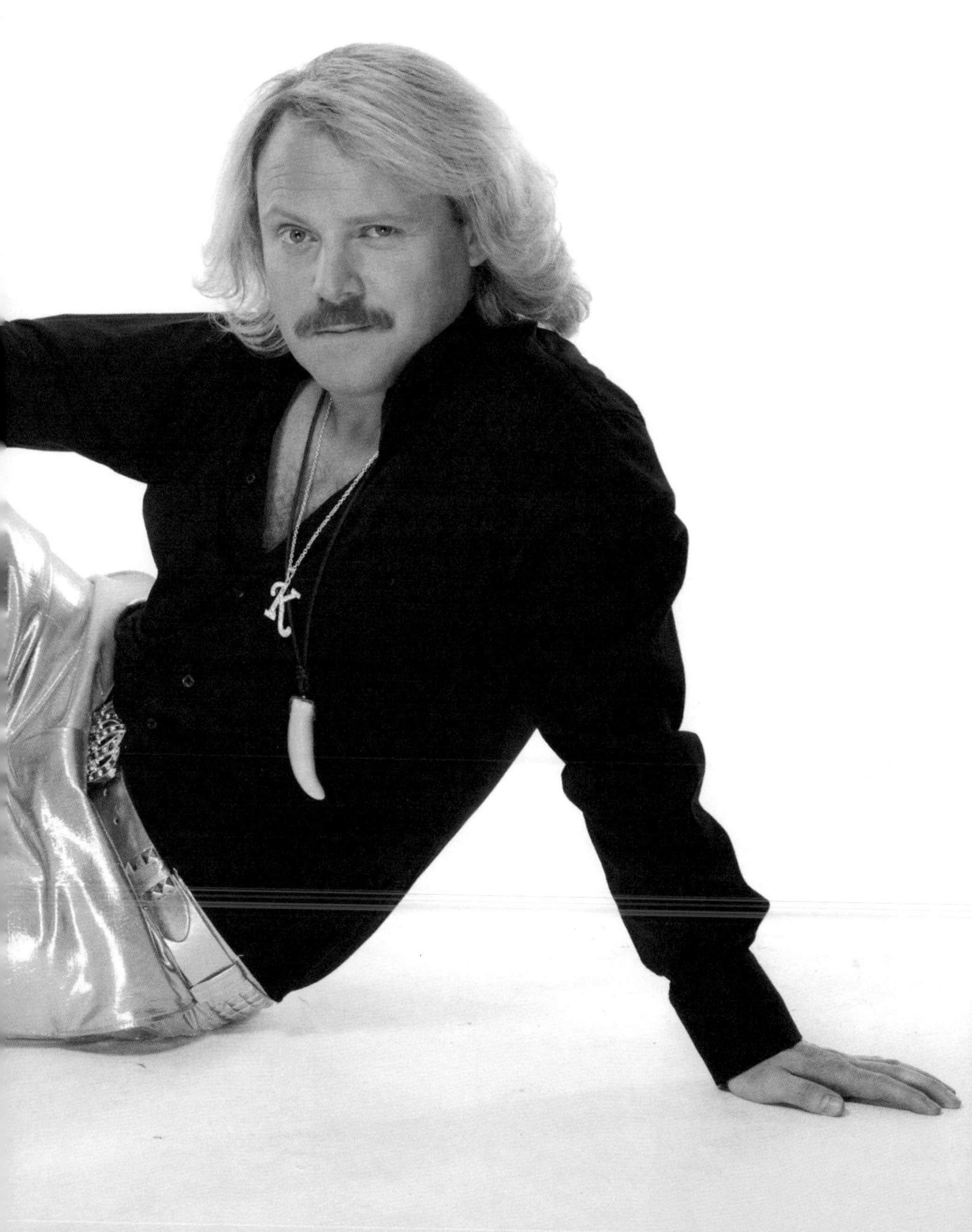

NTA
NATIONAL

Introduction fingy

Just got home from t' NTAs – the National Television Awards. It were the first time I've ever done t' red carpet with a girlfriend. I were quite proud when someone shouted they'd smash 'er back doors in. Rosie is lovely. She looks like a cross between someone from *Hollyoaks* and one of the fit nurses from *Casualty* and her out of t' *Office*.

Anywhere, it were a crazy night, though I were very nervous for some reason – which is very unlike me. It were a big do, like. Lovely to see Holly and Fearne. Holly's bangers looked as big as always and Fearne's nostrils looked even biggerer! We had a right laff. Fearne cudn't stop looking at me. There's no two ways about it. Fearne has got the hots for me and I fink Rosie could sense it. There were a moment of sexual rivalry in their eyes. I quite liked it to be honest.

F.A.F.

Anywhere, it comes to the category of Best Comedy Panel Show, the category we were up for ('we' as in *Celebrity Juice*). I had a feeling if the person that were presenting the award were somehow linked to the show, or a friend of mine, Holly's or Fearne's, then we might be in with a chance of winning. Would it be Rufus Hound? Cos he were nowhere to be seen.

Not sure where he were that night. Probably out with his prostitutes. He loves prostitutes! Just kidding, dingbats!

So, on walks Russell Kane, the lovely guy from *I'm a Celebrity Get Me Out of Here!* who looks like Jedward's older lesbian sister. I know Russell, he's a very funny, lovely man and has appeared on *Juice* a few times. This were all looking good. He called out the nominations.

'And the nominations are – *QI*, *Mock the Week*, *Have I Got News For You* and *Celebrity Jews*'. I fink he meant 'Juice'.

'And the winner is... *Celebrity Juice*!'.

I saw me face in t' corner of the screen looking nervous. I looked at Fearne and had sex with her three times in me mind, then looked at Rosie and had sex with her four times, including some oral and some stuff I better not say cos she don't like me talking about it. She's the one for me... For now anywhere, as Sam Faiers from *TOWIE* were sat a few seats away from me and her bangers were crying out for some TLC – Tender Lemon Cuddles. Anywhere, where was I?

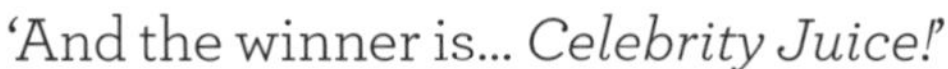
'And the winner is... *Celebrity Juice!*'

Shit me backwards, we'd won! After six series and lots of begging for votes on Twittor, we'd won t' big 'un. *Celebrity Juice,* a show on ITV2 on Thursdays at 10pm, were officially the Best Comedy Panel Show on telly. I were swallowed up in a vortex of joy (that sounds good, don't it?). I cudn't believe it. I were literally without belief. I dint even hug Rosie, which I fink I should've. (I did more than

SAM FAIERS

give her hugs when we got home that night though.) I jumped straight up for Fearne. Even though I give her a lot of grief on *Juice,* she's me mate and I do respect her a lot as a beautiful woman that has to carry those large nostrils on her face on a daily basis. Can't be easy for her. Then I hugged Dan, the executive producer of *Juice,* who is married to Holly (the spawny bastard), nuzzled into Holly's massive bangers and approached the stage.

I were overcome with joy and had to display me joy with t' power of dance. Dint have a clue what I were gonna say. I fought about me mam, me dad, me old school friends, me girlfriend Rosie sat in t' audience, the team. It were incredible. And what did I do? I sang two brief extracts from the songs 'When the Going Gets Tough' and 'Caribbean Queen' by Billy Ocean, who I often joke is me dad. But deep down it in't a joke. I honestly believe Billy Ocean is me dad. Ya can see it in both our eyes.

BILLY OCEAN IS ME DAD

Backstage at the NTAs were a total buzz, doing all those interviews and having the victory photoshoot. Mark Wright, another one from *TOWIE* seemed to crawl into our photo. *TOWIE* are like how So Solid Crew use to be. There's always one of 'em in ya peripheral vision as there's so many of 'em. They're like Gremlins!

Me, Holly and Fearne did a lot of laffing before I were whisked off back into me seat for another award that I were up for – Best Entertainment Presenter. God only knows how I got that nomination! Anywhere, Ant and Dec won it for the 11th year running and I were happy for 'em. I knew they were gonna win. I'm just lucky. I dint even know how I got 'ere. I were just riding a wave, being paid to mess about and have a laff. Now, if it were for somet like 'Best Hair', or 'Best Dressed Person' if they gave awards like that, I would've won, cos I looked Bang Tidy, even if I say so meself. But honestly, I find it hard to believe how I got 'ere. And if ya finking ya dint know how I got 'ere, well... 'ere's how I got 'ere...

I said I dint know how I got 'ere a lot then, dint I? Well, 'ere's how I got 'ere...

'Ere's how I got 'ere

I were invented in Leeds via me mam's womb. Anatomically gifted with a three-inch tally wacker, ya can only imagine how many inches I'm packing now. Said it before and I'll say it again, fick as a coke can.

I learn't nowt at school apart from how to control the mind of the female to convince 'em to do almost anyfing ya like. I'm not talking about getting her to cook for ya or do the cleaning and stuff as I'm metrosexually that way, very good around the house. I'm talking about erasicating any negative responses to sexual advances. Turnin a 'no' into a 'maybe' to a 'yeah' to a 'oh my god! There were an earthquake in me knickers!'.

Hold on! I'm just gonna look at me Twittor page. New series of *Juice* is on this week so I'm getting lots of tweets and I wanna see if Rosie has sent me a message. She's on holiday at the mo with t' girls, in Greece. I hope she don't cop off with some Greek bloke. Don't know what I'm I worrying for... She in't gonna go off with someone else. She's dating Keith Lemon from t' telly. She's winning!

OK, let's see what they're saying on Twittor...

@lemontwittor: Just been watching your dvd, your one hilarious bastard. Il be on your show one day and il abuse you.

That's nice in't it? Barry finks I'm a bastard and he wants to abuse me.

@lemontwittor bang tidy!!

That's one I get often. That and 'potato'.

@lemontwittor puberty started late on you then ha ha

Ha ha ha! Not sure what that one means...

Caprice Bourret @lemontwittor my designer at my office wants to marry u and have ur children :) xxxx

That's the actual Caprice from retro dreams' wetness! See, I know all kinds me. Ok. Let me just check if I've got a message from Rosie.

No. Nowt. Last message were 14 hours ago.

Rosie Parker @lemontwittor fought ya were being rude there and then realised you were being a different kind of rude!

That were in response to me telling her I met up with Kelly Brook, purely on a work basis. She replied 'Oh your job's so hard, in't it!' I told her it in't hard, but it would be if I were working with her – Rosie, that is. It were meant as a compliment, ya know. It's hard being with Rosie cos she's very FAF (Fit as Fuck or Flip,

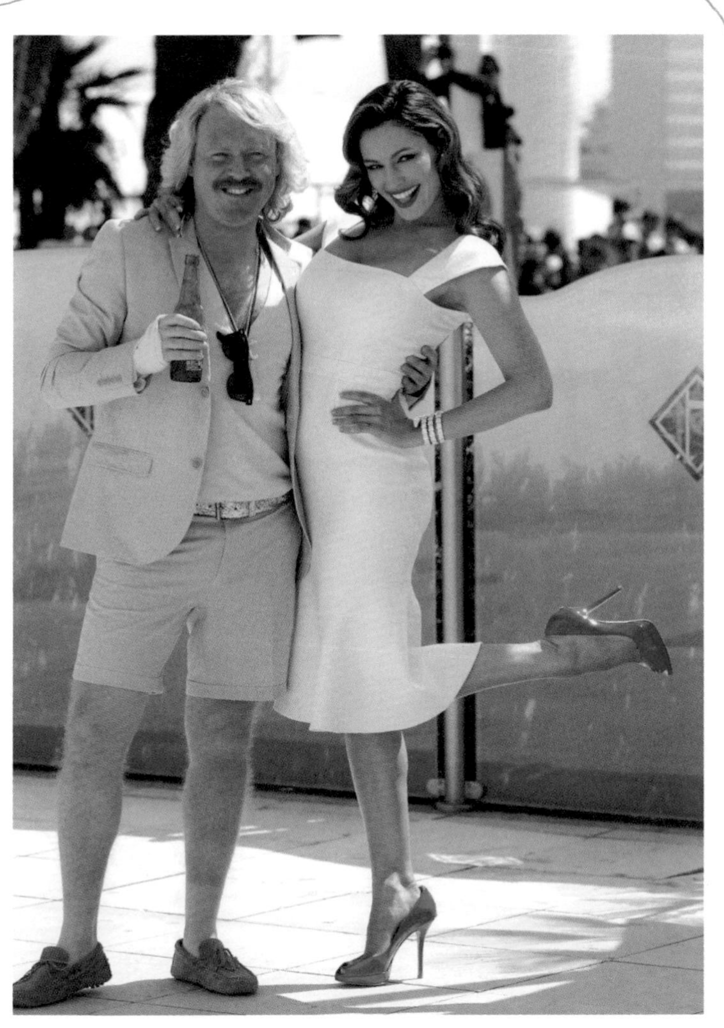

dependant on how naughty you're feeling) and I get a hard tally wacker. I fink that's how I often get away with saying rude fings. There's always a nice motive behind what I'm saying. Anywhere, back on track...

Little Lemon

So, I were born, went to school, learnt nowt but had a lot of initiative, had sexual relations at a very young age and thus were very experienced in t' field of lovemeking. I knew Rosie back then as well – we met in the youthclub. But I were thirteen and she were eight so I just fought I'd wait till she got bangers else it would just be moralistically wrong. But ya just knew Rosie were gonna grow up to be fit. I knew she'd be a banker for the future, so we stayed in touch.

I were a ladies man from the day dot. I remember charging girls for snogs in the wendy house, fifty pence a snog, which back then were like five pounds. Looking back on it, I guess it's easy to see that I've always been a entrepreneurerer in the meking.

I were youngerer back then and even though I left school with no education on account of all me messing about and cos I spent most of the day trying to get off with girls, I got a job on Leeds market and soon I were owner of me own business selling Rhino Jeans. Basically, I bought a loads of jeans off this man and stuck a label on 'em and called them Rhino Jeans. Rhino as in they were right strong, like a rhino. I basically saw a gap in the market cos I fink that jeans always get a lot of wear and tear around the happy area and that's where the material goes first. I don't know whether it's just cos I've got a big cock and balls but it always goes down there for me. But these Rhino Jeans were

Me Rosie

right tough so they'd stay strong, even for me. I've still got a couple of boxes in the spare room for memories sake. Some people would complain saying one leg were fatter than t' other, but I would say that's the style. It's encapsulating both the ragamuffin look and the emo look – which hadn't even been invented back then. The emo look, I invented that.

I lived with me mam and brother in Leeds and me family have always meant a lot to me, me mom in particular so I wanted to share a bit of the success I'd had with Rhino Jeans with her so I started saving to pay for her to get a new set of teeth. At the time they were right mashed up – like a picket fence in her mouth – so I wanted to sort them out for her. I weren't connecting meself to one woman at this stage as I had too much love in me pants for one woman.

Anywhere from Rhino Jeans I went off to Securipole which I won Business Man of the Year 1993 for. I were proper chuffed with that. And if ya don't know what Securipole is, let me tell ya what it is. It's a 2 foot reinforced aluminium shaft ya can have installed on your driveway to prevent evil scum buggers from stealing your car, or your auto-moto-vehicle as scientists call them.

And for me services to Securipole I was awarded the Business Man of the Year 1993 and that's where it all got a little more interesting. Not that me life weren't interesting before telly, it were! I've always had an interesting life.

But for now let's just concentrate on t' bits ya know me for. I'm gonna start in America because that's where I first found I had a face for telly on *Bo! In the USA*.

In the USA!

After the success of Securipole in the UK we decided to take Securipole to all t' needy people around the world. So I were over in America, LA to be pecific, trying to promote Securipole and I just so happened to be staying at the same hotel that they were filming Bo!, which were that documentary fing with those masks, that little penguin/monkey/bear fing and that ginger stalker from Transylvania who were married to his sister, the freak. It were a mad old time with all sorts staying there. Craig David, Elton John, Holly Valance to name but a few.

But let's talk about Holly Valance. Oh my god! She were Bang Tidy. I would've let her stick a digit up me and I've never let any girl do that. Me poo shoot is a deposit box only. She smelt of right nice perfume and had legs the colour of hotdogs. She wanted it, that Holly Valance. When I first saw her, she did that fing where she'd look at me too much, and she were obviously not looking at me shoes, she's gone beyond me shoes and she's looking right into me soul, via the eyes. So I said, 'Hello, my name's Keith, I've got me own business, I'm here in the United States of America promoting that business. I know who ya are, but I'd like to get to know ya more furtherer.' And she said 'I'm Holly Valance', and I said 'yes, I know that. You sang, "I wanna kiss your mouth mouth, kiss kiss your mouth"' and then we just took it from there. It's very strange that I never got off with her back then. She gave me plenty of come 'ere and back skuttle me looks. But maybe because the cameras were around all t' time. She were sunbathing by t' pool all t' time and I fink she enjoyed the admiration from all t'

blokes. She were right nice to talk to and I still talk to her now. She still has that look in her eye. When I came back from LA I bumped into her at The BRITs and she came over to say 'how do!'. I fink she were a bit surprised by all the attention I were getting. I weren't as well known as I am now, but I still had Pixie Lott and Geri Halliwell round me like flies on shit. (Did I just liken meself to shit then?). Anywhere, ya know what I mean! We exchanged numbers and that were it. I'll tell ya what happened with her later though. It's getting like *Pulp Fiction* this, in't it? Back and fourth with t' story line. I hope I dint forget to tell ya what happens. In case I do, I'll tell ya now, I fucked her. Tell ya in more detail later.

Okay, so back to LA. The weather were shite. It were cloudy a lot of the time, but I weren't there on a jolly, I were there to work. It just so happened that I had a camera crew following me. Nice enough lads they were. There were this gay fella Ben, who later turned out not to be gay (a bit of a shock) and this good-looking fella called James, who's nearly as good looking as me. We made a great pulling team. The cameraman, called Pete, looked like t' little lad out of *Jungle Book* but a grown up version with a job instead of eating bananas all day and singing 'I wanna be like you O-oo O-oo'. The sound recording recordist man, Joe, were a proper gonk though, one of those techno-nonces. Knew everyfing about computers and stuff. Turned out to be a sound lad in the end (no pun intended!) and he later

top bloKe

Avid Merrion

helped me build me phone app, Keith Lemon's Mouth Board. He lives on a barge now. I fink he's a sea gypsy or a pirate. Or a tax dodger. Only joking, Joe, if ya're reading this. Top bloke! Oh, and I forgot Roy! How could I forget Roy? He were t' oldest one out of us. We called him 'Yoda', among other fings, but all in jest.

I remember one night we all went to a nightclub. Apart from me, we looked a right set of dingbats. I had a nice off-white linen suit on from H&M. For some reason camera crews all wear t' same sort off clothes: army shorts, Abercomby and Fish, which is just Gap clothes all broken up. They wore North Space a lot as well. All dress t' same they do. We looked too old to be in there, again apart from me. Just a bunch of English dingbats. We all adopted American accents so people could tell what we were speaking about. Joe's American accent were ridiculous. Like Kermit t' Frog's granddad or somet.

Anywhere, we were meeting Jack Osbourne inside the club. Not quite sure how that happened, I fink t' crew must have been filming with him earlier in t' day with Avid Merrion. Once at t' door we just had to say 'six English blokes', that's what name they had down on t' door for us. Soon as we went in, one of the cameramen Dave went straight off on to t' dance floor, quite well spoken he were.

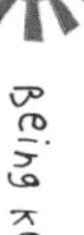

DOT AND KIRSTEN

'Excuse me gentlemen, I'm going off to have some fun.'

Tell ya what, he wun't have got through t' finals of Davina McCall's dance fing on Sky. They'd have just said live on t' telly, "Ere mate, fuck off!'. Funny moves he had, but he were definitely enjoying himself. I showed him how to dance proper later on. We met Kirsten Dunst from *Spiderman* in there. She were fit, but not a very sexy dancer, dint express herself in a positive manner. Bit hunched, like how I imagined Dot Cotton to dance.

We met Paris Hilton in there too. I'd have a go on her. I bet she's proper dirty. I've seen her sex tape. She did a good job! Lindsay Lolan were there too. Fit for a ginger bird! Anywhere, in case you're wondering, I got off with a few people people in the club. I can't remember their names, just faces. They all look the same, like they're all out of *Sweet Valley High*. We dint have too much of a late 'un cos I had a meeting the next day with a bloke called Fabio early in t' morning and they wanted to film that. If ya dint know who Fabio is let me tell ya who he is, or just show ya a picture.

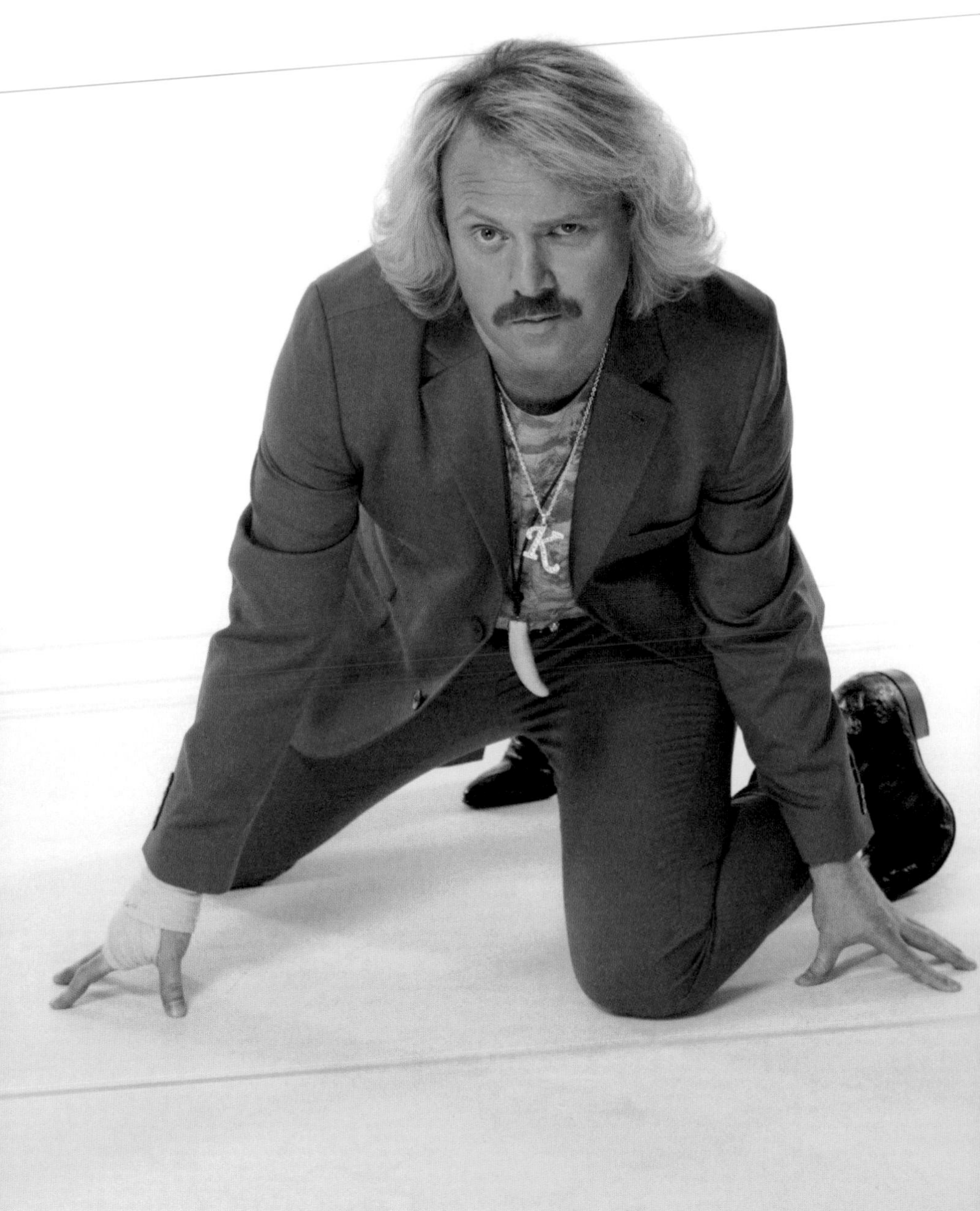

The mojo maestro

In t' 80s, Fabio were t' face of many love romance novels. He is the mojo maestro. He looks a bit like He-man and has biggerer tits than Holly Willoughbooby. I fink he later went on to not only be on't cover but write romance books himself, with such titles as *Pirate, Rogue, Viking* and *Champion*. Anywhere, he's also been in a few films – *Dude, Where's Me Car, Spy Hard* and *Zoolander*. In the United States of America he's also known for being in t' 'I Can't Believe It's Not Butter' ad on t' telly. And a goose flew into his face while he were launching a new rollercoaster in a theme park called Thor. He looks a bit like Thor as well. Which made him the ideal celeb to be the face of me Securipole campaign.

He's not very well known in t' UK but massive in t' United States of America. Women throw 'emselves at him. He's a bit like me. So I rock up to his gaff and a lovely place, it were. Dint know what to expect. I wun't sure if he'd wanna get involved in the project or not. Some people in the United States of America cudn't even understand what I were saying, but Fabio in't American, he's Italian and I've been out with an Italian bird so I knew a bit of t' lingo. They eat pizza don't they? I knocked on t' door. He answered, and I gotta say, it were like looking in a mirror, apart from I looked a bit youngerer, me hair were a bit shorterer than his and he dint have a tash – other than that it were literally just like looking in a mirror.

A novel of epic proportions

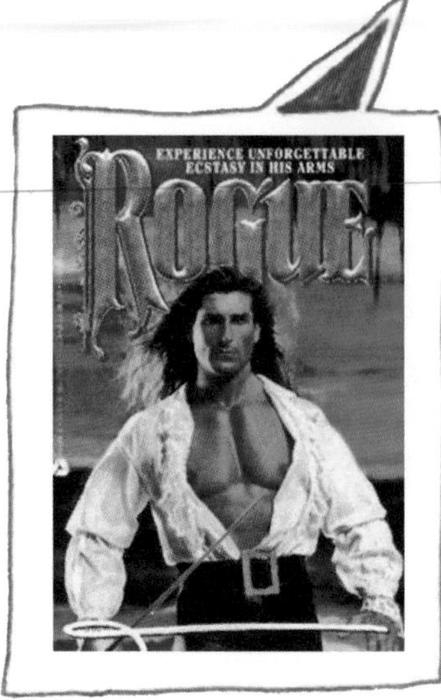

He asked me in and he were right nice. Not what I expected at all. We clicked straight away and were soon talking about our sexual conquests, just two blokes talking about shagging birds. Proper man's man, he were. He showed me around the place and it were like somet out of *Cribs*. Kinda place ya dreamed of having. His plasma weren't as big as mine though. His were 60" and mine's 62". But his speaker system were outta this world. Four fuck-off speakers as big as me mam's front door. Bet they threw off some wattage. They had a kind of mixing desk to work 'em that were like somet out of *Superman 3*. Ya know the one with Lionel Richie in it. Were't Lionel Richie? Not sure, anywhere. That big computer that takes over t' world and mekes all traffic lights fight. The one where the green man on't traffic lights has a fight with t' red man. Oh I know who it were! *Not* Lionel Richie, but Richard Prior!

So, Fabio took me to his garage. His hobbies include a passion for off-road motorbikes and he wanted to show me 'em. All 365 of 'em! Cudn't believe it. Christ knows how he gets one out from the back of garage. He proper loved 'em though. He got one out and showed me a few wheelies. He let me have a go on one, bearing in mind I crash anyfing with an engine me. Apart from cars, vans and stuff, I've crashed a snowbike in t' past and a few motorbikes. Anywhere, I get on this little fing, probably made for a six year old. All's going well and suddenly I lose control and crash into some bins, in America they call 'em 'trashcans'. I fink 'that's fucked it'.

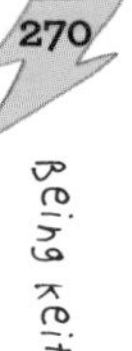

He's not gonna be part of me Securipole campaign. I were 'ell bent on getting him, as well. He were perfect. Women love him; men wanna be him. He were the perfect face for buying into the Securipole lifestyle. Plus, he weren't gonna be too expensive cos I'm sure he just wanted the exposure in t' UK.

I told him I were sorry and he said he'd fink about the campaign. He were worried he fought it were gonna come across a bit gay. Him being half-naked, holding a pole covering his knob. I assured him it weren't gay but sexy and the idea were to attract a female audience, but still keeping it manly. That's why it were a right clever idea. So, he said he'd sleep on it, but offered to take me out that evening. Now, I fought *that* were a bit gay. But then he said we'd be going out to get some minge. Well... he dint say 'minge' he said 'pussy'. But by the end of the time he spent with me he were calling it 'minge' and learnt lots of other youthermisms. Such as 'bangers and gash', 'ham sandwhich', 'mouse's ear' and many, many more.

Ooof! I've got shooty arse. Gonna go for a poo and call it a day. I'll write a bit more tomorrow. Just check if I've had a tweet fing from Rosie... No nowt. I wonder if I'll still go out with her when I've finished this book? Who knows, I could be shacked up with Kelly Brook. Super fit. I'd let her kick the crap out of me. Oooosh! I once had a dream about her and there were two of me. She sorted both of us out no problem. Can't believe I actually know her in real life. She's a lovely lass. Imagine if she were ya bird though. Every time ya left her stood at the bar there'd be blokes chatting her up. That's why it's nice wee Rosie's fit, but not insanely fit cos she's not got much in t' way of bangers. Similar to Fearne Cotton in some respect. Imagine if me and Fearne got it together. That might be good for me career. Fink people would like to see us together. We could do the *Hello, OK* magazine shoots maybe. Perhaps I'll ask her one day. I'll wait and see if Rosie tweets me. If there's nowt by 10 o'clock, I may ask Fearne out tomorrow. Me Nando's card an't expired yet. I could take her there. See ya in t' next chapter. Good this in' t it. It's very ferapeutic. Wish me computer had spellcheck on it though.

How do! I'm back! Had a crazy few weeks so I an't had time to write nowt. But just to fill ya in... Rosie did tweet me back. I knew she would. And when I said she weren't insanely fit, I were lying. She is! I fink this could be the girl that gonna be the cure to all those STDs. Joking! I always wear rubber johnnys. So anywhere, as I'm writing this I'm proper ill me. I'm freezing but sweating laid in bed watching *Tootsie,* Geena Davis and Jessica Lang were fit in that film. Love those naughty 80s birds.

Rather than just jumping straight back to the United States of America, I'm gonna give ya a brief summary of what I've been up to and then I'll get back to where we left off. When I were in mnsjwjndjksmkldmdsmmm boooooo''

Sorry! I nodded off on me keyboard. See, I'm proper ill me. So quickly, in t' past few weeks I've started me new show *Keith Lemon's Lemonaid,* which is for ITV1 Saturday nights . When I say 'nights', I mean just before *Britain's Got Talent*. I'm gonna have to get off me effs and jeffs out before I go on. We've started the seventh

series of *Juice* and got our highest ever ratings but I've been busy in and out of the edit for t' film.

By the time ya're reading this ya should know that I've got a film out, that's *Keith Lemon: The Film*. I can't tell ya how annoying it is that people keep saying, 'couldn't ya fink of a title?' Yeah... the *title* is *Keith Lemon: The Film*. What were t' Spiderman film called? *Spiderman*! What were t' Batman film called? *Batman*! Maybe we should call the film *The Amazing Keith Lemon* like that new Spiderman film reboot fing. Was good that.

OK! Let's get back to it. America! Back when they were filming *Bo! In the USA*, I fink that were the first time I'd ever been to the United States of America. Not many people could understand what I were saying while I were over there. I fink that's why I had a connection with Fabio. Nobody can understand him either. Cos I guess in the United States of America me and him are foreign. I like LA for a booze up but I don't fink I could live there. There's no centre to it, ya know like a town centre, and they don't really have proper pubs like, they don't even seem to like pubs. Madness! But it were handy that I made pals with Fabio cos he showed us round and stuff. When I weren't hanging out with Fabio trying to get him to be the face of me Securipole campaign, I'd go shopping and I found some good shops on Melrose Place , which to be honest I dint know were a real place. I fought it were just a telly show back in t' 90s. But ya can get some good clobber down there.

Sometimes I'd sit by t' pool and just look at t' birds. Well, I say birds, there weren't that many apart from Holly Valance, but she were Fit as Fuck. Sometimes I'd watch 'em film their *Bo' Selecta* fing. Proper mad. I remember I went with t' crew to watch that pervy little bear with t' dick interview Jenny McCarthy. I had her *Playboy* issue when I were a young lad. I wanked off to her one day so much that nowt came out. It were like the end of me tally wacker just coughed, looked up and said 'No more! No more! Go out and meet people!' I fink all teens go through that stage of constantly wanking. It's like a new toy in't it? A new toy that dint need batteries.

So anywhere, cos the bear were sweating a lot cos it were hot (I were hot and I'm not covered in fur), they built a marquee over where he were gonna be interviewing Jenny McCarthy. She turned up and she looked just as fit as she did in me jazz mag I had when I were a young lad. She were on good form, too, considering she'd already done 40-somet interviews that morning. She were promoting her book about how to be a mam or somet. It were hard to listen to her while she were titmotizing me with her big LA bangers. The bear and her were having a flirt off. She won the flirt off when she went down on him and sucked his little bear knob though. It sounds like I'm meking it up, don't it? But they put it all in t' show. Ya can see it with ya own eyes. My she were fit. A stereotypical Bang Tidy American beach babe!

They started off just filming me meetings with Fabio and then they started wanting to put *Bo' Selecta* people in me bits. I fink that's what they do with reality shows and documentaries and stuff. They meke shit up dint they so it's more entertaining for t' viewer? Like that *TOWIE* programme. That's not real is it? *The Vampire Diaries* is more realistic than that show.

One day they had me doing a scene with Craig David, but he were dressing as that scary Rabbit from *Donny Darky*, ya know that film? It were very odd like. They also had me with Emma Bunton. She were playing a psychiatrist. I know Bunton in real life now. She's one of me mates. Lovely bird. Drinks like a tramp.

It were good doing those little acting bits that weren't real. I fink that's what gave me the bug for t' telly game. Me brother always said it were show business I were destined for, rather than t' security business. In fact, on subject of 'R' kid. I remember we did a scene recreating 'R' Greg coming out. Me brother's hormone sexual, as I said. It weren't how it actually happened. I fink that'd be too rude to put on t' telly. He got caught out rather than coming out. But in t' show they had him played by *Some Chips and a Pint of Lager,* Will Mellor. Or if you're American, Will Mell–OR. Nice bloke. Well, he were playing Gregory – and Cleo Rocos were playing me mam. Have to glamourise it for t' telly dint ya. Mam, I'm not saying ya aren't glamorous but ya dint look like the funny lass from Kenny Everett, who often had 'em half hanging out. Lovely Cleo Rocos.

I remember the clothes that I wore in that scene. They were actually mine from t' 80s. The scene were a backflash see. We were having our dinner and Gregory were trying to tell us that he were hormone, which is not actually the way it happened, as I said. I remember I were working late and when I came home I caught him in t' kitchen with another man. He always said he weren't sure but I told him, man on man, means ya are. You're hormone! I'm quite liberal me, I like all kinds. I've always said that one animal is different to another animal but they're all animals and they all have to eat nuts so they're all on the same plane really. And since he has come out he's been happierer ever since. I knew he were troubled with somet before he admitted it. He's not with t' same lad but he's got a new fella and he's a top bloke. Gregory's got aspirations of being a dancer. I'm not sure if it'll ever happen for him. He's a bit tall. It's good that he sticks out when he goes for auditions but I don't fink he sticks out for t' right reasons. He can dance though! Us Lemons have all got the dancing jean, I fink. Ya may have seen me dancing on't telly, I've got some moves!

LOVELY CLEO ROCOS

Checking up on R Gary

I were in LA for six weeks. We shot me ad campaign with Fabio, but I weren't allowed to air it in t' UK. They did show it in t' programme *Bo! In the USA* though. Shame it dint come off proper. I fink it would've really put Securipole on t' map. Anywhere, I made some good friends there, and I've been back since.

To be honest, when I finally came back to the land of the Lemon it were a bit of a comedown. From the sunshine of La–La land to the pissing down rain tapping on me porta-cabin roof. That's where I use to run Securipole from, a porta-cabin. It were grim . We've got proper premises now like. I don't work there much any more though, 'R' Gary runs it. Gary's me cousin. I just own t' company.

Aye, I've come a long way from that porta-cabin in Leeds, when I won Businessman of the Year 1993. That were a proud day. I met t' Lord Mayor of Leeds back then. I know they're just a normal person wearing a big chain around their neck and I'm sure I'd be more chuffed if I'd met Mr T, but back then it were like meeting the King of Leeds! I say the King, but it may have been a woman. Can't remember now. Honestly it were a big moment though. Anywhere, I fink it were that time in LA that gave me the push to do telly. So that's when I got me finking cap on. How could I get me some of that telly action again? There were no one on telly like me. OK, Owen Wilson looked like me, but he were Hollywood. He were big screen. I wanted that

small screen, to be in t' corner of every room in t' United States of England. Then I'll have a pop at t' big screen later!

How do! Had a break from writing for a couple of days. Were too poorly. Ya fought I were poorly in t' last chapter, dint ya? Well, I got worse. I bet ya fink men like me don't get ill. I've got earache now. Doing me 'ed in, in't it. Feels like I'm under water. Maybe I should have me ears syringed? Ya ever had that done? It's amazing! Feels like the best shit in ya life. It's like an orgasm and a good crap all at the same time! Were shooting *Celebrity Juice* t' other night while I were still ill. Had to get a bit drunk to numb the flu feeling and it worked. We had Jason Donovan on. What a lovely bloke! Proper threw himself into the Juice World and were proper daft for two hours. He also admitted that he'd had a go on Kylie ... Lucky, lucky bastard!

Footballer Robbie Savage were also on. He's got bea-u-tif-ul hair, nearly as nice as Patsy Kensit's. Gotta call her to meet for lunch to talk about doing somet together. I'm always dreaming of doing somet with her... Always had a fing for Patsy.

Me best mate from Sheffield were on *Juice*, Gino D'Acampo. Were a good show! They dint show Rosie sat in t' audience though. She said she were glad, but I fink deep down she wanted to be on telly to brag to her mate, Hannah. I've never met Hannah. I bet she's right fit – and that's why Rosie's never introduced me to her.

Yesterday I were at a Q&A fing about this book. It were at BAFTA. Me editor, Jane, were interviewing me. She'd like a bit of Lemon, I can tell. I fink I can see t' desire in her eyes. She did a good interview though. Got onto the subject of Rosie. I could see disappointment in her face that I were hooked up. I were telling her how me and Rosie met. I've known her years – since she were about eight and I were 13. I dint go there then though, but I knew she were gonna grow up to be a sort. And as soon as she did I 'sorted' her a couple of times. It's a bit serious now, but I'm enjoying it. I can totally be meself with her. She knows that I look at other birds and flirt with 'em but I never stick owt in. Anywhere, back to the whens and wheres of me career...

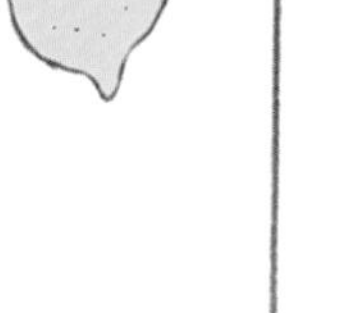

The Very Brilliant World Tour

So I'd taken Securipole to the United States of America and delivered it to the masses, came back but I'd caught the bug for being on t' telly from my guest appearances on *Bo!* So, I put some of the bits that I'd done on that *Bo! in the USA* programme together on a DVD and sent 'em to ITV2 with an idea for a holiday show. Ya get paid to have a right good holiday and a laff. What better telly idea than that?

Anywhere, a bloke called Zai Bennett got back to me and I went in for a meeting. I took him a little gift of some *Nuts* magazines. I remember one of the issues had Lucy 'Big Tits' Pinder on t' front. It may have been the first time Lucy Pinder had her nips out. For ages she kept 'em covered. We looked at those mags for a while before chatting about me telly idea. So, we did a bit of male bonding over some lovely jugs, and then we got down to business. My new mate Ben from the Bo! programme were with me. We put on a clip of me with Fabio, when I went to his house and he let me have a go on his little bike. I told Zai that's what I wanted to do. Not fall off bikes – I'm not a effing stunt man – but go around and meet people in different countries. He saw straight through me though and said:

'What ya want is for us to pay ya to go on holiday?'

I laffed and said, 'Yeah.'

I always find honesty is the best policy. If a girl is fit and ya wanna finger blast her, ya should tell her. If ya don't, ya might miss out. But it's all about timing. If ya want some more pulling tips like that, ya should get me last book, *The Rules*. You'll be reeling in the high class totty before ya know it. So, anywhere, I laffed a bit longer, then asked Zai:

'D'ya wanna do it then?'

He said: 'Leave the *Nuts* magazines with me and I'll get back to ya.'

So, I did. Two weeks went by and then we got it, t' green light! I were gonna be doing me own telly show, in which I just went around world. I cun't believe it! I were proper chuffed.

So, I set out a flight plan in the shape of a shark. Sharks are exciting and it were gonna be exciting! I were excited! Mexico, Japan, Las Vegas, Egypt, Iceland, Australia. One of those gap year fings like posh students have. Take a year off and just go bumming around t' globe. In fact, that's what it were originally called, *Keith Lemon's Gap Year*, but ITV2 fought it sounded too studenty. And I spose it did. But they wanted to call it *Keith Lemon's World Tour*, which I fought suggested I were a stand-up comedian, which I'm not. I don't tell jokes and I don't really laff at 'em. When someone tells me a joke I just fink they're clever riddles. So, I fought OK, if it's gonna be called 'World Tour' it's not just gonna be any old world tour, it's gonna be brilliant. So that were it, the title – *Keith Lemon's Very Brilliant World Tour*. But the title were so long that when it came up on the Sky menu, it just said: *Keith Lemon's Very Brilliant*. Which I liked betterer.

But before I did me own new show I got offered the chance to host *Big Brother's Big Mouth* – the show that Russell Brand use to host. I use to know him before he moved to the United States of America. I an't seen him in years. I can remember I use to take t' piss out of his ladies jeans. He said: 'You'll be wearing these one day, Lemon.'

I said: 'I effing won't!'

OK. I wear tight jeans now, but they don't belong to lasses. Anywhere I don't buy 'em, me stylist Heather does. Yeah, I've caught London. I've got a stylist. Ha-ha, me, having a stylist. Heather knows what she's talking about, though.

Anywhere, *Big Mouth* were gonna be a new experience for me and I had some big pointy shoes to fill in the shape of Russell Brand's feet. It were my first proper job on telly and it were live! I had a good time on *Big Mouth*. The team were lovely – one girl in it pecifically were really nice. Blonde she were. And when we were about to go travelling she gave me a bum bag, or if you're American, a fanny pack, and it had a little keyring on with a picture of her. I can remember she said she'd never given a blow job and I said 'ya can give me one if ya want, and ya can use me as a tool to practice on, so when ya fall in love with whoever ya're gonna fall in love with, you'll know how to give head'. So, I'm generous that way. I would often bump into t' Bang Tidy Davina McCall too. Davina is lovely, just like ya see on t' telly. She's right sexy, too. When she looks at ya, she just looks into ya soul. I'd smash her back doors in, but she's a good friend. A lot of people fink that I'm a right womanizer, but I've just got a lot of lady friends, that's all. I like hanging out with birds too. They

Shark-shape flight plan

seem to connect with me. I fink it is because I'm like a locket – hard on t' outside and soft on t ' inside. I'm a good listener. Listen to this... apparently Will Young is hormone sexual. Would've never seen that, me.

So anywhere as soon as *Big Mouth* were finished, we planned out what we were gonna do in each country for me programme – and me, Roy, Ben, James and Joe set off to our first destination for *Keith Lemon's Very Brilliant World Tour,* Japan!

I went home to Leeds to say 'Ta-ra!' t' lads and tell 'em the great news that I'm gonna have me own show. Dint fink they believed me though. Had a right good Sunday roast at me mam's, who were very excited about me trip. And finally, I made sure R Gary had everyfing under control back at Securipole HQ. Then I came back to London and the following morning – so early I still had a stiffy in me pants – I set off t' airport to fly to Japan, home of the inventors of egg fried rice. (Or so I fought then...).

In the land of the non-egg fried rice

If you've never been to Japan, ya may have seen it on t' telly in that Bill Murray film *Lost in Transfusion.* In accordance with its location, Japan is situated on the shark's tail rudder on me map or if you're touring the world following a shark-shaped flightplan.

Before I went to Japan, the fing I could picture in me mind is what I'd seen in London's China Town. Lots of Chineses walking around and little orange ducks hanging upside down in restaurant windows. But it's not like that at all cos the people in Japan aren't even Chinese, as it turns out – that's in China and Hong Kong. The people in Japan, they're Japanese and if ya fink they're t' both same ya being racist and ya wanna get over yaself and recognise it. It's far too easy to call somet that's not the same as ya names, and I'm not about negative shit. If that's what ya about, then ya can stop reading this right now.

Anyway, quick fact for ya, they say that the 'pan' element of the word 'Japan' derives from the word frying pan which is what Japanics used to wear on their heads before hats were invented. Me tour guide that tour-guided me round Japan were called Yujiro and I'm still in touch with him to this very day. In fact, he emailed me t' other day to tell me it were snowing there. I dint fink it snowed there. Apparently ya can go skiing in Japan! How effed up is that?

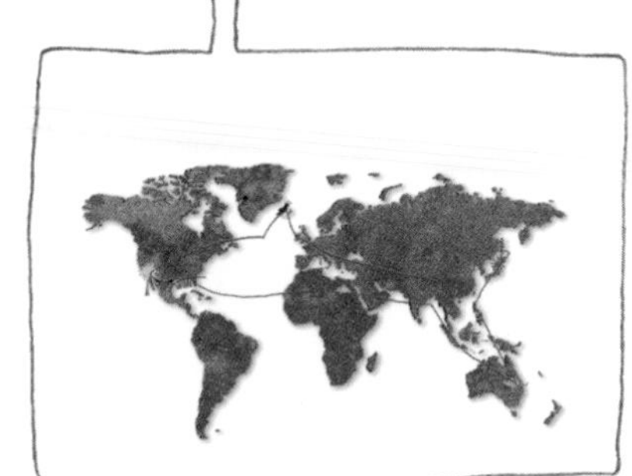

Anywhere, I weren't as intelligent back then as I am now so I cudn't say words as good as I speak 'em now, so I just called Yujiro 'Glenn' – as he looked a little bit like Glenn Medeiros from t' 80s, who sang 'Nowt's gonna stop me love for ya'. (He dint really look like him, but he did have arms and so did Glenn.) Top bloke Yujiro Glenn were. He also reminded me of me old mate at school Dereck Tooteager, who were a bit Japanese as it happens, but more like Eskimo.

First place he took us were a market called Ameyoko market. It were good. I ate all sorts or weird shit that in t' past I wouldn't never've put in me mouth. But I were there to have fun, do stuff I wun't normally do and fatten me horizons. It were there where we teached each other about day-to-day phrases that each of us use in our own countries. I told Glenn 'Bang Tidy' meant 'fit bird' or if somet looks good like. I told him it can also mean 'sexy'. He told me that 'sexy' in Japanese is 'sexshy'.

After the market, we dressed up as Monkey Magic. He were Tripitaka from t' telly show in t' past *Monkey*. I use to watch it when I were a kid. It were about a Monkey Ninja that flew about on a pink cloud. Mad as fuck, it were. Anywhere, this were the norm at Harajuku. Which apparently is the fashion mecca of Japan. It's a bridge where crazy bastards dress up. It's a lot of fun as I like dressing up, me. There were this one man that fought he were half-man, half-cat. A mad cat twat, if ya ask me. He were doing all these cat moves and licking himself. Not me cuppa tea, but each to there own, I say.

One day I remember we went techno-shopping, cos Japan is also the home of technological advances. It's very advanced in the realm of gadgetry. We found

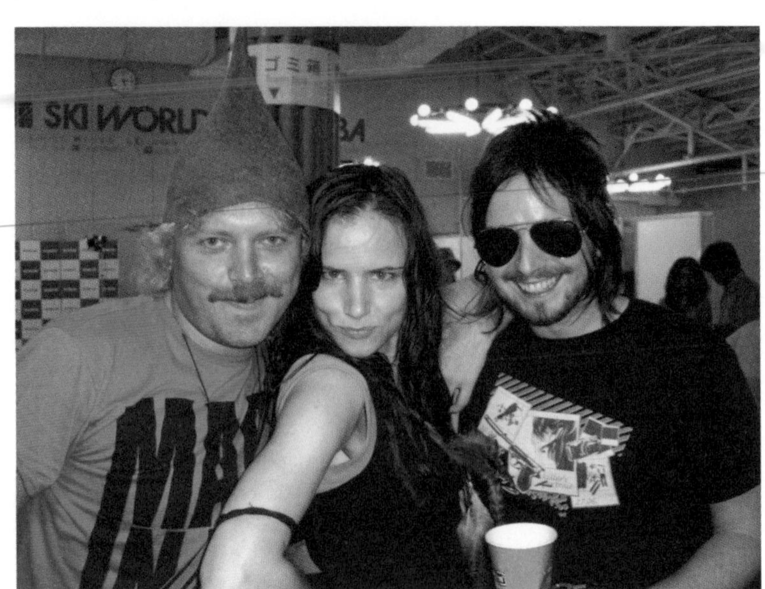

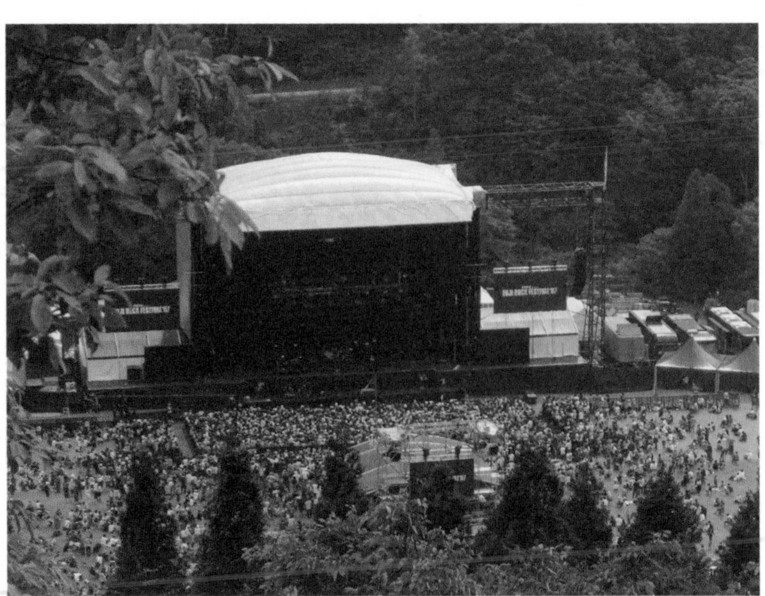

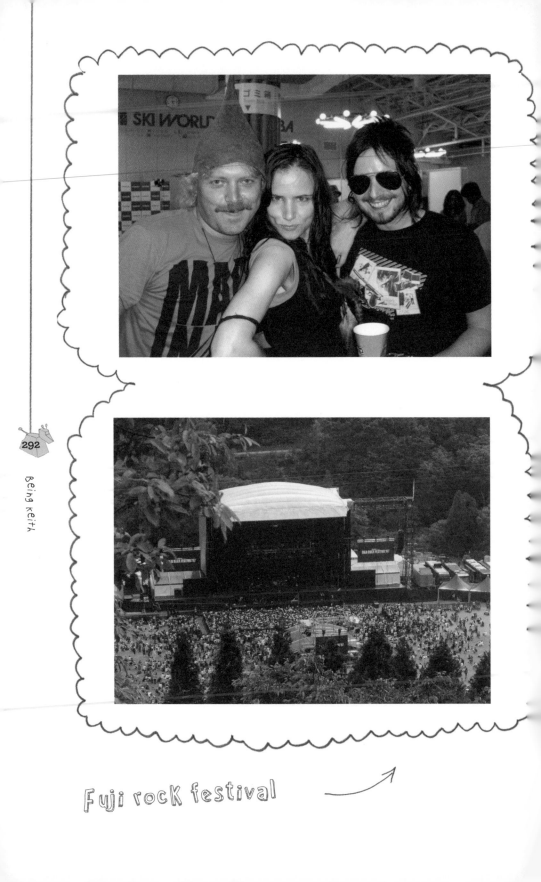

Fuji rock festival

this little robotic dog. Now, this were a few years ago ya gotta remember, but it were good. I fought it'd be a great tool to help the minds of kids who had no minds – or dingbats. I'm always finking how I can help others, I am. So, I bought the dog with plans to also buy the rights to it, and took it to the Fuji Rock Festival so I could get some quality pop/rock acts to help me come up with a theme tune to help promote the dog as a mind development tool for kids. Well, the responses were amazing! I'd written the lyrics meself and planned to get Juliette Lewis and the Kaiser Chiefs to sing the song for the ad selling the dog. It went somet like this...

Little Child
So Tender and Mild
But with the strength of an ox
You had a real dog
But you crushed him to Death
Now he's Buried in a box
But don't worry now you got a new Friend
He barks and he begs
There'll be no tears
When you Rip off his ears
Or Break his tiny legs
His tiny legs!
Cos he's more better
Metaller
More indestructibiller
Conan the Artificial dog
–For over passionate kids that
Kill their pets cos they're slow.

That were the slogan, catchy right?

I fink Juliette could feel how passionate I were about the project and congratulated me with a touchy-feely cuddle. It were lovely. She's a crazy bastard, but a lovely one. The Kaiser Chiefs were good lads to. Well, they're from Leeds, aren't they?

Since then the robotic dog hasn't gone anywhere. I couldn't get enough support to get it off the ground. But we did sell a calendar which raised money for autistic dogs. We got autistic dogs to paint pictures, and the more autistic these dogs got, the better they got at painting. I'd put the paintbrush in their mouths and they'd just paint. And some of those paintings were just beautiful, like I'd never seen. Better than Neil Buchanon on *Art Attack* could ever do, or even the man who replaced Neil Buchanon. Better than *Mister Meker* on CBBC too, yeah these dogs were really good. Some of these dogs dint even know they were dogs and would behave like other animals, it were horrible to watch. So, we raised a bit of money for that. I couldn't get any celebrity to promote the calendar so I just sold them on the street and from door to door.

I've always been an animal lover. Trust me the ladies love it if ya go a bit soft over animals, specially when ya combine it with a bit of charity.

Anywhere, while I were in Japan, I met Bruce Lee's brother, Dairy Lee. Great singer. Later in t' evening, I met up with Tamzin Outhwaite from *EastEnders, Red Hat* and some other drama fings on t' telly. After romancing her on a boat after a sushi dinner, I took her back to me hotel. I were staying in one of those little cubicle hotels. There weren't much room in there for both of us so we did get close. And if ya were wondering what she were doing over there in t' first place, I'd flown

麻雀
2F
24
1980

her over as I fought she'd be a nice bit of eye candy for t' programme. The next day she went back to the UK bow-legged after a night of passion with me in the cubicle, and I stayed in Japan and got all cleansed at a Buddhist temple before attending the international birdman rally. That's where people bring their mechanical flying machines they've made in order to jump off a cliff to win a trophy. I got it a bit wrong though and dint win any trophy. I turned up in a Bernie Clifton Emu costume.

I immersed meself so much in Japanese culture that I almost felt Japanese meself, accept I cun't speak the language.

Ooooof! Me ears are really aching. Gonna put some eardrops in. Ey up, I've got a text from Patsy Kensit. She were just asking me dates for shooting extra scenes for me film. Were hoping she were texting for a date. I'd go out with her, but I wun't do nowt. Not while I'm seeing somebody already. Honest, Rosie.

Right. I'm off out in a bit. Gotta go to a premiere of a Lionsgate film cos they're showing the trailer of me film at the beginning. So exciting!

How do! It's me again. So I last told ya about me trip to Japan. We were there for two weeks in total. Came back to London to pack different clothes and have me hair trimmed and then we set off to the United States of America!

Gonna tell ya about what happened in the United States of America very soon. But let's have a little catch-up first and let me tell ya who and what I've been up to more recently. I've been busy as a shitting dog filming me new telly show, which is gonna be on at 6.15pm on Saturdays which is very early for me. Hope I don't say 'piss', 'shit' or 'fuck' too much! If I do they can just cut it out though; it's not live, and anywhere, I have a swearbox that I pop on me 'ed if I feel a naughty coming on. The show's called *Keith Lemon's Lemonaid.* You'll know this by now as it'll already have been on t' box by the time you're reading this. In it, I spit in the face of people's problems and meke their dreams come true. I am the Dream Meker. Oh, and I've been working with Adidas. Who'd have fought it? Me being t' face of Adidas. Only sport I do is swing ball. Three hours of swingball a day though. Ya need to work for a body like this. They keep sending me clobber, as well! Sent me an ace gold biker jacket with wings on t' back! I wun't wear it to go shopping like, good for t' telly though. I like jazzing it up for t' telly.

All still going well with Rosie. In fact, we've been shooting our own reality show. She's moved down to be with me in t' Big Smoke. When she first moved down she were in my flat and there just weren't enough room, it were a small pad. And she weren't happy with just one drawer, and she cudn't have the wardrobe cos it had all my clobber in. And I've got loads of clobber. So we had to move to a new place. It's quite a nice normal place.

Odd living with a girl when I'm use to me own space. But it's going well. I've got blow jobs on tap and she's a great cook. She's told me not to mention too much of our sexual exploits in this, but she won't mind me telling ya I'm getting the odd blowy. That's why they give ya 'em. So ya tell people. I fink it's like a dog marking its territory. It's their ownership on ya. The only problem is that bloody programme *Sex and the City* is on constantly. I don't like that programme. It gives women too many ideas, it mekes them all independent.

So where were we in the narrative of the story – oh, yes, the United States of America!

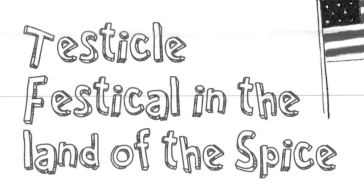

Testicle Festical in the land of the Spice

I fink, like most kids from me generation, I always loved the United States of America as a kid. It seemed a place where dreams could come true and Spiderman lived there and the A-Team. I'd been before as ya know, but I'd never been to Las Vegas and that were our first destination in t' United States of America. Las Vegas is basically the shady side of the American Dream and features an array and an abundance of spectacles to pleasurise your sensories. I remember we arrived smack bang on the shark's hooter early in t' morning like 1am or somet. It were still hot and the heat wolloped the back of me neck as I got out of t' car. The place we were staying were a lot posherer than I expected it to be. I were proper excited cos I knew some of the stuff we'd planned to get up to. I were gonna be hooking up with one of me old friends, Mel B, aka Black Spice, and the plan were to get up her! Fit!

First up, we filmed a little tour of the place. The streets were pathed with pissed-up party people holding glasses filled with brightly-coloured cocktails that looked like bongs full of booze. It were a total totty nest. Like Blackpool with a thousand times more lights. I knew I were gonna like it 'ere. We'd arranged for me to join t' Chippendales, who if ya don't know who they are, I'll tell ya who they are. They're a dance troop of strippers that were well known in the 80s, mostly for

20

taking their clothes off, but are still going strong today. A bit like the fellas in that film *The Full Monty,* but better looking and youngerer, in fact some of 'em were honestly as good looking as me. One of 'em looked like a youngerer Fabio. I bet he were a right fanny magnet. It was good fun for all the family because they din't reveal their peniseses or owt.

Anywhere, they seemed like a good bunch of lads and after an hour or two of going through the routine, I showed 'em what I'd brought to wear for that night's performance. I fink I'd left a bit of it at home cos there only seemed to be some blue boxing boots and a pair of blue rubber pants that dint really hold in all me tally wacker, so me nib and a left knacker hung out the right side. They said it were a bit inappropriate and lent me one of their costumes, which consisted of a long *Matrix*-style coat, cuffs and collars, a bit like what a male Playboy bunny might wear.

I'd put Mel B on the guest list. I hoped she dint stand me up. I were really looking forward to showing her what I were made of. She did turn up, even if she were a bit late, but that's Mel B, she's always late. I fink she were suitably impressed by me performance with t' Chippendales even though I forgot half the routine. Good job I'm naturally gifted when it comes to the power of dance. I met her after the show and we went for a drink at this ace bar before going back to me room to show her me knob. She fought it were beautiful so she gave it a kiss. What a lovely woman.

After the night of spicy black magic in every hole I were bought to an even bigger hole – t' Grand Canyon. We'd arranged a flight in a 'elicopter – or if you're American a 'chopp-or' – to fly us over the grandest of canyons!

You could throw 10 million marshmallows into t' Grand Canyon and it wun't even fill it half way. Unless those marshmallows were as big as the Royal Albert Hall where I once saw Wet Wet Wet. It were absolutely breathtaking. Then I fell asleep. Roy had to nudge me to wake me up. It were proper amazing, but I were sleepy! We'd done a lot of travelling – and filming for this show were 24/ 7. It were like a reality telly show. There weren't a script so they just had to film everyfing.

They dropped me off in t' middle of t' Grand Canyon and then flew off and left me to get aerial shots of me. There I stood all by meself in t' middle. I fink about it now and all I can fink is I wish I'd had a wank so I could just drop into an interview that the strangest place I'd ever pumped fist were in t' Grand Canyon. That's if that question ever came up. Which it does sometimes. That one, and 'what would ya do if ya were invisible?' I'd go round to Kelly Brooks' house to see what's going down or should I say 'who'.

Our next stop were Montana, passing briefly through Seattle. Ya know that place from the film *Sleepless in Seattle*, starring Tom Banks and Meg Ryan. Dint see either of 'em two there as we were only there for about an hour. Would've been nice to see 'em to see if they were still sleepless.

When we arrived the hotel, it were nofing like the one in Vegas. It were very strange, like a hotel within a hotel, and a bit scary, like somet out of a horror film, *The Shining*, or somet. In the morning we were due to go t' Testicle Festical, where lots of crazy bastards gather to eat

GTO
68 GTO

'mountain oysters'. That's what they call them ya know – mountain oysters are bulls bollox. Crazy bastards! It were a proper eye opener I can tell ya!

I fink we must have been the first there that morning. There were a few bikers there, which were a clue as to what kind of people were gonna be there. When I say 'bikers' I mean like proper film-style bikers from 'ell, wearing German helmets with raccoon tails hanging from t' back. I remember finking, 'It's gonna get a bit strange round 'ere', pecifically when we were sat just having a cuppa and a woman walked in wearing a cowboy hat, a bra, biker boots and some black lacy stockings and nowt else. I looked at her minge, then back up at Ben the Director. Then both me and Ben looked at the minge. Don't know how we kept a straight face. I knew this were just gonna be a crazy day.

As the day went off and t' Testicle Festical got busy, we got to see many other ladies' minges. Many of 'em had tattoos of butterflies or eagles down there, which they wanted to show off. And it got odder and odderer. I remember one bloke just walking around drunk, saying 'I've only got one nut' – and he weren't even lying. There were lots of different events going on, girls fighting in oil, horse shit bingo and, of course, the main event ball munching, the winner being the person who consumed the most within an allotted time. Don't know how many times I must of said that on telly. It's always an 'allotted time'.

Of course, I had to taste a testicle meself and it tasted a lot like chicken. A really shite chicken nugget. As it got later, the place got more drunken and wired. It reminded me of that film *From Dusk Till Dawn,* where they all turn into vampires so we fought it best to get

outta there before it got dark and they all started vamping out to try to suck and fuck us.

The little town we stopped at next were a real cowboy town. And the people on the farm that we were staying at were lovely. I really fitted in. Everyone had a tash! I fink cowboys are cool. Even the old fellas look cool. Nice smart jeans, cowboy hat and boots and lovely shirts. One cowboy I really hit it off with were Tim, and that's not just cos I wanted to have it off with his daughter, who were fit as a butcher's dog, I just really hit it off with him. Right nice fella he were, but I did want to have it off with his daughter and I fink she wanted to have it off with me. I dint have it off with her though out of respect for Tim. But I wanted to. She were Bang Tidy!

I really loved being a cowboy and hanging out on the ranch. It suited me. In this episode, I also did a sketch with Mel C from t' Spice Girls. I'd had a go on both of the Mels. The idea were that I'd got her up the duff and I had to come back from the United States of America cos she cudn't cope. Most of *World Tour* were real, but we had little fings like the Mel C sketch in there just to meke it that more comedically-led. (I fink that's the most serious fing I've ever said...) Anywhere, Mel were great. Brilliant actress. I have banged her, but I'm not the father of her kid and I'm willing to do a DMA test to prove it. She's a lovely lady is Mel. Bunton's another lovely lady, who I've also banged and I'm not the father of her kid either. She's got lovely kids and her fella is a top bloke too. Good for a booze-up!

Mexican midget wrestling

After America we flew to Mexico, which were located on the mouth of the shark. I never knew a country could be so highly and densely populated with old men with wrinkly tomato faces, old women with wrinkly tomato faces and old children with wrinkly tomato faces.

I were a bit nervous about Mexico. Not sure why, because when we got there it were right nice (parts of it, anywhere). We started off in a place called Cancun. It were like a right nice holiday resort really. Not what I expected at all.

There were lots of young funky people partying on t' beach. I hooked up with this bird. She had legs the colour of hot dogs and she were suffering for me! So I gave it to her. Only fair to put her out of her misery. Our tour guide looked like Penfold from *Danger Mouse*. We did a lot of interesting fings in Mexico. I watched Mexican wrestling, and then took part in a wrestling match meself. Not any old wrestling though. No, no, no! I did Mexican midget wrestling .Now, just because the midget I were wrestling were the size of a small boy, it dint mean that he dint have some serious power behind him. I'm not sure why he were being so rough with me, though. We only wanted a demo of a few moves for the camera. Little bastard.

'Ere's a bit of trivia for ya, if ya ever get in a mass debate about Mexican midget wrestling use these facts to dazzle the person ya are conversing with with your knowledge... The wrestlers can never be seen in public without their masks, even if they're having a day off and are playing out with their mates on their BMXs. They sometimes even wear their beautiful decorative masks in t' shower if they don't wanna get their hair wet.

If you're wondering what the PC term is for a 'Mexican midget wrestler' – it's a 'dwarf', 'umpa–lumpa' or a 'monkey man'. Perhaps, there in't a pecific term. They're not bothered what they're called, as long as they're being paid.

Indulging further into Mexican culture we went to a witchcraft market. They sold lots of voodoo trinkets, including voodoo balls, voodoo sheep, voodoo pigs, voodoo beards and voodoo Scooby Doos. Oh, and how could I forget? Voodoo trumpets, of course.

I went to the Mayan city in Mexico as well. It were fascinating. The Mayan city were a restored ruined city that were still a bit ruined, if truth be told, but apparently it'd been restored. It were where they filmed the Mel Gibson film *Apocalypse Now*, which were all about Mayans, I fink. It's a big shame that he got drunk and went all racist, but he's since said sorry so we've gotta forgive him, I guess. After all, he were once Mad Max and he were in *Lethal Weapon* which were ace too. More pecifically *Lethal Weapon 2* with Patsy Kensit. She is one of me favourite MILFs. She's got right blowy lips. Oooosh!

I went into the Mexican jungle, where there were poisonous trees. I got all dangerous and manly like when I saw the trees but when I went to see a bullfight I actually turned into a woman. I fink that were the first

CERVEZA
HUAMANTLADA

time I've ever cried. It really saddened me when they killed the bull. Poor bastard bull. I swam with dolphins, too, while I were in Mexico, but I'm not such a big fan of the dolphin, I prefer the bulls. Anyfing that laffs that much has an alternative motive. Plus I feel compelled to stick me finger in their blow hole. It's not just a dolphin's hole. Any hole. I always wanna stick me finger in them.

It were a valuable trip, Mexico, and I learned a lot. Apparently Mexicans dint discover shoelaces until 1946, so it's a country that's obviously gone through hardship, but it's still a very lovely place. A word of warning to ya in case ya ever go to Mexico. Too many chillies can wreck ya arse. It must have been the start of me piles cos by the time I got to me next stop, Egypt, me backside were like a scrap yard!

Me at the Mayan City!

Egyptian piles

So, there I were in Egypt, some might say funnily enough situated on the shark's rectum. I'd been there before and wun't right into it. But this time, I had a tour guide with me that should know all t' best bits of Egypt to show me. His name were Rami and he did. He also looked a bit like the guy from *Jurassic Park*.

The first place that Rami took me to were this market. It reminded me of Chapeltown in Leeds. It were full of keyrings in the shape of pyramids and sphincters. Many of the people seemed to have teeth like sugar puffs. I stuck out like a sore finger. And as we were walking through the market, Rami asked me to hold his hand. I were a bit uncomfortable with it at first but apparently it is a sign of manuality in Egypt and nowt to do with hormones.

After the market, we went on a desert safari. Din't see any elephants though. I travelled on a camel but now my behind were in excruciating pain. Don't think the camel ride helped me arse crack, and after having it inspected by a doctor, I realised that I had piles. It killed like no pain I'd ever experienced. Apart from an in-grown toenail. In fact, that's what it felt like, – an in-grown toenail in me arse hole.

I remember Roy saying to me, 'welcome to the world of piles! Once ya get them, ya have 'em for the rest of your life'. But, touch wood, I've never had 'em since.

The ones I got, just so happened to be external. I dint know that at the time. Roy told me if ya get piles ya should try to shove 'em back up ya crack. Now, at this time I dint know mine were external, so I were trying to shove 'em up where they'd never been. It were really embarrassing showing the doctor. I knelt on all fours like she were gonna put a strap on and do me doggy-style. She told me to lie down in the foetal position and told me to relax as she were gonna insert her finger. I couldn't relax. I told her if she shoved her finger up me, I'd snap it off with me arse flaps. No chance. She gave me a bit of cream and some suppositories and I were on me way. I remember I recorded the first time I stuck one up me for me video diary for t' show. At first, me arse just wun't accept it. Then, as if it had a mind of its own, it snatched the suppository off me and consumed it quicker than ya could say 'Ooooosh!'. The anus is an amazing invention.

Maybe the fact that I were having so much trouble with me bum were, and still is, the reason I have bad memories of Egypt. I remember the morning we were

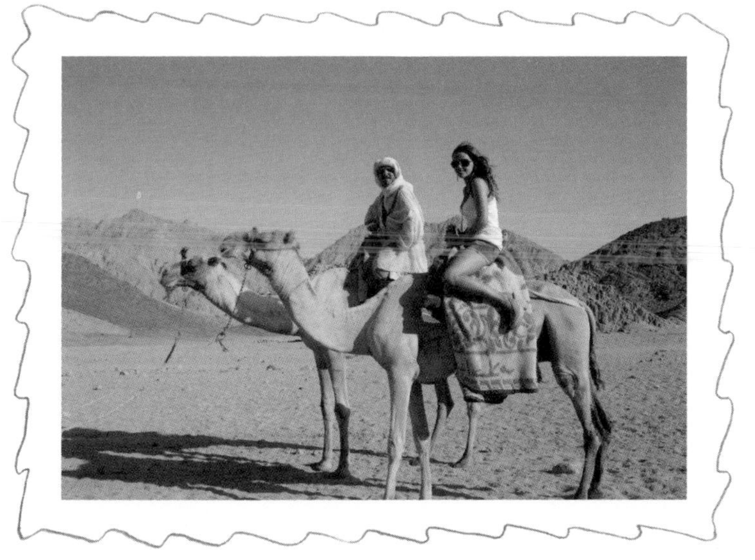

set to get a hot air balloon ride over the River Nile. It should've been amazing, but I were in amazing pain from the Dreaded Pile. I were in so much pain, I felt drunk. It were madness.

Me celebrity guest that were joining me in me Egyptian adventure were Samia Smith who plays Maria in *Coronation Street*. Yes, that's right, the fittest girl on t' street! Well, equal fittest with Michelle Keegan. I'd love to have a minge tout with those two.

We went on a camel safari together. Oh, the way she mounted the three lipped beast (yes they've got three lips!), it sent a quiver down me private sectors. But I'm not sure I'm a natural camel lover. Horrible creatures. They're like some kind of monster from *Star Wars*. Anywhere, after riding on the humpy bastards for I don't know how long, we settled down on a Bedwinner campsite (Egyptian gypsy camp, basically), where we ate a goat and I serenaded Samia. I sang 'I fink we're alone now' by Tiffany, a ginger pop star of the 80s with big bangers.

I wish we had been alone cos she looked fit, man. And the nice fing about Samia is that she's a lovely down-to-earth girl. Not one of those stuck up bints that knows they're fit. Her fella at the time had come along too. Top bloke! But like I said, I wished we'd been alone, then maybe I could've seduced her with me Lemony love sword.

I'm still in touch with Samia and I'm always running into her at dos and stuff. In fact, saw her only t' other week at the RTS Awards which stands for Royal... actually not sure what it stands for. I dint win, anywhere. I were against the legends of Ant and Dec, so they won.

Nowt against 'em winning anyfing though as they're good lads. I wonder if they'd sell me a couple of their awards...?

Rather than going to the RTS Awards, I could've done with staying in that night cos the next day I had a double recording of *Celebrity Juice*. Not easy filming with a hangover. Nearly as bad as filming with an arse full of piles. Jesus it hurt. I can remember Rami, the tour guide, getting me one of those Egyptian dresses they wear. Had a nice draft going up it to sooth me poorly bum. I also had one of those Tommy Cooper red hats. If it wun't for me fick Northern accent, you'd swear down I were an Egyptian. Dint 'alf look the part.

We had a backflash sketch in this episode, which had me auditioning for *The X Factor*. I'd got to boot camp stage and were at Sharon Osbourne's house. I were singing with me band 'Up North', featuring meself and one of me mates, Jonesy. We sang 'I don't know much' by Aaron Neville. Anywhere, Sharon fought he were good and I were shite so I decided to split up and go solo. I told her that I had a kid that were gonna die when it were a bit older and she still didn't wanna put me through. But Sharon din't really know what she were

Me and me guide

talking about. I knew I could sing because when I was youngerer one of me uncle's was pretty well off and he had a karaoke machine. We use to go round every weekend and have a bit of a sing song and everyone said that I sounded like Simon Le Bon. Anywhere, she might not have fought I had t' X Factor but Sharon's a lovely sexual woman. I bet she knows what she's doing in bed, or stood up in t' kitchen over t' sink or in t' garden behind t' shed.

So, anywhere, where were I? Oh, in Egypt.

What else did I do? I went scubby diving in t' Red Sea but I weren't right into that as when I were about seven I had a bad dream that my tallywhacker had a fish face on t' end of it so I weren't too keen to get in the water with those bastards. That's about it really. So, I'm gonna go now. Ta-ra for a bit.

Hello, I'm back! Just got back from t' hairdresser's for a trip and some highlights. That sounds a bit hormone, dint it?

Just tweeted Rosie a poem to cheer her up. She's hurt her foot. I fink she fell over drunk. Anywhere, I wrote...

Rosies foot's red
My mind is blue
I miss you so much
Wanna finger blast you X

We're gonna get take-out tonight. I'll unzip it – she'll take it out. Oooosh!

Australia, the Land of Priscilla and Neighbours

Well, from Egypt, mostly known for the adventure film *The Mummy* starring Brendon Fraser and *Jewel in t' Nile* starring Michael Douglas, it's onto Australia, known for the film *Priscilla Queen of t' Desert, Neighbours* and *Home and Away*. It's situated near the shark's back foot. Can I just point out that this weren't the order that the episodes appeared on t' telly but the order that we travelled in. That were just a bit of trivia for ya. Ya can use that to impress your mates.

I'd never been to Australia previously so I were very excited. Our first stop were a small town. I can't for the life of me remember what it were called, but it were in the bush district. It were very stereotypical outback Australia. We were staying above a pub. All made of wood in t' middle of nowhere. There were no lock on me bedroom door. But the owners seemed very nice.
I remember the first night being woke up by the sound of tap dancers. I went down stair to t' bar area and there were a pissed-up Roy (the camera man) clapping and enjoying what looked like Australia's answer to River Dance. There were a line of blokes tap dancing and Roy were loving it. I told 'em (in a raised voice cos I were a little bit pissed-off cos I'd been woken up) that we had to be up early in t' morning for a local poetry festival fing. We both went to bed. I quizzed Roy about his secret obsession for Ozzy tap dancers. Willy smoker.

Anywhere, the next morning I were a bit nervous about this poetry fing, but nobody knew who I were so I just fought 'Keith! Go and enjoy yaself.'

I had nowt prepared so I just freestyled it. They all fought I were shite, but I weren't shite. I just don't fink they understood me references. As ya can see from me poem to Rosie, I'm actually quite poetically-minded. Anywhere, this were a mad town, but fun and they were having some kind of sporting event in which all the town took part. Like a mini Olympics. So, in t' afternoon, in a bid to regain me dignity, I entered the dunny race, which basically involved a couple of young 'uns dragging a 'dunny' or a toilet on wheels. I lost at that as well.

Finally we went deeper in t' bush all dressed in drag to replicate *Priscilla Queen of t' Desert*. And then we had a flight booked out of there. Ya wun't believe how many flies there were, though. It dint pick up too much on

camera, but there were swarms of them. Weird how they feel so wet when they fly in ya eye. I fink I swallowed a few and all.

The pilot of the plane that were flying outta there to our next location were a top bloke and had hung with us while spending time in that little town. I purposely befriended him so he'd let me have a go on his plane. It were only a little plane and we were a bit worried that it weren't gonna get us up in the air. I were sweating buckets. It were hot on there. I fought I were gonna sweat so much I'd be reduced to the size of Prince.

Flying the plane were a piece of piss in the end. Ya just had to keep the fingy-majig in t' middle of the watsit. While I were doing that, the pilot were doing loads of maths to meke sure we were flying to the right place. I fink he had the harder job. I'm shite at maths. We landed in another part of Australia. Again I cudn't remember where we were. But it were nice little hotel, this time with locks on t' door.

We'd arranged to go and see a man called the Barefoot Bushman, who had an old run-down zoo full of monsters. Crocodiles, Kangaroos and worst of al Koala bears! They look cute, but they've got retractable razor sharp claws like little furry Freddie Kruegers, the little bstards. The Barefoot Bushman were nice enough, but a bit crazy. But I like crazy people. I fink they're interesting. He had me sat on a 14, no 16 – well, might have been 20 to 25 foot-long – croc. I were sweating and

absolutely shitting meself. There were a brown onion farm in me pants. I cudn't honestly remember how he got me to do it. The crew were egging me on and I guess I just fought, 'hey! While I'm 'ere, I may as well'. It's a very manly fing to do sit on a croc. And not many men can say they've sat on a massive croc!

The Bushman took me into what he called the 'Croc's Kitchen' (the pond that it lived in). He spoke about how crocs have bad press – ya know, like sharks have cos of the film *Jaws*. He said they're not really man-eating monsters and that crocs doing death rolls is just in films. A 'death roll' is where they roll around their prey and take 'em to t' bottom to drown 'em before eating 'em. He demonstrated that it were all just a myth using a dummy (which I named 'Nigel'). As soon as he threw Nigel into t' water, what d'ya fink 'appened? The croc death rolled it straight away. See... they're just evil bastards.

After that, we went to Sydney, home to the Sydney Opera house. Architecturally ahead of its time some say, its creamy concrete wings are the sails of the first fleet (see, I know some fings). To me though they looked like loads of chicken beaks. Good though. There were a lot of hot totty in Sydney. I fought I would bump into Kylie or Danni at some point, but I dint. I've since met Kylie and she were a vision of beauty. But back then she were one of the people I'd always wanted to meet and have sex with. She's a proper little spinner, in't she?

As well as the Sydney Opera House, Australia is famed for its many beaches, so quicker than Crocodile Dundee could say 'that in't a knife, this is a knife', I hit one of its many beaches. Lucky for me there were a

group of birds on t' beach who were part of a volleyball team. Cos I'm attractive, they let me join in. I learned how to surfboard while I were there, too. I've never done it since, but I still keep my surfboard propped up in the kitchen. Ya never know when you're gonna be able to drop it into conversation.

I also met up with Paul Robinson (aka Stephan Denis) from *Neighbours*. What a lovely man he is. I expected him to be taller than me, but stood next to me he looked like Frodo from t' *Lord of t' Rings*.

Australia were a lovely place, but I wun't rush back in a hurry – apart from when I'm appearing on ITV2's *I'm a Celebrity Get Me Out of Here!* It takes effing ages to get there. It's like time travel. On a plane for 24 hours? Madness.

Dint bump in t' Kylie once!

Right. Now I'm hungry. Gonna have to meke me a sandwich or somet. Hold on a tick. I'll be two minutes. Unless I've got nowt in t' fridge then I may have to pop out t' shops. It's gone crazy recently. People in t' street say 'hello' and I fink to meself, 'Do I know ya? Have I worked with ya?' Sometimes I'll even end up going for a pint with 'em before I realise I dint actually know 'em at all. It's mental. Can't buy porn from me local shop any more either. Mind, I don't really use porn any more. Got me lovely Rosie to be all dirty with. I remember the good old days when I were a little kid I'd find porn in t' bushes all t' time. Ya never find porn in t' bushes now cos kids dont steal their dads' porn anymore, they just go online, dint they? Wait till their mam and dad have gone to bed, then get on that computer and wank their little eyelashes off.

Right sandwich! Be back in a bit.

How do! I'm back. Had a ham sandwich, some of those salt and vinegar twirl crisps and some apple juice. That's healthy, in't it? Then I gave me right arm some exercise. I were feeling a bit horny. Martine McCutcheon were on t' telly selling good bacteria. Don't know how ya can have good bacteria. Ya can have a good bash when she comes on t' telly though. I don't know what she's up to, Martine McCutcheon, just doing telly ads. I wish she'd get back on t' telly properly in a film. I fought she were great in that film *Love, Actually*. Would love to bang 'er.

Magical Icelander tour

So, nextly and lastly in me Very Brilliant World Tour, I were in Iceland. Not the shop but the country named after it, situated on the shark's back flap, or fin as experts might call it.

Me Iceland tour guide were called Enrick. I expect ya don't spell it like that, but I expect he won't be reading this. If ya are, Enrick, I hope all's well and I've still got me fingers crossed for ya that they do a follow up to *Beauty and the Beast*. He told me that he did the voice for The Beast for the Icelandic version of *Beauty and the Beast*.

What were it he use to say? Oh, I know...

'If ya want me to, I can do it for ya, my lady.'

I would ask, 'do what? What is it ya can do for her, Tom?' (Although he were called 'Enrick' I called him 'Tom' cos he looked like Tom Hanks from *Big*, *Bachelor Party* and *Forrest Gump*. Good film *Forrest Gump*. 'Life were like a box of chocolates. Ya never know what ya gonna get'. Well, that's not 100% true, is it really? It's likely that if you're eating a box of chocolates, ya know what ya gonna be eating is a chocolate. Ya hardly gonna buy a box of chocolates and find a crabstick in there, are ya? And if ya did, I expect you'd take 'em back. But yeah, it's a great film. It'd meke more sense though if he'd said, 'life is like a shopping trolley filled with different food and if ya pick somet out of there

Poor Dermot is terrified of puffins

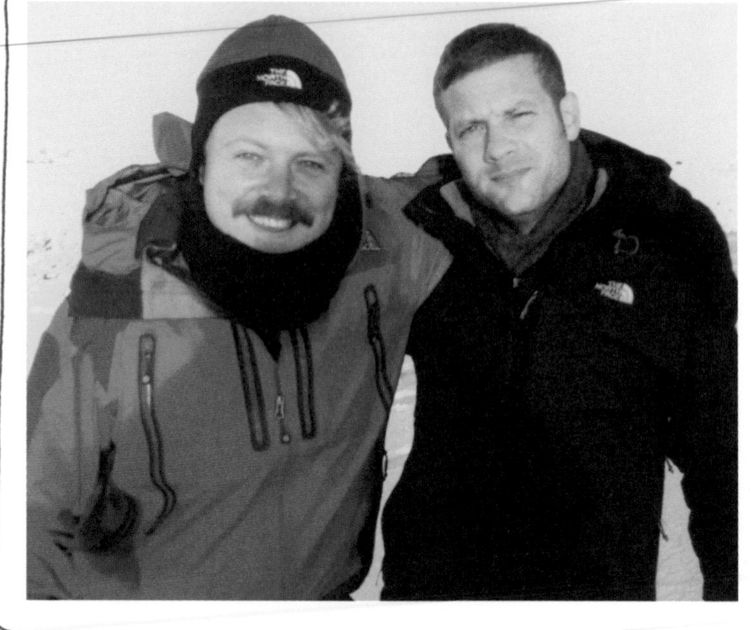

blindfolded, then ya probably never know what ya gonna get.'

Anywhere, here are some basic facts about Iceland: (If ya know lots of fings ya can impress the ladies by showing them you're much cleverer than them, they love that!) Firstly, the postal service is reliable and efficient and rates are comparable to those in Leeds or other northern cities.

Secondly, to say 'Hello' in Iceland ya say 'Hello'.

First stop to experience true Icelandic fings were a visit to the Blue Lagoon. A manmade lagoon, made by men, the Blue Lagoon is known as the social mecca of Iceland and the pulling rate there is equal to that at the Playboy Mansion. Ya can pull there even if ya like computers. As well as checking out birds and having a little paddle, one of the features there is this troff fing filled with silica mud. People put this on their face like a 'mud mask' sort of fing and it is said to possess magical powers and turn a munter into a Bang Tidy bird. Which is the reason there's lots of fit birds in Iceland that look like models. Apart from Björk. I'm not saying she's a munter, I actually find her attractive. I've always wanted to have a go on her, but she dont look like a model, does she? She's fit though. An't seen or heard from her for a while. When she did that song 'Oh, So Quiet', I liked her. I bet she's crazy in bed. I've always said that one of me good mates Paloma Faith looks like the bastard daughter of Björk and Billie Piper. I'd have it off with all three of 'em at the same time.

I remember when Tom took me to see a geezer. I don't mean a man about a dog but a geofermal hot spring that shoots into t' air. Very exciting! I don't mean that sarcastically either. It were ace! Although I had to film it meself cos me and Roy had a fallout. For some reason, he kept talking while I were doing me opening link about the geezer. Going on and on about the battery on t' camera running out. Don't know why he just dint stop and bang another in. Anywhere, he accused me of being ageist, which is not true at all. It's not me fault he's so old like Yoda and I dint hold it against him. In fact, I pity him that he's so old, he's going daft. Apparently he said he got on t' computer and sent an email to his lawyer. I dint hear owt though. Fing is, I dint fink Roy could use a computer. He's too old. (I love ya really, Roy, if you're reading this. He knows that. Silly old bint.) Anywhere, we made up and we continued on our magical Icelander tour with Tom Banks.

I'm terribly hungover at the moment. It were the *Celebrity Juice* combined with *Lemonaid* wrap party last night, and me back is aching. Fink it's with all t' sex I've been having recently. And cos I'm a bit older. Can't believe I'm gonna be 29 next week. That's me real age – on telly I always say I'm 27 and a 'arf. I fink I can get away with it. Young at heart, young in visual appearance.

Just found out that *Juice* is up for two BAFTAs! The Best Entertainment Programme and the YouTube Audience Award. It's at the end of the month, so I should still be writing this book. I'll let ya know what happens.

I loved Iceland, but it weren't 'arf expensive. Ten quid for a pint! So, we took our own sneaky booze in t' pub with us. I'm not paying ten quid! I use to have a full night out for a tenner when I were a lad, and still have enough left over for a kebab.

After a night of drinking our own sneaky booze in a posh bar full of model-like quality totty, it were the morning and we planned to hook up with the headmaster of the Fairy School. The headmaster came onto me, but the school he were headmaster of weren't hormone sexually related. It were 'Fairy' as in Tinkerbell. In Iceland, a large majority of people believe in the existence of fairies and trolls. Piles of rocks are piled up among the wasteland and it is said that fairies and trolls are responsible for this. Meself, I don't believe in fairies and trolls and there were nowt the headmaster could say or show me to meke me believe otherwise.

At the end of showing me his pictures of said fairies, the headmaster asked whether it were now time we took our clothes off and had a look at each other... I told him it were *not* and were outta there quicker than ya can say '*Sha-ting!*' (For the sake of accuracy, that's actually a word I'd not yet start using yet; that word were born during a rehearsal for *Juice*).

So from fairies, I went sailing in an iceberg water forest, which is what other people call a lake with some big ice cubes in it. Apparently it were used in *Superman 2* featuring Terrence Stamp as General Zod (I fink that were his name). Best baddy ever, General Zod. I can do a wicked impression of him. It doesn't work in writing though so there's no point, but if ya bump into me on t' street or in t' boozer ask me to do it and I will.

The next day, I went to a penis museum. Not that I'm interested in looking at cock, but we fought it might meke for good telly, edgy like. It were full of animal cocks, mostly whales. Some of 'em were terrifying. They looked like weapons. The man who owned the museum were called Mr Ciplin and it's the only tally wacker museum in the world apparently. They dint have one minge in there. Mr Ciplin had a really small cock. It use to belong to a cat. Apparently it's the only cock with a bone in it. And there was one so small you had to have a microscope to see it! Poor bastard.

Of course, Iceland is known for inventing Vikings, as seen in the film *Lord of t' Rings*. I went to a Viking Hotel to learn about the history of them. One of the phrases that they teached me were 'a man is a man and a word is a word'. I confess, I an't got an effing clue what it means, but it sounds good, don't it?

Joining me in Iceland were me pal Dermot O'Leary. He's terrified of puffins. He shared a bed with me, he were that scared. I dint mind cos I don't really like puffins that much meself, and the place where we were staying were surrounded by them. Imagine somebody shoving a puffin in your mouth. Horrible.

We went on a glacier on snowbike fings. That were ace! I stopped for a piss and almost froze me dick off. It were freezing then it got even colderer when we sat down to do an interview. It were ridiculous. There were a snowstorm just as we started the interview. This were back when Dermot had just started *The X Factor* so I wanted to get the lowdown on Cowell. He's a very mysterious character, but me being me, I just came out and said it.

'Tell me somet about Cowell'

I fought Dermot could interpretate that question however he wanted and we'd find somet out. But he dint tell me anyfing of interest really. Very nice like that is Dermot. He ain't a gossip. He's a proper gent...even if he is scared of puffins!

We headed back to the place we were staying at and watched the Northern Lights. Well we dint really. We cudn't see em so they put 'em in t' sky in post-production special FX!

It were great doing *World Tour* and I learnt a lot. I often get asked if I'm gonna do another, but it in't really up to me. It's up to the telly bigwigs.

Anywhere, before the show were released on DVD, I had to do promotion for it on t' telly. Then promote it on DVD. One of me most memorable appearances that I can remember were when I went on *Loose Women*. I've been on a few times since then, but it were me first time and I remember it well. I were a bit nervous. It's weird when the nervous fing happens cos normally I don't give a crap about what people fink of me. But now and again this nervous fing happens. I guess deep down I do care what people fink of me. Maybe that's why I spend three hours in t' hairdresser having highlights done. I'm naturally strawberry blond. I just have it enhanced now and again to meke it betterer. So, anywhere there I were stood backstage and I dint have a clue what I were gonna say.

I rarely plan owt. I just say what I'm finking at time. Then I fought to meself, 'I know! I'll just tell 'em me piles' story. Is that appropriate for daytime telly?'. Turns out it went down a storm. They loved it!

People always fink I'm gonna eff and jeff when I'm on daytime, or they say 'were it 'ard for me to control meself?'. I don't have tourettes though. Yeah, I swear on *Celebrity Juice* cos it's past t' watershed fing, and I've swore in this book a couple of times already, but that's cos I'm a bit childish and I like seeing swearwords written out on t' paper.

Fuck, bugger, tits, arse hole, wank!
See. I use to put swearwords in me SAs at school just to see what the teacher would say.

I never swear in front of me mam though, and cos she watches *Loose Women*, there's no way I were gonna swear on it. So I told 'em about me piles and me trip to the docs, but a daytime edited version like. I demonstrated how the doctor looked at me arse on t' bed, using the *Loose Women* desk as the bed, and I'm talking 'em through it when suddenly I felt the desk go. I broke it! I shit meself and so did Andrea McLean, bless her. She's lovely is Andrea McLean, like Snow White. I bet she's dirty in the sack too. Lisa Maxwell is fit, an' all. Like Emma Bunton's older sister. Not too much older, like.

Talking of which, I were out with Bunton last night. I went to t' Soap Awards and presented the award for Sexiest Female to Michelle Keegan. She is Bang Tidy! She's more classic beauty than sexy though. It's like Jesus laid an egg and out crawled Keegan. She's visually perfect and has a lovely personality to match. So nice and grounded. I'd definitely bash her rat. I met Jacqui Dixon from *Brookside* too. Use to love her when *Brookside* were on. She were always in a shellsuit carrying an oversized handbag coming back from t' swimming baths. Love to take *her* swimming! I tell ya what, she an't changed. She were lovely. If me romance with Rosie weren't blossoming so much I might have got me heels in there with 'er... Yeah, I'd have a go on her, and Keegan and Samia Smith. But, it dint matter as it's going well with Rosie. She gets me, I fink. I flirt and say a lot of shite but she just takes it on t' chin...

I also went on *The Paul O'Grady Show* to promote the *Very Brilliant World Tour*. I use to love that show when it were on. Haven't seen O'Grady on t' telly for a while. I fink he's brilliant and a right nice man. It's so strange when ya meet these people that ya right like and it turns out they like what ya do, too. So, yeah, I went on there and I'd just come back from me holiday and had an eye infection. I looked like Rocky (hero!). It'd proper swelled up. Looked like I had a twat growing on me eye so I figured if jizum can meke humans, surely it can cure me swollen eye. So I pumped fist and put a bit of me man milk on me eye, and d'ya know what? It cured it. I told Paul O'Grady I were gonna bottle it up and sell it to Boots. Who'd have fought me jizum had magical healing powers? I mention all of this on t' show, but just editing out certain words so I could get away with it

on daytime telly, while also saying *Keith Lemon's Very Brilliant World Tour* on ITV2 10pm a lot. *Cha'mone motha plugga!* I pride meself on me pluggin skills. I've got no shame when it comes to promoting fings. When I've made somet I'm proud of, I wanna tell everyone about it. Been that way since I were a young 'un. If I'd had a right good perfect poo, I'd shout me mam and say 'Come 'ave a look at this pipe I've laid!'.

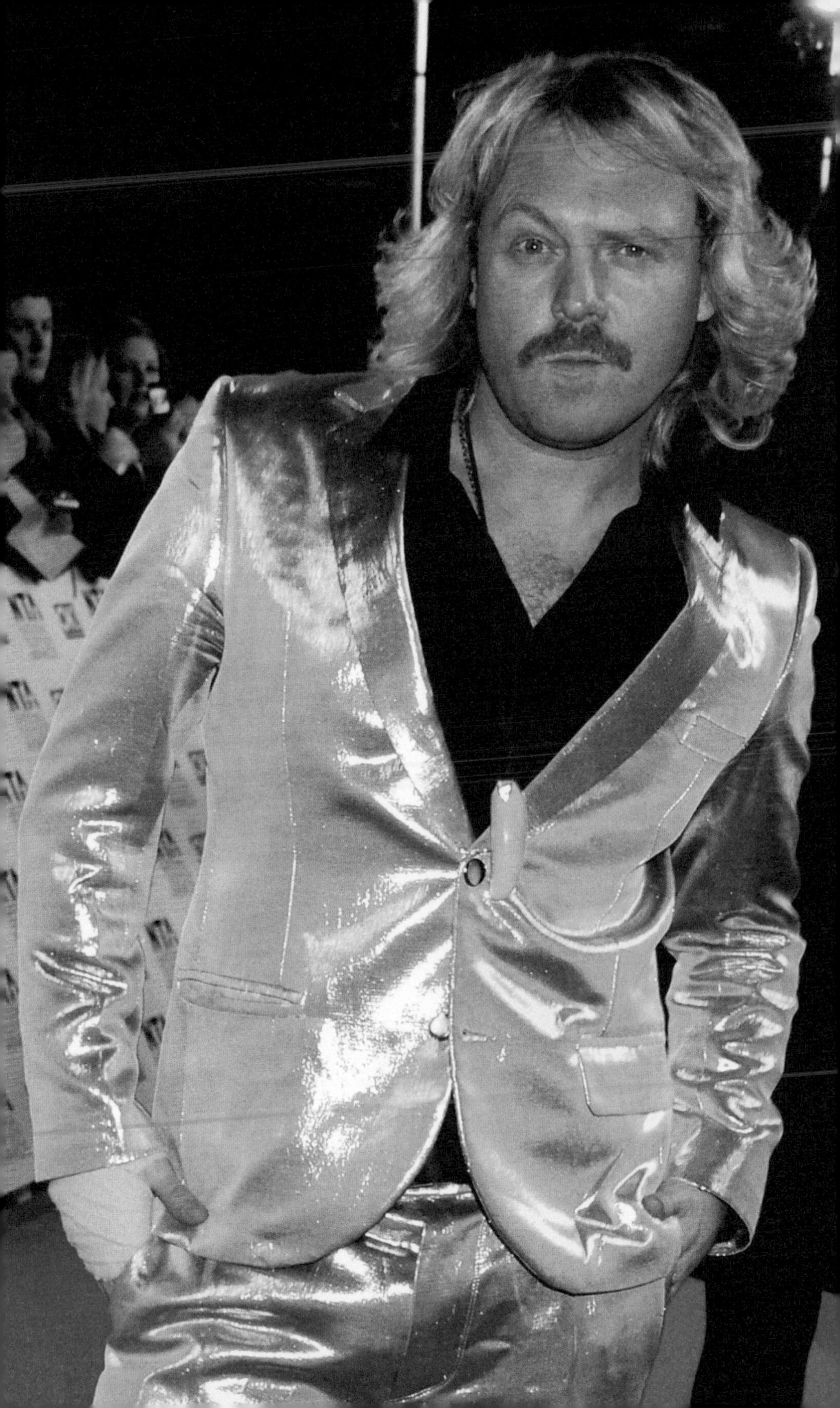

Moving t' big Smoke

When ***The Very Brilliant World Tour*** came out on DVD, I were off again this time on a small regional promotional tour, going to local radio stations and stuff and doing a bit more TV and signings. I went on Channel 5's *Studio Five Live*, I fink it were called. Did that a few times. Matthew Wright were a nice bloke – *not* Matthew Wright, I mean *Ian* Wright. Matthew Wright is a nice bloke, though. I like him on t' *Wright Stuff*. I'd like to do a show like that. Or like Jeremy Kyle. I fink I'm good with people. I watch that Jeremy Kyle and I fink one day one of those loonies is gonna crack him.

I did a photoshoot in *Heat* magazine with me mate, Olivia Lee. That were fun. Olivia is as funny as she is fit. I fink it's rare for someone to be that funny and fit, cos in the back of t' mind their fitness distracts from their funniness. But Olivia always seems to pull it off.

Anywhere, then I went on a signing tour up and down t' country. I went back to Leeds and did a signing in HMV. I weren't sure if anyone would turn up, but they did and they were all right nice. A few birds there that I would've finger blasted too! Still fink it's odd when someone asks ya to sign a lemon. What are they gonna do with it? Good when they ask ya to sign their bangers though. When they ask me to do that I get a right good hold and spend some time on it. I draw a self-portrait and put 'Keith woz 'ere', with an arrow pointing down t' tit slit. At this point in me life I decided that if I were gonna meke a go of it on t' telly as a TV host or an entertainer or whatever it is I were, I fought it best to move to London. It were a big step but I knew a few people there. I weren't seeing Rosie back then. We'd got off with each other now and again, but she weren't me bird yet so it weren't like I were leaving her behind.

Me mam encouraged me to go live me dream. She were always behind what I did apart from when I were a kid and I got done by the police for filling a school toilet with stones through a skylight window. Got bolloxed then.

So, I left Leeds to live in t' Big Smoke. I got a right nice place in the centre of town and even MTV's *Cribs* wanted to come and see it! Madness. I were a bit dubious about doing *Cribs*. It's a bit showy offy in't it? I heard someone once did *Cribs* and two weeks later they got robbed. Not sure if that's true but it is a word of warning. But in the end it were good to do, it felt a bit like I'd arrived. In a small way. Not like those American *Cribs* ya see with their big fuck-off houses... Me place were nowt like that. In fact none of the English *Cribs* are like the Americans. Caprice's *Cribs* were good though! Don't know if ya saw it. In her basement, she had a dance floor. Apparently she did a bit of DJing on t' side. Somet I've been asked to do but I always say no cos I'm not a DJ. I tell a lie. I did it for a *Heat* magazine party once. That's only cos Lucy Cave asked me. I like 'er. She's got hair like me. In fact if she had a tash she'd look like me, apart from she has a bangers and gash. Anywhere in Caprice's dance floor, she had a massive disco ball, too. The floor were lowered into the ground and water came in turning the dance floor into a pool. She must've made some money to afford a gaff like that. It were truly amazing.

Obviously I've got a right nice gaff too, I just an't got a dance floor that turns into a pool. I fought about having a pool put in t' garden, but it's the up keep.

And the British weather is shite, in't it? I wonder how much I'd actually use a pool. I got a treadmill. Used it for six weeks every day, then never touched it again. Boring as fuck is fitness. Ya wun't know it to look at me, but I've never been to a gym in me life. Just three hours of swingball a day.

So yeah, moving to London were exciting, although there were a bit of a language barrier with me accent. For some reason nobody could understand me when I tried to order a glass of coke. I can remember going to a pub and saying 'can I have a glass of coke, please?' and the barman said 'erm, sorry?' and he looked at me like I'd asked him to put his ass on me coke. So I repeated myself, 'can I have a glass of coke?'. Again he said, 'what did you say?' and I fought, 'what does he fink im saying? It don't sound like I'm asking for a bottle of Newquay Brown, 'can I have a bottle of Newquay Brown...' Then I heard someone say, 'can I have a glass of cewk?' and even to this day if you're in t' pub with me, you'll hear me voice change. Ya know how people have a telephone manner, I have an ordering a glass of coke manner.

Anywhere, enough of that! I had a little break before me next telly project. Not by choice, it were just coming up. Sexually everyfing were coming up. I kept myself busy in the meantime – there were plenty of fings to distract me. There were loads more birds in London than in Leeds. I'd already scored with most of 'em in Leeds. I went back to LA on holiday where I stayed at Avid Merrion's hotel again. He were still a crank and had become obsessed with her out of *Charmed*... ya know, Shannon Doherty. He spent most of his time outside her house asking her to spit in his face. Weirdo. Don't fink his wife were too happy about it. She's also his sister. All very strange.

The Spice Girls had also just got back together and were doing a tour so I popped along for a few of 'em. By 'eck they are all FAF. I were right proud of me mate Bunton. It were nice to see her on stage holding a mic instead of a pint of lager for a change. Boy she can drink. The after party were nuts – just Spicy Girls everywhere. Fink Geri fancied me, I could see it in her eyes. I fink we had a strawberry blond connection. Emma introduced me to Victoria and David. I fink she fought I'd be more excited. I'm not right into football, me though. I saw a charity match with Page 3 Girls once and that were amazing. I had a stiffy so long it ached. Cun't wait to get home and bash it off. Victoria were right nice though and she's very funny. David were a top bloke, too. Very polite. One night after the show we went back to Mel B's. She had a lovely gaff – could have been on *Cribs* too! Fink she were quite proud and chuffed to show us round. This right normal Leeds lass from Leeds had done so well. I can remember Mel B from years ago when she use to be a dancer in a place in Leeds called Yell Bar. She were just as fit back then as she is now. One of me mates actually worked with her in a jeans shop as well. I won't go into any of the stories that she told me about Mel cos she might get arrested and I'd hate this to be one of those controversial books like that Ulrika book years ago. I actually saw her a few weeks ago, she were right nice.

arqiva

Introducing Celebrity Juice

Then one night full of fate, I were out with me mate Kate Thornton celebrating her birthday. I went out with Kate for a bit, but nowt came of it. We went bowling once. I remember her bending down and seeing her fong pop out of her trousers, looked like t' Yorkshire Television logo popping out of her pants, nice. She's fit Kate Thornton. I always fought she looks a bit like Billie Piper, which means she must also look a bit like Paloma Faith and Bjork. Each one of 'em has got the essence of each other in 'em, d'ya know what I mean? I knew ya would. Anywhere, as I were saying it were a fateful night as it were where I met Dan Baldwin, executive producer of *Celebrity Juice*!

It's like Yorkshire television

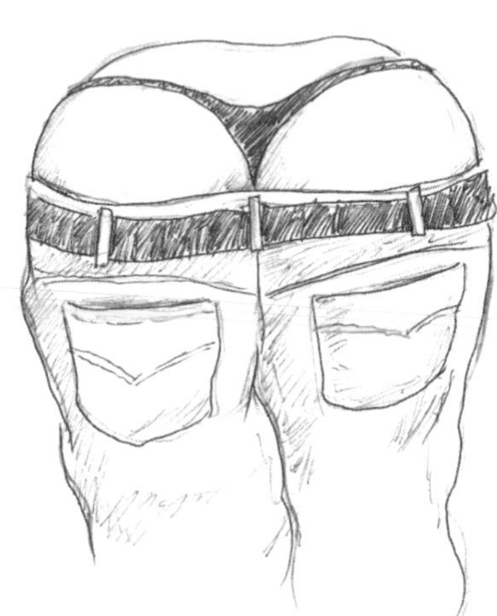

Dan introduced himself to me and said that'd he'd like to work with me, and would I be interested in doing a show with Fearne Cotton and Holly Willoughbooby, who just so happened to be his wife, and still is. He's done well there cos he's not a hunky bloke like me, but he's a good lad and knows his shite. Obviously, I'd already met Holly when I did me *World Tour* and she were lovely. I dint know Fearne. I only knew what I'd seen on telly and I liked her on t' telly. She were proper. Now that I've worked with 'er I can only tell ya that she's the most professional person I've ever met. The most professional person with the most professional nostrils. Her and Holly both, they're brilliant. I would never have fought about working with 'em but I guess that is the genius of Dan putting us all together.

He gave me a treatment for the idea. That normally consists of a piece of paper with what the idea is on it and a cover sheet. Producers like to have a name for the show lined up before they take it to a channel and beg for a commission. Funny fing were I'd just written an idea for a panel show meself called *Keith Lemon's Big Heads*. But I really liked Dan and his idea of *Celebrity Juice* so I gave him me treatment and they took a couple of fings from it and included them in the *Juice* show. I had the late Amy Winehouse in there with different categories for games in her beehive. That went in the first episode I recall.

I tell ya what, I've just been watching *Britain's Got Talent*. Fuckin 'ell, Alesha Dixon is fit. I've met her before like and I always fought she were the fittest when she were in Mystique. But she's just getting fitterer!

It's like magic. If I weren't with Rosie, she'd get it. Can't believe she's never been on *Juice* – or Martine McCutcheon. If you're reading this Alesha or Martine, ya should come on t' show!

Before we actually started the show I went to the V Festival with Holly – not sure what the 'V' stands for. I fink that were a great bonding weekend. Somehow Holly had blagged a Winnebagel. It had a toilet in it, which were a big bonus. I remember seeing a shit pyramid in a toilet at Glastonbury once. I can still see it when I blink me eyes. So Holly says we can only use the toilet for weeing and no solids. If we needed a shit we had to go use the civilian toilets with the civilians. But I remember hearing her in t' toilet. She sounded like an old tramp. Sounded like she were having a fight with her arse and then there were a big fallout. I fought the Winnebagel were gonna tip over. Then she came out with her little angelic face. Face of an angel, arse of a tramp.

I had a great time that weekend. It were exciting to talk about the new show that we were gonna be doing together. I remember while we were drunk, saying it's gonna be good this show, and saying 'I fink it's gonna be big'. Then I told Holly that it is common for most women to have one breast biggerer than t' other and normally it's the left one. I asked her if I could check and she said 'no'. Still, it were a great weekend.

The first time I met Fearne I remember finking she seemed like she were up for a bit of fun and I did fink she had incredibly large nostrils. I fink she is actually a mix of Madonna and Beyoncé. If ya merged them two together, take two photographs and get a computer wizard to put them together and you'll see, it looks like Fearne.

So we started out doing *Juice* in the basement of the TalkBack offices. Fink we did it about three times, once with just a basic camcorder filming it. The guests were different back then too. There'd be a journalist from a tabloid or celebrity magazine a Richard Bacon-type person (who's a good lad and been on *Juice* a few times). I fink Jodie Marsh were on the panel. She's a lovely lass and meke what ya will about her with her new Bruce Lee muscles , when ya see her in person it's quite impressive. She fancies me, but there's never been a window there for me to smash her back doors in. Either she's always been seeing someone or I have. But I'll always be here if she wants some TLC. She's got shit loads of tattoos now, more than Fearne. Fink Fearne's got about 16. They say having tats are addictive, once ya have one ya want another. Bit like wanking, I suppose.

So I fink TalkBack sent a copy of what we filmed in the basement to ITV and they liked it. The people at ITV liked what we filmed! Peter Fincham (The Boss of ITV) and the poshest man I've ever met came to watch us do it live and he liked it! The chemistry between the three of us were there. Both Holly and Fearne were already hooked up with fellas, but they were still giving me the eye. Holly still can't stop touching me and I can see Fearne's nostrils flare with excitement when she sees me, but it weren't the onscreen chemistry we see now. I fink the three of us went to an awards ceremony, fink it were Vodafone, and that were the first time we all got a bit drunk. I can remember pushing it with both of 'em to

Bruce Lee
Muscles
Jodie
Marsh

see where the line were. Fearne had her mouth sucking on me balls whilst Holly stroked and kissed me penis. Just joking... They're both really good sports, with great senses of humour and I get away with murder. Fink that were the first night I mentioned Fearne's massive nostrils. She din t' teck any offence. If I wink at her though she hates it. I fink it's cos it turns her on and she's finding it increasingly hard to fight her emotions for me.

Right, I fink its dinner time. Gonna have a breck. It's me birthday tomorrow so I'll report back to ya what happens and hopefully remember to take some pictures.

Oh my god! It is now the day after me birthday. I am fucked! Just got home from some meetings and put me leopard print PJ bottoms on. Feel mashed up. I had a great day and night though. Went to me fave restaurant in Camden, which is right posh and food is amazing. Ya get a lot of FAF totty in there too. Most of 'em were sat with me: Holly and Fearne, Bunton, Kate Thornton, Cleo Rocos and me boymates. Got a great set of mates in London now. Would've been nice to have some of me Leeds massive down though.

So it were 2008, I fink. We were about to start the first ever *Celebrity Juice*. There weren't too much in the way of a script – 'Sha-ting', 'po-ta-to' and lots of the fings that people fink are catchphrases of the show, they all pretty much happened organically. I fink that's the right word. Sounds good anywhere.

The first show featured Dermot O'Leary (top lad, but scared of puffins as ya know!) Laurence Llewelyn Bowling, a tabloid journalist and me good mate Paddy McGuinness!

In the first episode, I'm not sure Laurence knew how to take me. I don't fink he'd met a Northern person before. I fink he were a bit disgusted with me. He should come on now, it's ruderer than ever. Last time I saw him he were lovely, though. I've always admired his wicked hair. I said 'wicked' as in 'right good' to one of me mates in Leeds and he looked shocked. Fink he fought I'd caught London. I don't fink I'm ever gonna catch London though. I'm Leeds right through to the arse hole.

I remember me outfit as if it were yesterday. I had on a beautiful silver suit what I bought from a shop on Oxford Street called French Eye. Not sure what that name means. Top Man is obvious, it means if ya shop there you'll look like a 'Top Man', and when I do shop there I look like a 'Top Man'. But I also look top when I shop at Zara or H&M or River Island. Not sure what their names are supposed to suggest. But I had this silver suit on and I honestly felt like a million pounds. Before the series I were given a clothing allowance. I cudn't believe it. I just went on a shopping spree buying clobber. I felt like I'd won a competition.

People ask me if I watch *Juice* go out on t' telly when it's on and the answer is if I'm in, I watch just to see what mekes the cut. It's so strange to watch back old episodes. Not that I normally do. When they released the *Celebrity Juice* DVD I watched it again when I did the commentary fingy. The show were a lot tamer back then. I fink I only swore once. I can remember Fearne giving me some jip so I said to her:

'D'ya know what that "F" stands for on t' front of ya desk?'

She said 'What?'

I said, 'Fuckin shut up!'

Ya should've seen the shock on Holly's face. Everyone's face, in fact. It were like I'd punched a baby in t' face. The rest of the series were a lot cleaner back then, but still now and again I'd drop an 'F' bomb 'ere and there. I never set out to be nasty with Fearne, not nasty, just winding her up like. It just happened like that naturally. None of it were planned. Same with Holly, calling her 'Holly Willoughbooby'. It were all a natural process. Her name is Holly and she's got massive boobies. Even her mum calls her Holly Willoughbooby now! Ya can see that we're all really enjoying ourselves. Holly often says that it's her 'night out'. That's what happens when ya have kids I suppose. Holly, she drinks like a tramp. She comes in t' studio with a bottle in a brown paper bag. But I really like it when she says that. Although I dint like it when Fearne started with all that ginger shite. The first time she said it I fought to meself 'Are ya blind? Me hair is the same colour as yours, ya dingbat!' Bigging up Julie from me hairdressers that mekes me hair look so good and strawberry blond!

I fink the first show got around 360 thousand viewers, which apparently were a respectable start. But if we got that now I fink they'd chuck us of air. It's crazy how it's grown.

I don't fink Jedward joined the show until Series 3. Of course back then we had no idea we'd get to Series 2. We were proper chuffed that ITV2 went with it and let it grow. But before I talk about Jedward, who to me are such an integral part of the show, here's a brief run down of some of the people that have been memorable on *Juice,* if I can remember 'em.

CELEBRITY
JUICE

The Juice hall of fame

Rufus Hound

Rufus is a lovely man that were so lovely he became a regular panelist. It were great to have Rufus on t' show, nice to have another bloke on to talk about tits and minge. Rufus loved prostitutes and would often wanna go out and pay to smash back doors in. I'm kidding ya dingbats! The whole prostitute fing with Rufus came about when we'd been out for some award fing or other and a prostitute came up to him and asked him if he wanted business. When he said to her it weren't really his fing, she said that she knew some boys that'd suck him off. I were in the taxi about to go home while this were happening so I just saw him talking to the lady of the night, and I've ruined him ever since. To be honest I'm not even sure if it's ever been in the show me talking about Rufus and his prostitute addiction. Anywhere, Rufus is always a good sport. I remember in one show me and Rufus actually snogged. I fink we were playing 'Get ya coat, you've pulled.' It's almost like a game of 'Chicken'. He went to kiss me I fink and I just fought: 'Fuck it. Ya cun't mock it till you've tried it.' It were horrible, but I fink it helped Rufus overcome his curiosity. Rufus has taken his top off a couple of times in the show, too. He's got incredibly big nips and colourful tattoos that match his colourful underpantage.

Jedward

The first time I met Jedward were the weirdest day of me life. All they kept on going on about were 'let's go to Tescos, there's a Tescos near here. Let's go to Tescos, it would be really cool to go to Tescos'. So I asked 'Why would it be cool?' and they said 'I don't know it just would be really cool.' Weird.

On the way back home on the fun bus, no one were speaking and I just piped up and said 'Were that weird or what?' And that got everyone talking. I'm not saying I dint like them but it were weird. But now, I know them right well and I love those boys. At Christmas they phoned me a couple of times going 'Hello Keith, it's Christmas, yayy!' at whatever effing o'clock. 'Santa has come, get up! There's a whole world out there! Let's go get it Keith, let's do this'. But I do love them. I'm sometimes envious of them because they're so close. Imagine ya don't give a shite what anyone finks of ya because your brother, who's just like ya, loves ya so much. I'd bum him I would, and is it a bad fing to bum yourself? If ya could clone yourself, would ya get off with yourself? I would. Just to see what I'm like.

I fink I'm a bit of a mentor to them, I'm like their older brother. They don't drink, they've never had a drink. I want to take them out t' Rhino, get them pissed and get them a lap dance. I'd love to do that, it would break them in to manhood.

The Hoff

The Hoff dint know who I were so I fink he fought I were a bit crazy to begin with, same as Kelly Brook when she first met me – she looked at me like I were a murderer. But he kept trying to copy my accent which I took as a compliment. And now we're proper mates. He's a bit like Jedward in the respect that he don't care too much.

I fink he enjoys being 'The Hoff' and the memory of what's been and gone, but I'm more obsessed with his *Knight Rider* years. I fink he likes to be remembered as Michael Knight, and who wouldn't? Black leather jacket, red shirt... I remember when we filmed with him the second time and we asked what he were wearing and it were a black leather jacket, a red shirt and jeans like Knight Rider and I said cool and turned up with the same gear on.

Emma Bunton

It is always good having Bunton on t' show. Whenever anyone asks me who the best guest is we've 'ad on I always say anyone who is a mate in real life is best. When you've got someone on that ya know ya can take it further, ya know where that line is and, often with mates there is no line cos they know yer just joking. Emma's lovely and has a great sense of humour and lovely bangers. She's been on so many times now she can more or less deputy captain. If Fearne or Holly aren't on for some reason, I always want Emma there. She's very much like Holly, in fact. Really pretty 'girl next door' but with a dirty mind. I'd love to have a Spice Girls' Special one week. Mel C's been on and she's really nice. So down to earth and Mel B's been on a few times. Mel B always acts shocked by some of the naughtier fings I say, but she's one of the naughtiest women I've ever met. She loves talking about sex. She once asked me if I liked chocolate star-fish. I still don't know what that means.

Eamonn Holmes

He's a lovely warm, funny man. Eamonn has been on *Celebrity Juice* a couple of times. I fink he enjoys himself. He laffs a lot and has a good sense of humour. He's from Belfast and I can talk Belfastian 'Situation'. It's funny with Eamonn cos when I appear on *This Morning,* he mekes out that he don't like me, like that's our on screen chemistry. But he does like me really, I can tell. I fink me and Eamonn should have a night out at Spearmint Rhino.

Claudia Winkleman

I've known Winkletoes a while, although I an't seen her recently. She is so funny, and sexy. I fink she were the first person I ever said 'I would destroy ya' to.

Eamonn likes me really

Saying that were quite shocking back then. I'm not sure the channel knew what it meant cos they used it in a promo that went out pre-watershed. Obviously 'I would destroy ya' is a sexual reference. It's basically saying 'I would sex ya up so vigorous, ya won't be able to walk for a week.' Passionate loving, like. Yeah, she's really cool is Claudia. Got good hair, too.

Paloma Faith

Paloma is brilliant. Right good singer and very creative. Some people confuse that creativeness with craziness. But she an't crazy. People fink I'm crazy, but I'm not. I just like enjoying meself and just like Paloma I sometimes don't have an edit button. Paloma just says what she finks and that mekes for a great guest on a panel show. I fink the first show she were on were with

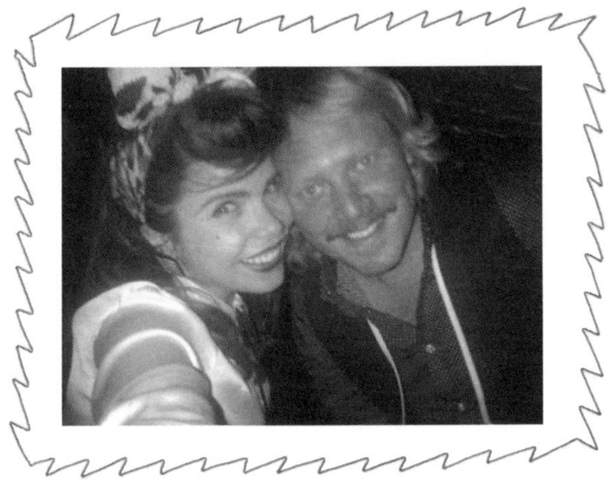

Tamzin Outhwaite and Bunton. They were all pissed up! It were brilliant. Paloma had a fruit bowl hat on. I had me own, which the props department had made that squirted water from a banana. It had plums at the bottom of the banana to represent bollocks. Obviously the banana were the cock. Yeah, she's great, Paloma. The next time she came on she were slightly quieterer. Fink she'd not drunk as much. She told me she's not really a drinker, a glass of wine and ya can smash her back doors in. I did a charity fing with her once. Me and her hosted it and she'd got loads of music acts involved. It were a great night. Ricky from t' Kaiser Chiefs were there. He's a nice bloke from Leeds! Apparently he bought me a drink once when I loved in Leeds, but I can't remember. Don't worry, Ricky! I'll buy ya one back.

Joe Swash

A right nice ginger lovable dingbat. He says no wrong about anyone, Joe. Top bloke, good for a night out, even though he's so cockney I can't tell what he's saying sometimes. Talks about bouncer balls a lot. Saw him at the Soap Awards t' other night. He were hosting the after party show for ITV2. He had similar light-coloured trousers on like meself. I don't fink he shuck his willy enough after he had a wee. He had a little crop circle. That'll teach him!

Verne Troyer

I class Verne as another good mate. He's in me film, which I'll talk about when we get to that bit. One of the smallest fellas I've ever met, too. I fink woman just wanna breastfeed him and he's always hungry for the tit. A great sport too. I hope to work more with Verne. I'm finking of writing *Gremlins: The Musical,* he'd be great as Gizmo. I actually did a pilot with him, but nowt happened. Not a *Gremlins* pilot but more like a late-night chatshow fing. Maybe we'll rework it though. He just sent me a copy of his *Playboy* issue. *He* were in *Playboy*. Funny, as he's dressed as Hugh Hefner, surrounded by naked women. He's just at the right height for some good old motting out! Ooooooosh! I fink one of the most memorable bits of *Juice* were me chasing Verne like a T-Rex. We were acting out scenes from famous films and the panels had to guess what the film were. I know it were one of Fearne's favourite bits. It were nice to see her laffing, miserable cow. Joking, if ya reading this Fearne. Although she probably in't. She's probably too busy painting her bedroom black or somet morbid like that.

Paddy McGuinness

A very good mate of mine, who later became me dancing partner in *Let's Dance for Comic Relief*. Love having Paddy on the show. He's so funny and we have a similar sense of humour. He's a proper man's man. If he weren't married up with an incredibly Bang Tidy wife, I fink Paddy would be me pulling partner when he comes down London. If I weren't with Rosie, of course. I don't go out on t' pull now – just have a little flirt now and again. I'm a bit cheeky but I'm not a love rat!

Dermot O'Leary

Another top lad! Fink he'll be married up by t' time this book is out. So congrats to him. Shit me! Everyone is getting married up. It's great having people like Dermot on t' show cos ya get to see the real them rather than what ya see when they're doing their own shows what they are known for. It's a kinda release as they can do and say what they want and that's me job – to bring that side of 'em out. Of course everyfing is all done in jest. There's no better hug than a hug from Dermot O'Leary... apart from a Kelly Brook hug or a Davina McCall hug. Or a Pamela Anderson hug. Or a Cheryl Cole hug, I mean a Cheryl Tweedy hug, or let's just say a Cheryl hug. Saying that, I don't fink I've had a hug from Cheryl. Have I? Of course, in me dreams I've done all sorts of fings with 'er. Once I had 'er sat on top of me while Kimberly from Girls Aloud were sat on me face. One of the best dreams I've ever had, I fink, pecifically as Sarah and Nicola were lezzing off with each other. Great when ya have those sort of dreams.

man's man

Janet Street Porter aka 'Margret'

First of all, what a fantastic name! Although for some reason, I always wanna call her 'Margret' or 'Aunty Margret'. I love Margret. She's so opinionated and funny. Easy to wind up, but she plays on it sometimes. A great woman. Apparently Janet likes 'rambling', which is what she calls going for a walk, but in me book it's going 'ra, ra, ra, ra, ra, ra', which is what she does a lot on *Loose Women*. I wonder if she can piss standing up. I bet all those Loose Women can piss standing up! Denise Welsh can for sure. She's a great woman. After she were on *Juice* she flashed me her bangers. I knew she were gonna get 'em out when she were on *Big Brother*. Chuffed she won that. She's a right good egg is Denise. Sexy too! I bet there in't owt she wun't do. Good lass!

I'm just gonna have somet to eat. I'm starving me cock off. I might bash one out as well. Let's just see if Rosie has tweeted me.

Rosie Parker @lemontwittor soon soon soon! Long as I get you to meself soon. You spend more time with Cotton than with me at the moment!

Ooooh, see she finks there's somet going on between me and Fearne. I like that she's a bit jealous. Nice that. Now dinner...

Well, that dish weren't that exciting, but it were healthy. Me healthy oriental meal, as featured in me workout DVD, a lot later on from t' period that we're in now.

But if ya want the recipe 'ere it is:

UNCLE BEN'S RICE!

Bang it in t' microwave for two minutes.

While that's cooking chop up some white cabbage and add some red peppers if ya feeling posh.

Empty a tin of tuner fish on top of that.

When ya rice is done mix it up with the tuner, peppers and white cabbage.

Then add some zing with soya sauce for a healthy taste of the Orient!

Oooosh...

Anywhere, where was I?

Memorable guests that I can remember. Of course how could I not remember Louie Spence...

Louie Spence

He's such a funny guy. He were a dancer for t' Spice Girls back in t' day. So that programme *Pineapple Studios*, that show had started getting really popular. One week Louie were in t' big magazine we have when we do the cover story round. Most of the people in t' magazine are people that aren't doing as well as they once were, or are meking a comeback, or are just coming up. Well, one week Louie's in there but the next week he were doing so well that he were on the panel, doing the splits and spitting and doing all his Louie Spence-isms. Louie's got a potty mouth so fits right in with the *Juice* gang.

Louis Walsh

From one Louie to another, but this time spelt a bit different. Louis Walsh has been on a couple of times. I love 'R' Walsh, he gossips more than me! I remember the second time he were on he were saying, 'I've got all your DVDs.' I only had one out back then. Then he said 'I don't know what I'm doing. What's this show again?' I said, 'It's *Celebrity Juice*, remember the last time you were on? Well it's that.' I fink when Louis came on it were the first time I said, 'Po-ta-to!' He gave me the phone to Jedward's mam and I just ended up saying everyfing I could fink of that had an Irish link. *'River Dance, U2, Christine Bleakley, Graham Norton, Commitments, PO-TA-TO!'* And it seemed to stick. Every week after, I felt obligated to saying, 'Po-ta-to!' I still get it all the time now if I dint say it in the show they ask, 'WHY?' But I cudn't say it if there's no context – d'ya know what I mean? It's mad when I'm actually buying potatoes in t' supermarket and ya get a chorus of 'Po-ta-to!' from folk. It sometimes feels like a bunch of turkeys following ya. 'Potato, potato, potato!' Or owls.

Peaches Geldof

I remember when we had Peaches Geldof fill in for Fearne while she were away doing one of her many charity fings. Fearne would eat dogshit if it were for charity, she's so good like that. She won't suck me off for charity which is a shame, but I really got on with Peaches. I fought she might have been a bit awkward, but she were right nice and very flirty. Fink she'd've right liked some of me Lemon Juice.

Caroline Flack

I always enjoy it when Caroline 'Tiny Hands' Flack is on *Juice*. I'm quite built but ya cock must look massive in her little hands. I know Caroline right well. She's a lovely little spinner. I've got a bit of a festival history with 'er. She's a right goer, festival goer. I knew it were gonna be a little awkward when she came on the show after she'd been doing whatever she'd been doing with that young lad from One Erection, err, I mean 'Direction'. When t' audience are there I cudn't help but sometimes be a little bit naughty and just ask the question that everyone wants to know. Anywhere,

there's an age gap between me and Rosie so I'm not one to talk... except Rosie can buy fireworks and rent *Nightmare on Elm Street* from Blockbuster. Well, he should be able to now, shun't he? Fink he's 18 now. Age in't nofing but a numerical figure. Love is a very powerful fing. Look at *Dracula*. She were about 24 when he were 400! It's none of our business who Flack's banging.

Davina McCall

Lovely Davina has been on *Juice* a couple of times and she's great. A great inspiration who I'd also like to have full penatratitititive sex with her one day. Nofing dirty just to say fanks for all t' support she's giving me. With televisual advice and direction and given me an erection watching her workout DVDs. I have nowt but professional admiration for that sexy goddess and her big French nose. When she were first on *Juice* I remember wearing a white suit that had Velcro down the side so I could rip it of and reveal me gymtastic outfit so she could teach me some moves for when I'd finally release a fitness DVD. She got right stuck in and I eventually ended up simulating a good back scuttling with her. She's such a good sport. I love her.

Matt Horne

Matt Horne were a lovely guest and he taught me how to rave, then I gave him a lesson in Russian Kossack (how the fuck d'ya spell that?) dancing, which is me signature move.

Barbara Windsor aka 'Babs'

Always remember Christopher Biggins passing me on to the phone to Barbara Windsor. I fink ya could see I were a bit startled and starry-eyed about it. Love Babs. She told me I were a bit naughty, which I liked, and she said that *Juice were* a bit like *Carry On*. I were chuffed as I loved the *Carry On* films. I hope *Keith Lemon: The Film* follows in the footsteps of the *Carry On* films. That's what I've tried to create as such. Let's see how it goes. I remember asking Barbara if her bangers still made the honk noise they use to meke in t' films. She said that they did. I were thrilled. It were one of me Leeds massive that first did that noise. I remember 'em saying, ''Ere Keith can ya do this noise? *HONK*!' I said, 'I dint know. I'll have ago. '*HONK*!' – and I've been doing it ever since.

Chipmunk

Chipmunk were a good lad, although I fink he were a bit shocked by some of the behaviour. Especially me and Rufus snogging. The look on his face looked like he'd just seen a murder. He were a great sport when we changed his voice into the voice of an actual chipmunk though. Good on 'im. It's good when guys like Chipmunk, Tinchy or N-Dubz loose their street bravado and just become... well, less 'street' for a moment. It's nice to see that side of 'em. Instead of arms crossed, word to ya mam style all 't time.

Philip Schofield aka 'Uncle Phil'

He's another one that drops his street raga-muffin bravado when he's on *Juice* and we get to see the real Philip, whose hair is silver but pubes are as black as a raven's wing, so he told me. We had a great time with Philip. He's been on twice and the second time he were on I fink it were our highest rating episode, just beating the Ant n' Dec one. You've still got it Phil! Never left ya! Oooosh! The second time he came on he told a story about a guest (who I said I wouldn't name) who showed him and Holly her flange all t' way through t' interview. Classic!

Gino D'Acampo

Not sure how many times me mate Gino's been on, but he's lovely and everyone loves him. Of course I always joke that he's in character and that he's actually from Sheffield, but it's not a joke really. He is actually from Sheffield. He does a great Italian accent though, sounds proper. And cos the women love all that Italian stuff he gets away with saying stuff to women that normal fellas can't say. Like the time he said to Fearne with nostrils like she has, 'I bet she can suck like fuck'. I could get away with it, but again I an't normal – I'm just a bit betterer-looking than normal. Gino's a good-looking fella too, so that helps him get away with stuff too. I loved it when Gino and Uncle Phil were discussing Twittor and Gino were saying he weren't gonna follow somebody who had a picture of a bird for their profile picture. 'I'm not gonna follow a bird! Why am I gonna follow an effing bird?' I pissed meself. His theory that if they dint have picture of 'emselves then they have to be ugly. Chris Moyles and Comedy Dave were on that episode too.

Michelle Keegan

One of me all time favorite sports has gotta be Keegan though. Lovely Michelle Keegan. We've had her limbo-ing, she drank a pint of lager that had jizim in it. She's great fun.

Chris Moyles

Chris Moyles is a Leeds lad. Big up! Just been on t' Chris Moyles' Show today actually. Had a great time. Had a good laff playing 'Guess the TV Theme Tune'. There were a couple I dint get but I'm pretty good at that sort of stuff. Cun't believe I dint guess T*ake Me Out*? though. Got *Benson, Knight Rider* and *Airwolf* straight away! He an't 'arf lost some timber, Mr Moyles. Not sure how he's been doing it, but good on him. He seems a lot happier. Not that he weren't happy before, but ya can hear it in his voice on t' radio. He just seems happier! Well done, mate! When you've finished with this getting fin stuff let's go for some jars and a kebab.

George Lamb aka 'Lady Killer'

Lady Killer (not that he's actually killed a woman but ya know what I mean). George Lamb were a good sport when he came on and played *Silence of the Lamb*. I had to get a reaction out of him using different methods of getting a reaction in a series of different rounds. For example, 'A Joke', pulling a funny face, doing a dance, insults, or anyfing goes.

...and then the soap stars

Most soap stars are great fun. Jack P. Shepherd is a good lad. He plays that right cocky little bastard in *Corrie*, but he's actually right nice! Antony Cotton is lovely too, as is Kim 'Fit as Fuck' Marsh. Dave Berry has been on so many times we did a montage of his best bits. I fink when Dave were on it were the first time me willy ever popped out while I were doing some sort of strip. I get a lot of people ask me if it really were me willy that popped out. Even me mam phoned me and asked me. Well, I'm not telling. It's a secret. Speaking of willies, I remember in a series later down the line we had a naked old fella on in a game called 'I'm coming'. Again it were like a game of 'Chicken'. I fink it may have been Gok Wan and Fearne that were playing... yeah it were. He were a right nice old man who I fought would meke a great Santa Claus if he'd put his cock away, but he insisted he weren't fat enough. Not sure how he knew how fat Santa's cock were. I remember Dan talking to me in me earpiece saying, 'slap his knob!' I fought 'how can I do this?' I dint wanna hurt him or really touch his dick to be honest. But I'm like Marty McFly in *Back t' Future*, when someone dares me to do somet or calls me 'chicken', I fall right into it. So I said, 'And the scores at the end of that round are... *Sha-ting*!' Then hit his knob.

'Ere's a bit of *Juice* trifia for ya. When I say 'Sha-ting' I mean it like the sound of a bell or a microwave when ya food is cooked. I don't mean 'Shitting', as in having a crap. It all came from the pilot in t' basement we shot. When I did the scores saying 'and the scores are' I asked will there be a sound effect there, so I just said 'Sha-ting' and rather than have a sound effect we just ended up with me just saying 'Sha-ting' and that's where that came from.

One of the stand-out moments that stands out for me were the time we had Dick and Dom on t' show so we had a kids TV theme show. The losing team got gunged and that week it were Fearne's team and she had Thomas Turgoose on, the little skin 'ed kid from that film/TV show *This is England*. I threw the bucket of gunge on 'em and proper went flying. Went for a right burton I did, smacking me head on t' floor. I fink I were out for t' count for about a second and when I got up I could see stars. I slurryly said, 'If I dint see ya through t' week I'll see ya through t' winda', a saying that me mate's mam use to say as I left his house when I were a kid and I'd been playing round there. Afterwards I were asked if I need to see a doctor cos I proper walloped me head. I said 'no', then about 20 minutes later I felt a bit odd and me head were killing. So the doc came to see me and I ended up in a neck brace for three days. Reminded meself of that old weirdo Merrion.

I fink *Celebrity Juice* gets better each series. The chemistry gets better and as a team we just get closer and closer. Me and Fearne often get off with each other at the wrap party – although she'll deny it cos she just can't remember as at the wrap party she just gets wrecked. It's not very often she goes but when she does she really enjoys herself and gets right pissed. Whereas

with Holly she gets pissed all t' time if she in't pregnant. So as the show got more popular, I got invited onto more shows and to more functions and stuff. I love going to dos as I meet people that I never fought I'd meet. Like Knight Rider, who's such a close personal friend I can call him 'Dave' now.

Going to premieres is crazy, doing that whole red carpet fing and people shouting ya name. Sometimes I feel just like Rick Astley! And I promise I'm never gonna give ya up, never gonna let ya down, never gonna turn around and desert ya! That's a personal message t' fans! I love you!

I did a podcast at some point again. While I were doing the podcast I can remember not even really knowing what one were. Still don't really. I invited me mate Paloma t' studio for a chat and on the phone we had Dermot O'Leary and me mam. We had to do a sound check and I remember the sound engineer saying to me, 'You just spoke non-stop for 72 minutes.' I weren't

sure if that were a long time or not enough. But the sound had been checked and we were ready to record. I dint fink too much would come of it cos as I said I dint really know what it were. But for the two podcasts that I did I won a Loaded Lafta award, which were great cos I got to meet Vic and Bob, who I fink are funny as fuck.

As I slowly became a face of the telly, I'd often go back to see me mates and me mam back in Leeds. Always got asked who I'd met especially by Rosie, who I'd see in t' pub. She always had time for me and I'd always have time for her cos I knew at the end of the night if I hadn't pulled, Rosie were a dead cert. I know that sounds arrogant of me. But I dint know back then what I know now. That why I put it about a bit. But I always used a rubber johnny cos me mate who lived life on t' edge more than I did never wore a johnny and once got some kinda STD and green pulp dispersed from his cock end. Said it stung like he were pissing nettles and I never wanted to feel that pain. He's right. No way!

I came back to London and I were asked to go on the ITV2 show *I'm a Celebrity Get Me Out of Here! NOW!* hosted by Caroline Flack, Joe Swash and Russell Kane, all guests on Juice. So, a trip to Oz to do a bit of telly with me mates. Fair dos. It took an effing lifetime to get there. 24 hours to be pecific. I fink I switched planes in Dubai. I would of missed me second plane, if it weren't for a nice bloke I'd met on t' flight who said he were a fan. I were a bit of a dingbat travelling by meself. Once I got out there it were great even though ya get picked up at 4am do a bit of telly. The other guests were Janet Street Porter, Mel Blatt, Donna Air and Scott Mills.

I mainly hung out with Flack and Blatt, both Bang Tidy. Mel Blatt is great for a piss up, which is all we did really. Eat pizza and get pissed. One day we went to somet called Movie World, I fink it were called. Did the funniest fing – we sat in a booth with a green screen cape wrapped around us so only our heads were showing. Then they keyed our head onto the bodies of some dancers dancing to Beyoncé. For $30 we all got a DVD of it each. We went back to Joe Swash's and watched it on a loop about 20 times pissing ourselves with both me and Joe finking any minute now one of 'em is gonna put their tits in our face. But it dint happen.

The following year I went out there again. I would of done again if I hadn't been busy shooting *Keith Lemon: The Film.* Craz-ey times. But before that I were gonna do my workout DVD with Lionsgate. And before that even, I were gonna perform a dirty dance for Comic Relief with Paddy McGuinness.

Dirty Dancing with Paddy

So I were sat watching telly one night. Not sure why I weren't doing out. I were just teking it easy on t' sofa, hands down me pants, twisting me ball sack with me fumb and forefinger. That's enough detail, I fink. Suddenly Paddy McGuinness calls me up. He always starts with somet funny – 'Now then ya cheeky badger', 'Ey up cockle', 'Ummm I like veins me, big blue veins'. So he tells me he's been asked to do a new show called *Let's Dance for Comic Relief* and that they're looking for celebrities to do classic dances from films. All I can fink is 'Me a celebrity?' Anywhere, he'd told 'em that he'd be up for it if I were and if we could do the last dance from *Dirty Dancing*, ya know the one with 'The Lift' at the end. It were nice to be asked to do somet for Comic Relief. I'd done a photoshoot for 'em the previous year, but they'd not asked me to do owt on t' telly. It's good to help out I fink and to have fun while doing it – well that's a bonus in't it. So, anywhere, I said yeah. I put the phone down and fought for a bit and then I fought, 'what have I just said "yeah" to?' So, I phoned Paddy back up and said, 'What are we doing again?'.

It weren't a simple sketch like I fought it were. No, of course not. They wanted us to properly learn the dance and perform it live in front of a studio audience – LIVE on t' telly. This were mini *Strictly Come Dancing* so it meant rehearsing everyday to compete in a competition against other celebrities. I panicked a bit, composed meself and fought, 'Well, as it's gonna help starving kids, it's a good fing to do.' And there's another

tip for ya: do a bit for charity and the girls will be putty in your hands.

Paddy started the rehearsals. He were the lead – Patrick Swayze – and I were 'Baby' – Jennifer Grey. If he were gonna be the lead, surely he needed more rehearsal than me and I'd just take his lead. I can dance a bit anywhere. As a child I use to dance as a means of communication as I cudn't speak till I were about eight. I were a wicked break dancer back then and I can still body pop like a good 'un. We were given two weeks rehearsal of which I missed the first five days cos of *Juice*. So when I joined Paddy, he already knew what we were doing. We did a run through and I fought, 'Fuck! I'm not gonna remember this.'

It were so odd dancing with a bloke, feeling his chunk on me thigh, and looking so closely and intensely into Paddy's eyes to replicate what they did in t' film. Ya can only imagine how many times we started laffing. First few days I hated it and suddenly, when the penny had dropped, I started to really enjoy it. We both did. We said the only way we're gonna win this fing were to fall in love but have no puffery. We rehearsed the shit out of it and word had started to spread that we were a bit good. Robert Webb (from *Peep Show*) had already won the first episode, which meant if we got through we would be competing against him in t' final. He were very good, performing the routine from *Flash Dance*. In our episode, me and Paddy were against Jo Brand (lovely woman, really liked her), The Dragons from *Dragons Den* (they were right nice, especially Peter Jones who later were a guest on *Juice* in which he got ripped for being an actual giant), Dr Fox (who in't really a 'Dr' or a 'fox') and Nancy Sorrell (Vic Reeves' incredibly fit wife, who is also a great singer).

There were also *Blue Peter* presenters, including Peter Duncan (Legend) and Janet Ellis (who's basically Sophie Ellis-Baxter but older. She'd get it, both of 'em would actually), Mark Kury (nice fella), Dianne-Louise Jordan (she were really nice), Anthea Turner (I fink she is so sexy, always liked her) and Helen 'Fit as Fuck' Skelton (fink she's brilliant, she's always doing great stuff for comic relief – I wonder if she'd like to do a sex tape with me for charity?).

I remember everyone sat backstage. All teking it far more serious than ya could ever imagine. None more than me and Paddy as we wanted to win like mad. Whenever we could, we just went through the routine. I can remember one night even practising it by meself in me garden. I dint know how many times I watched *Dirty Dancing* that week and I use to hate that film. Chick flick in't it? It's all about *Rocky, Rambo* and *Back t' Future* for me. We weren't too worried about the lift. That were the first fing we got down. Although if we'd have effed it up on the night it would've been a right shambles. That lift were our secret weapon. Paddy were in his Swayze get-up and he looked really good! I can remember moaning that my wig weren't the right colour. But the dress looked proper and I even had heels on. Those effing heels! Bastards, they were. They cut the shit outta me. But it finished the outfit off just right.

As the curtains went up, me and Paddy were sat at a table just finishing off our pints of lager. I picked up a watermelon and we walked on stage. Fink we were both shitting bricks. There were no choreographers there anymore to help us (and they were brilliant!). I dint fink we looked at anyfing or anyone else apart from each other's eyes. Just like Jonny and Baby in *Dirty Dancing*. All were going well, then came t' lift.

We'd done it a thousand times and it cudn't go wrong while we're live on t' telly, could it? We were doing this for those starving kids after all! I shot up there like a majestic eagle and Paddy lifting me with all t' strength of the mighty Thor! Well, it weren't really like that, more like a short-arsed strawberry blond man in drag being lifted up by him from *Phoenix Nights*. I fink we pulled it off though. T' audience went mad. It were amazing. We dint really focus on anyfing else apart from each other. We stayed in character all the time and we got into trouble for the little kiss we did at the end. It were probably the most hormone sexual fing I'd ever done. Paddy had wanked someone off before, so it were nowt for him. Joking, Guinness!

We felt really chuffed with ourselves. Jo Brand came second which meant we both had a place in t' final. It were a good week that week. Had a lot of press and loads of hits on YouTube. I've always said it – I'm like a locket, I have a hard exterior but inside I'm soft and juicy, so it felt good to help out with Comic Relief. I were honoured and me mam were right proud.

In the final show, I fink we came on second. We fought, 'That's it then. We aren't gonna win.' And ya know what, we dint. But we had a great time at the wrap party and did the dance again, this time pissed up! Girls were queuing up for Paddy to lift 'em up, while I tried me best to get off with Claudia Winkleman.

After *Let's Dance* me and Paddy decided we should do some work together again. So we started writing stuff. We had an idea for a show recreating our favourite films on a budget. It were all inspired from the *Dirty Dancing* fing we did. So we wrote a half-hour version of *Dirty Dancing* called *Dirty Prancing*. We had a few meetings about it and it nearly happened but in the end it dint. I fink it would've been really good. We were gonna spoof a different film in each episode. It might happen one day but if it dint you'll find the first draft of the *Dirty Prancing* episode we wrote together at t' end of book.

Keith Lemon's FIT

So with my dancing career behind me, I had a bit more time to focus on finally getting me film off the ground. I got invited to a Lionsgate premiere so I went along with a mate from me Leeds massive. It were Sunday, I fink, and it were the premiere of a film called *Righteous Kill* starring Al Pacino and Robert DeNiro. I like 'em two. Pecifically Pacino in his Carlito formation and DeNiro as Rupert Pupkin in the cult classic *King of Comedy*. It's ace! I like *Taxi Driver* as well. When he makes a gun holster fing that shoots out of his wrist, out of a bit of sofa... Imagine 'em showing ya how to do that on *Blue Peter*. Janet Ellis eat ya heart out. '*Yo yo yo! Welcome to a special mutha fuckin' Bronx edition of Blue PetOR. Check this. This week we're gonna be showing y'all how to make a bad ass projectile gun holster that pops out of your sleeve like some terminator shit right there. Y'all know what I'm talking about. You dig? But first, here's what happened when one of my main brothas went kayaking down some white water rapid shit. That dude be ruthless! Let's see what went down...*'

Anywhere, me mate Paul had never been to a premiere before so took advantage of the free bar at the after show party. Why not? I bumped into an old friend of mine that I hadn't seen in some time and he told me that Lionsgate were gonna be meking his next film. I actually dint know he'd made one before. In fact, he hadn't. It were gonna be his first. But he knew how to talk fings up. That were one of his talents. A bit like me. It's not lying, it's enhancing the truth to meke

for good pub chat and for chatting up the ladies of course. Anywhere, I were right happy for him and he introduced me to his acquaintance at Lionsgate.

Paul said that me and him should meke a film! I said, 'Yeah I'd love to meke a film.' I'd always fancied meself as the next Owen Wilson. Get told I look like him except me nose in t' shaped like a penis. So we chatted about t' film for a while and kept on getting more and more excited. Then me attention were drawn to a certain Katie Price that were sat in t' corner. I said to me mate, 'Don't look now but that Katie Price is over there.' So what did he do? He looked now.

I forgave him cos as I said he'd never been to a premiere before and he dint realise ya have to play it all cool. It's like when you're on t' beach with your bird and you're checking out all t' other ladies with dark glasses on. To be honest though, I fink he were more bothered that the drinks were free and that they were serving these tiny, tiny burgers and fish and chips that were so tiny it were like they'd had a shrinking serum injected into them. Imagine, a whole burger in one bite. It blew his tiny little mind. Between us we must 'ave polished off about 15 of those little bastards.

It were a great night and nice to see me old mate Paul. We stumbled out of the party pissed up and full of tiny burgers and carefully looked for a place to have a slash without getting caught by the law. I were finking it were the best outside piss of me life, until I looked up to find that I were pissing against a police station. With the speed of haste, I shook it and put it away and speeded off. Then, by the Wednesday I were in Lionsgate having a meeting about doing a film. Cudn't believe it. Keith Lemon in glorious flat 2D.

I sometimes get asked who would play me in a film about me. It's like when ya go to a super hero film, the question ya most often get asked is, 'What power would ya have if ya were a super hero?' I always say the power of flight – although once when I appeared on *Richard Bacon's Beer and Pizza Club,* I said me power would be to shoot Scotch eggs from the palm of me hand. I fink a projectile Scotch egg in the face would hurt but it wun't kill me nemesis, cos if you're a super hero and ya kill someone you've crossed over t' dark side. But that's irrelevant, in't it? What is relevant is who would play me in a film about me? Erm... I would, of course! And that's the plan.

We had meeting after meeting developing the story for the film. Scriptwriting lasted almost three years. That's not solid writing obviously. I were doing plenty of other fings while it were going on. But the basic premise for t' film were it were to be an origin sort of fing.

So whenever I were filming *Juice*, or doing whatever, I were also writing the film that I never actually fought would happen. But it were through the film meetings that another project came about. One day in a meeting, a Bang Tidy bird from another department came in and said they had two more DVD entities left, and would I be interested in meking a workout DVD? I weren't sure what an 'entity' were apart from I'd seen a film called *The Entity*, where a woman were getting molested by a ghost. Horrible film, I hoped it weren't gonna be anyfing like that. But I sure as hell knew what a workout DVD were as I'd wanked off to so many when I were a kid. So, I considered it for less than a short second and then said, 'Yeah! I'm up for a workout DVD.'

I know I don't have the body of a god but I am fast. I'm robust. It mekes a lot of sense me doing a workout DVD because people will listen to me because I've got me own problems too just like everyone else. Well, I haven't really but sometimes I wear a verucca sock at the swimming pool – I don't have a verucca, I just want to look normal.

All I could fink of when I fought of this workout DVD were that music video of Eric Prydz's 'Call On Me' with that F.A.F. bird with the naughty body. What if I could do my workout video with her? That'd be worth doing. That video were amazing. More amazing than meat and po-ta-to pie! Don't know if ya've seen that video, but basically they're all fit and wearing 80s gym gear. A great video to pump fist to if you're away travelling and have got no babe station – apart from there's a man in t' video, but just block him out with ya mind.

Anywhere, if I were gonna do a fitness video, she were the perfect girl to do it with. So they got in touch with her, Deanne Berry her name were. Deanne is Australian for Diane. Now that woman has an arse! You'd let her use your face as toilet paper. You'd let her fart in your face. It is proper incredible! She were interested in doing it and came in for a meeting. Now I'm not gonna name names cos I don't wanna embarrass anyone – ya know who ya are, and ya know what I mean – but when she came in there weren't a bloke in that room that could stand up. And this were her just in normal clothes, not even the leotard fong fing she wears in t' video which we were obviously gonna get her to wear in our DVD – *Keith Lemon's Fit*.

She were actually right nice. I had no idea how to meke a workout DVD so I asked 'er to drag in some of 'er mates and basically she led and I followed. That's why I dint bother going to the rehearsal. So the weekend before we were shooting it – in the exact location used in t' Eric Prydz video – I popped up to Leeds to see me pals and a certain Rosie Parker.

While in Leeds, me mate Paul were badgering me to get him on t' telly. I told him when the time were right I'd try. He's like a mini Alexei Sayle crossed with Bruce Willis. He is right funny, though.

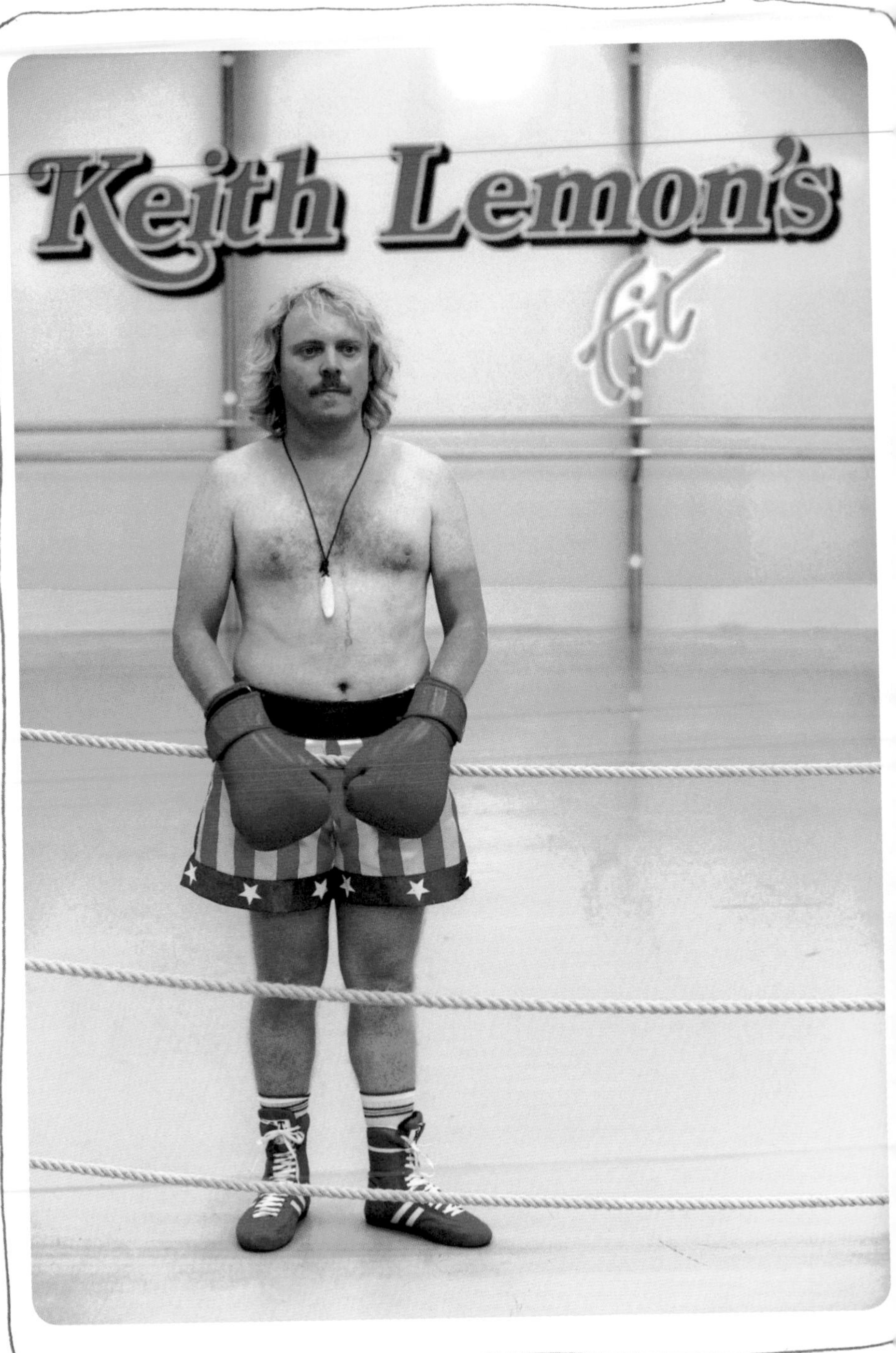
Keith Lemon's
Fit

Had a good chat with Rosie about how fings had changed in me life. She never seemed like one of those birds that were interested in me just cos I were on telly, and there were a lot of those, and I can't lie, sometimes ya just fink, 'Bollox let's have a go. If she wants to go around telling everyone she's had some Lemon juice then so be it.'

Rosie's different though. I'd often end up with a cheeky snog at the end of the night and then some. But I never wanted to say she were me bird, even though she were acting like me bird a bit. But we never said we were 'boyfriend and girlfriend'. I fink she knew that I wanted to get out there and explore before I settled with one lass. I were a lot naughtier back then.

Anywhere, it were Monday and I were back in London to do the workout DVD. It were gonna be a two-day shoot. Two days of dancing around with sweaty F.A.F. dancers. Every single one of 'em were fit. In me head, I fought the kids are gonna love this. I wanted it to be like an old school workout DVD that young lads could watch when their parents were out. It were me gift to 'em before they got into pumping fist over porn. I'm not right into porn meself, but I much prefer softer stuff such as a workout DVD or somet like *Basic Instinct*. After two days of dancing around I were proper fucked, but it were a lot of fun.

If you're wondering about the secret to my great body, I'll tell ya. I've been working on the theory that it's all about quantities, in't it. For example, I believe in binge drinking. I fink to binge drink is better than drinking shit loads every night. I know that scientists say to have a glass of wine a day but don't binge. But what a waste of time! You're not gonna get pissed as a newt like that are ya? I say, save it all for Saturday night and get hammered.

Anywhere, while this were happening I were still writing the film with Paul the Director. I'd just stand up and walk around sensationalising fings that had happened to me in real life, adding total fabrication for the purpose of filmic entertainment. When we laffed, then that'd go down in t' script. It were a lot different approach to working on *Celebrity Juice*. I write nowt for *Juice*, just turn up, have a drink and a laff. I've always said that I fink the success behind *Juice* is that folk like to watch us enjoying ourselves. The day we're not enjoying it anymore is the day we should stop doing it. But I fink we all still really enjoy it.

When my fitness DVD came out, I remember it being number one in the Fitness chart on Amazon, while Davina McCall were number six. I were a bit embarrassed by that, cos Davina's were a proper workout DVD and mine were just a bit of fun.

I really enjoyed doing the promotion for the DVD as Deanne did a lot with me. It were nice doing it with someone rather than by meself. It's like sex in't it? A wank is fun, but it's more fun when someone is doing it for ya. Sometimes I wish I were doing it with her. Boy, she were fit.

We did magazine stuff together – *Nuts* and *Zoo* and stuff. *Love It* mag were a funny one. We had photos done around the *Love It* van and they'd interview us as though we were in the van, but the interview were actually in an office. Not sure if you've ever read *Love It*, but there's a lot of sad tragic stories, then an interview with a celebrity. For example, in this week's *Love It*, there's a woman, pregnant with twins, involved in a punch up; there's the guilt of a mother that fell in love with a pedo; an interview with Abbey Clancy, who's 'skinny, but not happy' and the chance to win a trip to Alton Towers for four! What's not to love about *Love It*?!

We were also asked to perform a routine from the DVD at T4's Stars of 2010, which were a lot of fun. To start with, I were gonna be sharing a dressing room with five Bang Tidy birds. Result! And there were lots of stars there – The Saturdays, Olly Murs, Alexandra Burke, Example, Pixie Lott (best legs ever) and Professor Green. It were a big event! We had to show the producers the routine before we actually performed it, but apparently it were too rude and what the girls were wearing were not enough so we had to change it for a T4 audience. No thrusting. No thrusting, me arse! We did it anyhow and got away with it.

I remember I had to shoot some pre-title sketches before it with Frankie from t' Saturdays, Alexandra Burke and maybe Olly Murs. It were the first time I heard the phrase 'You is jokes' from Alexandra Burke. Fink that's her street lingo for 'Hey, you're right funny you!' Keeping it real, see! All in all I fink it worked. I'd done T4 stuff in t' past and there's always a worry that ya not gonna be able to say or do what ya want cos it's a younger audience. But I'd trained meself when to rude it up and when not to. I never swore or owt in front of me mam. In fact, t' first time me mam heard me swear were on t' telly. Never swore in front of her. Respect, in't it? She knows a lot of what I say on telly is just for jokes. And as Alexandra Burke says, I am 'jokes', an't I?

I never had it off with Deanne Berry. Dint even cup her tits in t' end. Oh, actually, I may have cupped her tits. But she had a boyfriend and were planning to get married. So, while she fucked off back to Australia, I continued to do PR for the DVD. I were doing a signing at an ASDA in Derby and I'd seen Katie Price do her signing on t' telly at the same ASDA and it were packed. I were worried I'd not be as popular but in t' end I signed for three hours, so it were a good turnout and everyone were happy.

Then I were asked to present 'behind the scenes' at the Comedy Awards with the lovely Emma Willis. I weren't nominated for one so I fought, 'Fuck it! Yeah, I'll do it!' I know Emma and she's lovely. I'd been on *Big Brother's Little Sister's Uncle*, or whatever they were calling it then. Emma hosted it with George Lamb. Another top bloke and I'd say, apart from me, the best-dressed man on telly. George's been on *Juice*, but to this day I dint know why Emma hasn't been on. Not sure if ya follow me on Twittor @lemontwittor, but as I say on there, *I DON'T BOOK THE GUESTS*. I'm forever being asked when will One Direction be on? When will Lady GaGa be on? When is Jessie J on? When's Rihanna on? Hey, they're all welcome! But it an't up to me!

And you, too, Gary Barlow! Who apparently is a big fan of the show. I've recently struck up a text friendship with him. I'd only spoken to him via text, until a few weeks ago, when he agreed to do a cameo in the film. Right nice fella he is and I'd love for him to come on *Juice*. Imagine that – a Take That Special! You can only hope. As I said... *I DON'T BOOK THE GUESTS.*

Speaking of Twittor, let's have look at some of me most recents. This is a shout out to all ya tweeters! Fanks for all your support. I hope there's no horrible ones like the one I had the other day. A young girl wanted to throw a brick in me face. Don't know what I'd done to upset her. Bint.

audra armsden @lemontwittor god,what a guy,celeb juice, lemonaid, and your film, now a book whens that out is it about you? any juicey goss in it lol xxx

That's nice, in it! Yeah, the book is about me and if you've bought it, you'll know it's about me. Cheers for buying it!

Tiff Foster @lemontwittor its me birthday today, could I have a RT please so I can brag :-)

Get these all the time too. 'Appy birfday Tiff!

louise jacobs @Nandos_Official I'm on the case of the renewal of @lemontwittor nandos card seein as it were said on national radio that he'd b getin a new1

That's nice, too. I said on Chris Moyles' Radio show that me Nando's card had run out. I use to be the Chicken Master!

It's really odd when ya get angry tweets from bitter people. I don't know how they can be arsed. Sometimes I wanna retaliate and tell 'em I hope they get impetigo all around their mouth and eyes or their dick falls off or they get mutilated by a fox or they get some sort of minge infection. But I'm just not that angry. I'm nice me! And niceness works! Just the other day I got some free shoes cos I'm nice and if being nice gets ya free shoes then I'm sticking with nice!

Working with Emma Willis were really nice. I fink she gets me sense of humour. She weren't scared of me or anyfing. A lot of people get all scared. I don't know what they fink I'm gonna do. But Emma were really cool. I'd like to work with her again or at least have a hand job from her if fings go wrong with Rosie. Emma's got the craziest blue eyes, beautiful.

It were a little odd interviewing a load of drunken comedians that I knew. It were funny running into Kevin Bishop. He's a good lad. We had a cheese throwing competition. Well, I say 'competition', but it weren't really. I just asked Kevin if he fancied throwing owt as the previous year I fink he were a little drunk and decided to throw fings. All in jest though. He's a top bloke (I know him even better now after t' film). So, we threw a bit of cheese on't stage.

The highlight though were meeting Pamela Anderson for the first time. Little did she (or I) know that she'd be a guest on *Juice* in t' future doing a pole dance for me. Incredible! I honestly can't believe me life sometimes. There I am sat in front of t' telly, eating a packet of crabsticks, the next minute I'm looking into Pamela Anderson's eyes finking, 'Ya know what love, you're aging pretty well! I'd love to meke vigorous love to ya.'

I fink we all do that with people we fancy. We shake their hands and say 'How do', and then we imagine 'em naked and before ya know it, we're smashing their back doors in, their front doors, maybe even in t' mouth... Sometimes I say too much me. Me mates say it's like an evil wizard has injected me with a truth serum. If I offend, I never mean to. I just fink honesty is the best policy. And from experience, if ya say everyfing with a cheeky nod and a wink, nine times outta ten ya get away with it!

My pulling methods are more maturer these days. Before I were like 'Hi, I'm Keith Lemon, wanna fuck?' but now I get 'em to notice me much more subtle like. Ya can tell if someone fancies ya, they'll look ya straight in t' eye. And what I'll do is, I'll stare back, trying to intimidate them a bit, not looking away, not even to look at all t' other fit birds. I always do that. I can remember one of the researchers on *Lemonaid* who were a body double for Jennifer Aniston in the film *Derailed* and I did it to her and she goes 'Stop it!' and I'm acting all innocent like, 'Stop what?' and she's like, 'You know what you're doing!' And I did cos I were gazing into her eyes like a predator, not like a *sexual* predator, more like a really focused leopard. She were dead attractive but I didn't act on it because I had a bird already. And I've changed that way. Faithful you know.

Before Rosie moved in, I were faithful but not as faithful as I am now. If she caught me cheating though she'd understand cos she knows that it's hard for me because I have so many women throwing themselves at me feet. It's hard, and sometimes I'm weak. But if I'm flirting too much, she'll drag me away. We had a dinner party a couple of weeks ago, Stacey Soloman were there, Chris Fountain, Toby Anstis and Jenny Powell. And Jenny Powell fancies me, that is scientific fact, and when she kissed me goodbye I got sucked in dint I, and kissed her a bit more than I should've and Rosie fucking dragged me off and then just snogged my face to bits in front of Jenny Powell then said 'Goodbye,

Jenny Powell'. I said to Toby, 'You better go, cos we're gonna have sex' and he told us to get a room but we already had one cos it were our house and every room were ours. Good night that.

Just had a little break and watched some Jessie J clips on YouTube. Very rare a bird looks fit even without make up. I fink she's lovely Jessie J – and she can sing like a bastard! Proper good singer. I had a dream about her a few weeks ago. Boy, she were naughty. Not sure it's true or not I heard see were bisensual? Whatever. Even if she's full blown lesbican. She's ace! Cool as Fuck and Super Bang! Fink she's me new favourite.

Ask Uncle Keith

Fings cun't have been going more betterer when I got a call asking me if I wanted to do a weekly slot on *This Morning* as an Agony Uncle. Of course, I did! I love *This Morning* and the fact that Holly's on it made it even more attractiverer – we could go into work together in the morning after the night before. And I know some fings about life and its problems. I've got a gay brother and had a fucked up toe before, so I were well up for it and more than qualified. I'm like a wise owl.

The first week I did it, I could see the worry in Uncle Philip's eyes. But I fink Holly must've reassured him that I'm not a mental. It went really well. I really enjoyed helping people with their problems. I fink I actually really helped them. Here's a sample of me wise pearls.

Agony Uncle Keith's Advice

If your boyfriend in t' giving ya the attention ya fink ya deserve then trade him in get a new 'un.
If your wife finks you're cheating, hey go ahead and cheat! She finks ya are anywhere, so ya may as well give her somet to be suspicious about.
If ya can't lose weight stop being a salad dodger, maybe get one of those elastic bands on your arse like Fearne Britton did. She looks well on it!

I did the Agony Uncle stuff for a while and then I went onto reviewing fings such as bouncy water slides and trampolines. The girl I were doing that item with were F.A.F. I suggested to her that later that afternoon I went round hers to see how bouncy her bed were!

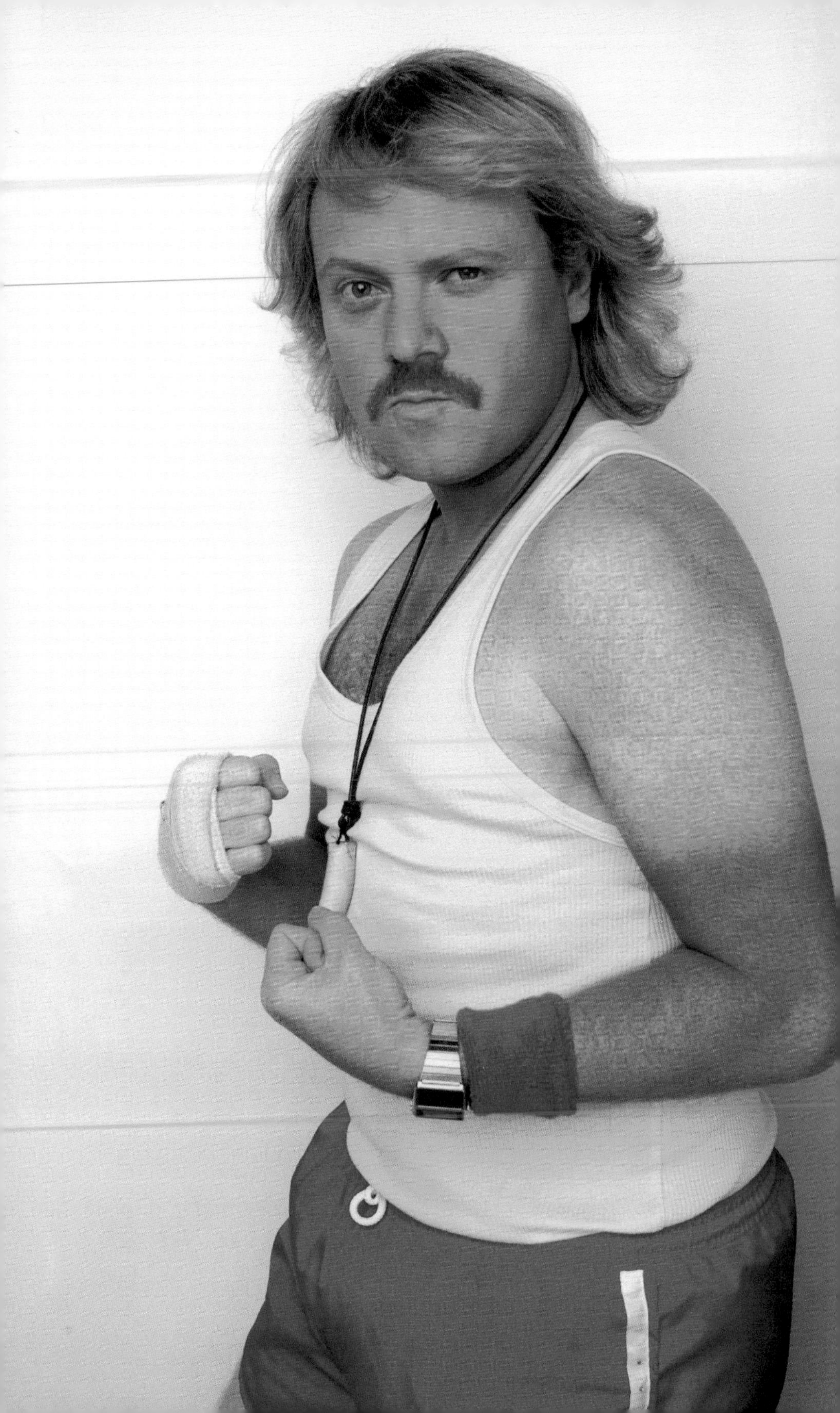

I also do a bit of cooking sometimes with me mate Gino D'Acampo. We made a peach Alaska in Christmas jumpers, it were ace! Gino's a great cook and I like the way he tries to put a naughty word in 'ere and there. Never says 'couldn't', it always sounds like a naughty four letter word. Similar to me accent. I always say 'cudn't'. 'He could but ya cudn't!'

Jenny Powell were there one week, too. She's F.A.F! I fancied Jenny Powell for years. It's strange cos she looks a bit like Michael Jackson but also like a super fit, Bang Tidy bird. I'd let her kick the shit out of me and I'm not really into that kinda fing as ya know. I gave her the eye and flirted with her but I dint do owt. Fings had started getting serious with Rosie. Again, we never said we were an item, but it were blossoming into somet and I fink we both knew it. So out of respect for Rosie, I never touched Jenny Powell. But in me mind, I finger blasted her to bits.

JENNY OR IS IT MJ?

Sometimes I did *This Morning* on a Friday with Ruth and Eamonn, when Phil and Holly weren't there. They're all right nice down at *This Morning*, which is why I enjoyed doing it. Alison Hammond is always nice to cuddle, Dr Chris is a lovely man and I class Gino as one of me pals. Phil Vickery's always nice to me, too. I always end up hanging out in t' pub when I'm down there, whether it's with Coleen Nolan (bet she gives a good blow job, massive bangers!), Stephen Mulhern (that evil wizard can pull a wine bottle out of a napkin, fuck knows how he does it), Matt Johnson (lovely Welsh bloke, nearly as good looking as me) or lovely Samantha (quiet at first, but ya know what they say about the quiet ones).

Sharon Marshall's always good for a bit of crack, too. I shared a cab home with her from the NTAs. I won't say what went on cos I don't wanna wreck her marriage, just that she's *very* giving. I were at the NTAs with *This Morning*. I felt a bit of a dingbat, to be honest, cos I'd only just started working there and there I were hanging out with 'em all like I'd been doing it for ages. But they invited me and what a great night it were. I bumped into someone who knew me old pal Patsy Kensit. When I say 'old', I don't mean she's old. Cos if she starts reading this, she'll get a complex, finking she's old. She looks as fit now as she did when she use to meke records, back in t' past. I only bought her records to put the cover up on me Wank Wall. Although I did like one of her songs 'I'm Not Scared'. I fink she does a French version of that song. Very sexy.

Yeah, it were a fantastic night. I remember when they announced *This Morning* as the winners and I went up with the team. They told me to!

When I were up there even me mate Dermot O'Leary said, 'What you doing up 'ere?'

So I said, 'I do *This Morning* now, don't I?'

I could see the look of disbelief in his eyes so I said, 'Watch this.'

Then I just stepped in between Uncle Phil and Holly and smiled right at the camera while they did their speech. I were basically looking at all me mates and Rosie and me mum to say, 'Look at me at the NTAs! Effing madness. I cudn't believe it.'

It almost felt like ITV had embraced me. I hope they're still embracing me when this books out and I an't been given the boot cos I've said somet I shun't. Cos that's what I always feel like when I'm on live telly. Any minute I'm just gonna shout, '*Your mam's a slag!*' And it'll be all over. Maybe I have got a mild case of Tourette's. Any commissioners reading this, don't worry I'll never shout 'Your mam's a slag!', I promise. But, yeah, I felt part of ITV and felt even more a part of it when the asked me to host a Saturday night show called *Sing If Ya Can*. Ooooosh! Lemon on primetime!

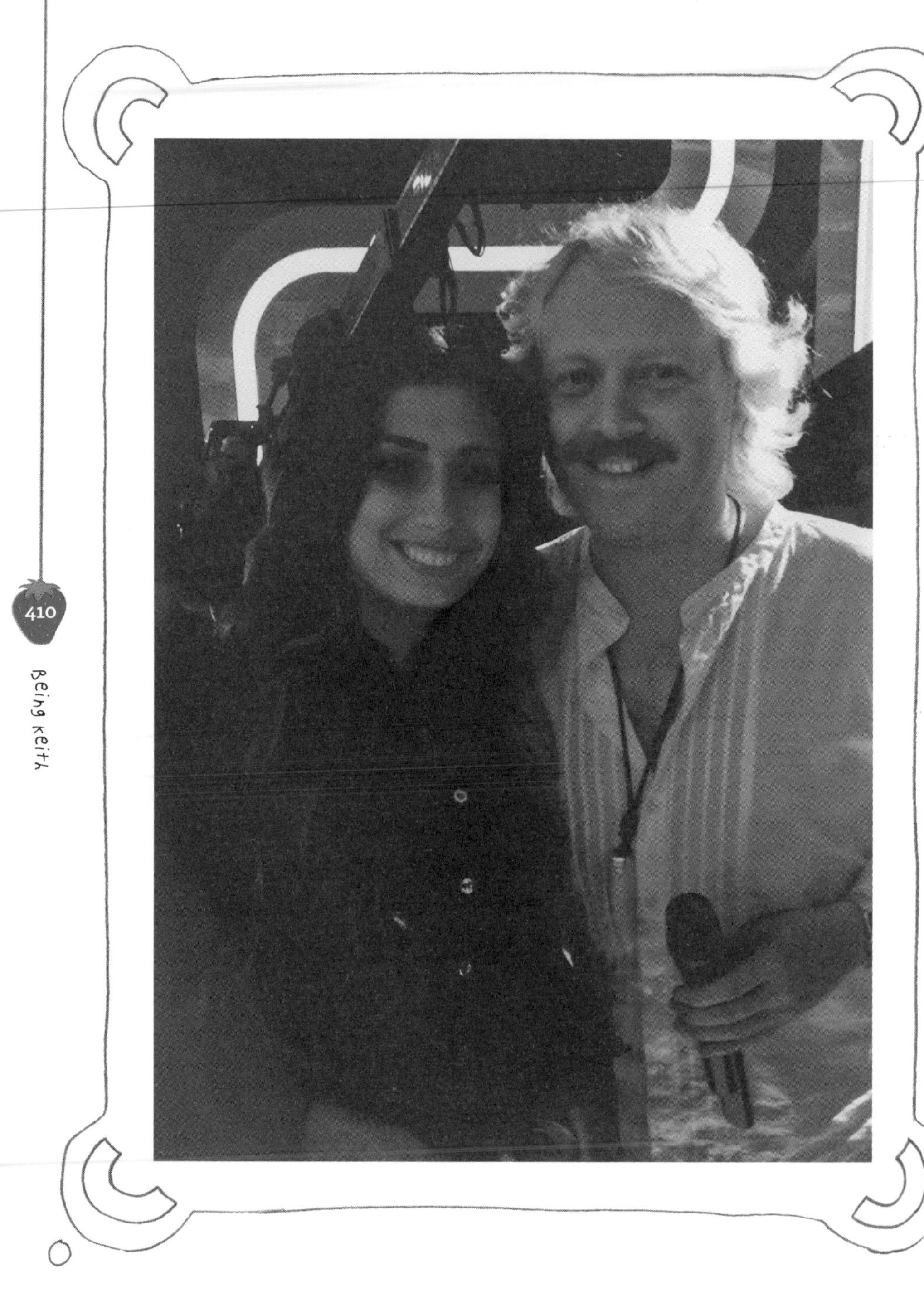

Sing If Ya Can

Anywhere, I get a call from me agent, George, who is fit as is her assistant Lara and they're both very good at their jobs. I love introducing 'em to blokes. Ya can see it straight away in their eyes, 'Ya said that your agent were fit, but I dint believe ya.' Well, believe it! Me Reps are fit boi. I'd destroy 'em both, but it would ruin our working relationship. And mine with Rosie. Oh, and their's with their other halfs. So let's just all keep it professional and keep the sex part in our minds, right George? She wants me so bad. One day I met up with her for a meeting and she had a bandage on her hand. Gave me some nonsense about a car accident. She wants me so bad, she wants to be me! I'm joking. Sort of – ish.

So, I get this call. ITV have done this pilot and want me to be a judge on the panel. I said, 'Yeah, why not?' Then they asked if I would be a judge every week? I weren't 100% sure but I fought it might be good for a laff.

Anywhere, I got another call a few days later just after I'd been having me barnet done (just a few highlights to enhance me strawberry blondness) and this time I were being asked by me fit agent if I'd *host* the show. I were flattered, of course, but I were also curious. In the pilot, Vernon Kay were the host. So what had happened? And I cudn't possibly do it like Vernon, we're different animals. If we actually were animals he'd be a giraffe and I'd be a Jack Russell that's how different we are. The show were a format that already existed. A crazy singing show in which celebrity contestants sang to win money for charity. They showed me the pilot,

Vernon's a giraffe and I'm a jack russell

but not the bits with Vernon in. Not sure why. It looked a right laff. Later Vernon told me, while he were in t' dressing room about to be a guest on *Juice*, that it were him that suggested me to do it. Which I fought were right nice of him. What a lovely lanky Bolton bastard he is. Vernon's a top lad. All t' best Vernon!

So me co-host on the show were gonna be none other than sexy Stacey Soloman. All I knew of Stacey were she were a good singer. I'd seen her on *The X Factor*, which is one of me favourite shows, and I'd seen her eat a kangaroo's pink bits on *I'm a Celebrity Get Me Out of Here!*, one of me other favourite shows, so I knew she were gonna be up for a laff.

The show were being shot at Pinewood Studios. So, cos I dint know her that well, I made a point of befriending her as quick at possible. As soon as I got there, I went to Stacey's trailer and said 'How do!, I'm not leaving till ya know everyfing about me and I know everyfing about ya. I'm circumcised and this is what it looks like. Smooth as a dolphin's beak. Do dolphins have beaks? Who cares! Now show me ya big bangers!'

So I made a point of becoming her friend right quickly so once we got in front of the cameras we would get on and have wicked chemistry. She is lovely and before ya could say sexy Soloman I were calling her names and we were the best of mates. I remember her telling me she fought she had rodent like features so from then on I called her a 'Sexy Rat'. She has a great sense of humour. Did I already mention she has great bangers, too? Well she does...

I fink this were her first big presenting gig and it were me first time doing family entertainment. We were happy with it and the audience figures were great but it did get a bit of a slagging. I knew it would cos it were fun and silly. Great Saturday night telly. It were mad as fuck. I remember Sinitta were on it. She came on in a wheelchair cos she'd done her leg in and sang, 'So macho', while being rained on. Hailstone, bricks, snow, all sorts of shit were thrown at her. Jedward were on as well. They had what looked like tar poured on 'em while they were singing. They're nuts those two!

It were off its 'ed and the response to it were cut right down t' middle. Like I said, the ratings were good but a couple of critics slagged it off. Anywhere they're paid to be nasty, I guess. I always fink of critics as panto baddies. Boo, hisssss! Panto baddies that are too scared to be guests on *Celebrity Juice*!

Got to meet a lot of nice people on *Sing If Ya Can*. One of me favourite judges on it had to be Sarah Cox. She's really funny and got the show immediately. Big up ya chest, Sarah Cox! I fink everyone that were involved in it enjoyed it anywhere.

Living by The Rules

It were a busy time. While *Sing If Ya Can* were going, *Celebrity Juice* were still on. Then I were asked to write a book. I honestly cun't believe what were going on. How mad it were! Still can't. Can't believe I'm writing this second one now. But, I'd always wanted to write a book. I'd had a lot of experience with ladies so I fought it'd be good to share me knowledge of the opposite sex and the same sex. I asked me brother for his tips on that sort of fing. I comprised all those facts in a little red pocket-size book called *The Rules, 69 Ways To Be Succ-sex-ful*. Oooooosh!

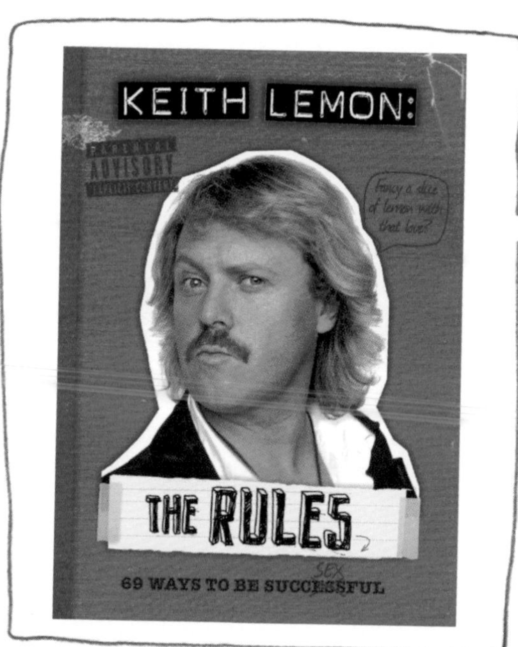

Me book

Right I might go have somet to eat now. I'm starving. Gotta write me *Now* magazine column, too! In't that funny that I have a column in *Now* magazine. It's proper like me diary. Is very liberating to look back and see what I were up to. I dint keep a diary when I were a lad. I had a great Black Book though, full of fit women. It were me Wank Book! Should publish that! Anywhere, I'm gonna go have me dinner, then I fink I'm going out with Rosie, who will remind not to put too much explicit info in her about me and her. I'll not write owt.

Be back in a bit...

How do! Well, it's a new day. A sunny one at last – but the weather has been shite. Of course, the day it's finally sunny, I'm sat in an office writing, when I could be outside in t' sun checking out the totty. Just looking at it, Rosie.

Anywhere, just to update ya on what I've been up to since I last wrote, a few days ago I met up with me old mate Caroline Flack and we went to meet Jack Osbourne, who'd made a documentary about his dad. Proper good it were. Maybe I should meke a documentary about me dad, ya know The Great Billy Ocean. Hopefully, we gonna be doing a remix soon of 'When the Going Gets Tough' for t' end credits of *Keith Lemon: The Film* and I fink I might be doing some rapping on it, with special guest Rizzle Kicks. I hope it happens, I fink it will be ace!

Since I wrote anyfing last, I've been doing a photoshoot for a fancy fashion magazine called *Rollercoaster*. Right posh clobber it were, ya know Versace, Prada, Dolcy and Cabanna. On this photoshoot I had Jay Jay (or Justine) with me. She's the make-up lady from *Celebrity Juice,* who does Fearne a lot. She's got her work cut out when she's with Fearne though with those massive nostrils. Anywhere I were telling her about me book and she said, 'Have ya mentioned me in it?' I said, 'Yeah I fink so.' But I cun't remember if I have so I'm mentioning her now. Jay Jay is right good at make-up. She's a lovely woman that dresses like she's from the past. Wears all that 50s clobber. Looks good though. She's right good at her job and has massive bangers that she likes to press upon me while she's trowelling on me clart. I always ask for 2% less on me clarted-up face than Jodie Marsh to meke me look healthy. She does a grand job! Cheers Jay Jay.

So all were going well and I were working on me first book. I wanted to have lots of pictures, cos to be honest I dint read a lot of books. In fact, the only books I've read are film books – *Rambo, Return of t' Jedi, Gremlins, Lost Boys* and *Back t' future*. All of which have glossy photos in t' middle. So I'd read up t' pictures and often never the rest. Not sure why I dint just jump t' pictures in t' middle; I fink it were cos I'd paid for t' book.

I don't read a lot but I've read Geri Halliwell's book from t' Spice Girls. Fink I picked that up at an airport. Hey, she's had some hard times her. Lived in a squat and everfing apparently. So, well done her for doing so well now. I use to fancy her a bit. Not when she went all fin, I prefer her when she's carrying a bit of timber. Her bangers look betterer... I wish she'd come on *Celebrity Juice* though. I fink she'd be a good guest.

So once I'd written *The Rules*, which were published by Orion, the same people that've published this 'un, (they're all nice and have some tidy birds there too), I were asked to do all t' drawings for it (like this one). I right enjoyed it cos I fought if there's any people that have bought the book but cudn't read well, they can just look at the pictures. Some of them I did on me iPad, although not many of them were used. I love drawing on me iPad, although people often don't believe that I've done 'em. There's a popular miss conception that I'm fick. But I know some fings and I know how to do right nice pictures on me iPad! At one point I wanted to do an exhibition of me iPad art, but that were one of those fings that dint happen. So have a look at some over t' page.

Anywhere, before too long I were back on t' road again, this time doing some book signings for *The Rules*. There were a few dates in London, where I bumped into an old pal of mine, Cleo Rocos from t' *Kenny Everett Show*, which I use to love when I were a kid. I remember Kenny doing a sketch where he were Spiderman and cudn't find his fly so he ended up pissing himself. I've known Cleo ages and she speaks like no one else I know. She don't say 'I'm off for me haircut', she says 'I'm off for me hairs cut'. I'll say 'Ya "hairs"? Dint ya mean ya "hair"? She'll say, "Well no, because there are many of them, so surely it's "hairs"?' She's got a point I guess.

Celebrity Juice

Jimmy Carr
drawn on't ipad obvioosly

Keith Lemon
on't ipad
Bang tidy

the Bafta winning Mr Cowell
i-Pad art

Then I went onto t' Bluewater shopping centre. It's always a bit scary doing a signing cos ya don't know if anyone's gonna turn up, but in t' end it were a great turnout. I'd say an even better turnout than when I were signing me fitness DVD. But nofing would prepare me for going back up t' North. It were total madness there. I felt like Harry Styles from One Erection. They had barriers up, massive bouncers and everyfing. Of course, some old school mates popped down and me mam, of course. I were a bit disappointed that Rosie dint come though. I fought she would've.

It were Halloween when I were up so I were in costume. Of course I like to embrace the festivities so I dressed as the Joker – Heath Ledger's Joker to be pecific. I looked The Dog's Bollox. I remember bumping into Batman and Robin on a train platform. Oh aye, I were dressed up on t' train! It were great as people dint recognise me as much. I were in Glasgow, Liverpool and then Manchester and people were right nice, giving me gifts and stuff. Including a beautiful pair of knitted bangers that I then gave to Fearne on *Celebrity Juice*. Better to have knitted bangers than no bangers! A lot of people asked me to sign their potatoes or lemons, as well as the book. Not sure what they'd want with an old mouldy potato or lemon with me name on, but I did it anywhere.

Somebody even gave me a silver leather jacket, which had the words 'Mr Lover Man, Mot, Mot, Mot' written on t' back. I wore that on *Celebrity Juice* that week. That were the first episode that we introduced 'Indian Keith', who's actually a Geordie. Yeah, I really enjoyed those signings, although me hand hurt after cos I had to sign me name I don't know how many times.

Keith Lemon: The Film

So, now I had a travel show out, *Celebrity Juice* were in its sixth series and I'd won a Loaded Lafta and a TV Choice Award. I'd written a book and now finally, after many rewrites, three years of development and thousands of meetings, we'd got the green light to actually go ahead and shoot a film.

I kept finking about all those telly appearances and red carpet moments where I'd spoke about meking a film. I swear people fought it were just part of me banter. 'Yeah! Yeah! I'm meking a film. Look at me.' But it were true; I were gonna actually be in a film that'd be at the cinema!

I'd not worked on the film script for a few months cos I'd been busy taking the piss out of Dot Cotton on *Juice* and promoting me book. But it were good that *Juice* were on air cos it gave me more of a sense of what the tone for the film should be like. I told Paul the Director that we had to give it far more edge, rude it up like.

Anywhere, I hadn't seen what Paul the Director had done to the film script, but it were already being sent out to potential cast members as I found out when I had a call from Holly Willoughbooby.

She said, 'I've just received a copy of your film script.'

I said, 'Oh aye?'

She said, 'You know I'd do owt for you...' (She wun't though, she'd never suck me off while tickling me balls and letting me seagull her bangers.) 'But I can't do this. It's disgusting!'

I said, 'Hold on! I aint seen *this* version!'

Turns out, when I told Paul to 'rude it up', he had got a little bit carried away and turned it into a porno! When I finally saw it, I said t' him I weren't happy and I wanted to rewrite it. And that's what we ended up doing like, just three days before shooting it. We also still had no cast.

In the film I have a girlfriend called Rosie. It were loosely based on Rosie, me on-and-off bit on t' side that were a bit more than just a bit on t' side. So we had to find a girl to play her. Originally Paloma Faith were gonna play her, but she were tied up with work and cun't do it. What a bastard, as who were now gonna play Rosie? Lots of girls auditioned and there were one girl that in me mind were perfect! Only problem were she looked nowt like Rosie. She were a big black lass and it just dint look right. She were about seven-feet tall. I looked like a hobbit next to her.

So, after finking I said I know someone who can play Rosie better than anyone. Me Rosie from Leeds, of course.

But there were lots of concerns that she weren't an actress though. She weren't, but it seemed silly to me cos she dint need to be. She were gonna be playing herself, just like I were playing meself. I weren't totally sure she'd do it though. She weren't really one for t' limelight. But I fought I'd ask her and all seemed right. Maybe this were all meant to be, after all t' others that I'd been sticking it in over the years some of them were right dirty.

We were supposed to be shooting in a few weeks time so I legged it up to Leeds and arranged to meet Rosie, who were temping at time. We met up in a wine bar, I fink it were, in t' centre of town. She looked Bang Tidy. She always does. She looked... like she should be in a film. Me film! So I just asked her. Initially, she weren't keen. She'd lived in Leeds all her life and I don't fink she'd ever even been to London. And she'd seen the looks that people from *Emmerdale* get when they walk in pubs in Leeds. People would look at them like 'Who do they fink they are? I bet they fink they're somet, them.' I'd fought it meself to be honest. It might not be like that now but it certainly were back then.

That's why I were chuffed the first time I went back to Leeds after I'd been on t' telly and I dint get that. I were expecting that glare though, that 'D'ya fink ya Billy Big Bollox now cos you've been on t' telly?' glare. Luckily everyone just wanted to buy me pints. Which most of t' time I accepted.

So I told her it wun't be acting cos she'd just be playing herself. More than that, if it all went well she could be playing with me too! All t' years when we'd just have a bit of slap and tickle at the end of t' night. I said to her, 'Why don't we kinda date properly and see how it goes?'. Sure, it were gonna be odd for her. I were now as famous as probably Richard Bacon and I had a Nando's card just like he did. When ya got that black Nando's card, ya know ya cudn't be doing too bad. I told her that we were gonna be shooting in Belfast, so whatever temp work she had she'd have to drop and go there with me – that is, if she were up for it. She said she'd fink about it.

TROYER
KEVIN
THE

LAURA
AIKMAN
AND KELLY
BROOK

All I could fink were, 'What's there to fink about? D'ya wanna be in a film? D'ya wanna be me girlfriend in me film and maybe be me girlfriend in real life if the spark is there like I fink it might be?' I know everytime I came back to Leeds, she were giving me t' eye. Maybe she dint want people finking she were just going out with me cos I were on telly... I dint know.

Anywhere, I went back to London on t' Sunday and on t' Monday morning Rosie called and said she were up for it. At last, I had someone to play Rosie, and also I were gonna have a proper grown-up relationship, but this were gonna be odd. Especially as in t' film I have two girlfriends and t' other were gonna be the FAFest of all t' FAF birds. I'd go so far as t' say The Fittest Girl in The UK and Woman of Me Dreams Kelly Brook! Super Bang!

Then, somet happened in the time before I went to Belfast to shoot the cleverly entitled *Keith Lemon: The Film*. I'd been asked to feature in... wait for it an ad for... wait for it... *ADIDAS!* So, I said 'Yeah' straight away and went along for a meeting with Lara, one of me fit agents, to see a fella called Steve. Top bloke he were and looked like Spiderman. Right nice and all. Told me about all these Olympians that I knew nowt about that I'd be interviewing. He also told me about 'finger blasting'. Which I also knew nowt about at time, but is a term I've used ever since, including 'ere in this book already. If ya dint know what it means let me tell ya what it means. What it means is meking love with ya finger vigorously with the speed of haste! Simple as peas. Everyfing in me life right now were moving at that same speed, the speed of haste!

So, I were doing an ad for Adidas and I had a dawn of realisation... Rosie who I'd known since she were about eight, I fink, were gonna be me bird. Like *me bird*! I were a bit scared of it, but I fought maybe it were time to have somet steady in me life. I fought It'd be nice to have someone to share the popcorn with. I proper liked Rosie and I knew she liked me. To this day I've never said the 'L' word to her though. I do in t' film but that's just script in't it?

I know I'm right good looking and I dress real good, I've got nice hair and I'm good at sex but I'm not sure what Rosie sees in me. I mean enough to be more than a one-night stand. She really gets me, ya know? And has a great sense of humour. I can take piss out of her all t' time and she just takes it on t' chin.

I had to fly out to Belfast before the rest of the cast which now includes Verne Troyer, as Archimedes, Kevin Bishop from the *Kevin Bishop Show*, as me mate Dougie, and Kelly Brook from naughty calendars, Piranha 3DD and me wet dreams. She were playing herself, just like Rosie from Leeds were as me bird Rosie. Kevin and Verne got on so well Kevin ended up putting his ball sack on Verne's head, can't remember why. But he's a proper wind up is Bishop. Fink I'm meeting him next week for a jar or seven.

As soon as I got there, the airport staff asked me for a photo. Never had that before. Nice for t' ego like. And they were lookers. I went straight for a costume fitting and while having that fitting I called Paul (who'd been out there a couple of weeks and already had a Belfast twang in his voice) and told him we'd gotta meet up in a room and sort the script out. We were staying in right posh apartments next to each other and he said come round to mine.

Aidan, one of t' producers, were in the same block as us. He's a nice Geordie fella. Not so Geordie that ya cudn't tell what he were saying like some of the locals. I remember, before me and Paul got in that room to look at the script, the first Belfastonian that spoke to me said... well, I *fought* he said, 'What has ya hair?'

I said, 'Eh?'

He said, 'What has ya hair?'

I said, 'Me hair has highlights.'

He looked at me confused and Aiden started laffing. 'He said "What has ya here?"'

I said, 'Oh, erm... a plane. A plane has got me 'ere'.

The Belfast man laffed, 'Ah Keet,' he said. 'Ya funny one, so ya are! Can ya talk to me friend on the phone?'

So I spoke to his friend on t' phone. Cudn't really tell what he were saying apart from, 'How d'ya find Belfast? What's the situation?' I told him it seemed nice but I'd just got 'ere and the situation were Nando's! I were off for me dinner!

I did notice they had a lot of tidy birds in Belfast though, which made me wonder if I'd made the right move getting hooked up with Rosie. But I were gonna be there for five and a half weeks and it were either gonna go terribly wrong or not terribly wrong.

The next day me and Paul locked ourselves away in his red hot apartment. He had his heating on full whack, cos he were scared he were gonna fall ill. Ya dingbat,

Paul. And we spent three days and nights rewriting before t' cast arrived. We worked so hard, me brain felt like it were gonna fall out. Now and again Paul'd pop out with me Nando's card and come back with mountains of chicken and we'd get back on it. Me pacing up and down talking and Paul typing away like a mad man, but we did it and were happy with it, although I knew we were gonna change somet once we got on set. It always happens cos ya come up with better ideas when ya shooting.

The day finally came for a table read. Kevin, Verne and Rosie had all arrived, but Kelly hadn't turned up yet and I were worried that she might pull out. I'm not sure why. When I saw her calendar above mine in HMV, I fought maybe that were a good omen. I bought one and took it back to me apartment and totally destroyed it!

Eventually Kelly did turn up and me, Rosie and Kevin, who'd already starred alongside her in a play and knew her, went to meet her. She were smaller than I fought – apart from her bangers, which were a lot biggerer. I kept on clocking Rosie looking at me to see if I were giving Kelly the eye. The fact were, I were! But Rosie weren't skilled enough to see it yet! I were a pro at this. But when Kelly got up to get a round in when we were having a drink at this nice little boozer, I got it in the ear from Rosie.

'I can see you ya know,' she said.

I knew how to play it. 'I can see ya too, and ya look Fit as Flip'. That seemed to keep her quiet for a bit.

The main fing were Kelly Brook were really nice and easy to get on with. I wun't of minded getting on her and all, but I were keeping it all professional like. The fing about Kelly that not many people realise is that she's not fick but she sometimes she just acts it. She's fick in certain areas, her breasts, for example, are very fick. But she's not really fick like a dingbat is fick; it's a cover. I bet she could invent somet like a rocket, I'm not saying she's an engineer but she could meke somet and people would be like, 'who invented that?' and they'd be like 'Oh, that? That were Kelly Brook'. Anywhere the next day I were gonna be banging her. It were in t' script that I wrote.

Doing the film were totally different from doing telly. I remember the first day's shoot had me in what were supposed to be a grubby shit-stinking bedsit in London. It were horrible and cold outside. It were always cold and rainy in Belfast. A nice city, but so fucking cold. The film were supposed to be set in London, but we were shooting it in Belfast cos the production company Generator were based there. Plus, I think it were cheaperer. The people were lovely and we all got on, but it just took ages to do anyfing. I might do a scene where I'd only say four lines and that'd take about two hours. Setting up, lighting... blah-blah-blah–blah.

Been off it for a few weeks. Lots has gone on since I last wrote owt. Been on me mate's stag do, been stalked by a Danish bird and won a little fing called a BAFTA. Cudn't believe it! *Celebrity Juice* were up for two: YouTube Audience Award and Best Entertainment Programme, which went to Derren Brown. Met him a few times and he's a good lad. Right nice wizard. But *Juice* won the

YouTube Audience Award, voted for by t' public so that means a lot. Cudn't believe we beat *Sherlock*. It felt very odd sat there. It felt like we'd sneaked in through t' fire escape.

We met *Doctor Who* and all and asked him if he'd come on *Juice*, so let's wait and see what happens. Fink it'd be good to do a *Dr Who* special, where we're all dressed as different Doctors, even though I know nowt about *Dr Who* really. I'm more into *Back t' Future*. My fancy dress costume of choice. T' kids like *Dr Who* though, don't they? Perhaps rather than do a *Dr Who* special, we could do a sci-fi special, all dressed as different sci-fi characters. Fearne could be Zelda from *Terrahawks*, I could be Han Solo from *Star Wars* or maybe Luke Skywalker as me hair's more like his, Holly could be Super Girl or Jabba the Hutt (she's got the tits for it). I swear her bangers are getting biggerer. I were

watching her on t' telly t'other night on that *Voice* fing and it looked like she'd bought the Mitchell brothers along, lovely Holly Willoughbooby!

Other week I were asked to introduce Jonathan Ross on stage at the Channel 4 Comedy Gala 2012. Personally asked by him and all, which is nice in't it? He were on the last series of *Juice* and were a great guest. He filled in for Fearne while she were on holiday doing some charity fing or other. So of course I did it. I got down t' O2. That's right! The effing massive O2. I saw The Spice Girls there, and Peter Kay. I saw me name on t' poster and I fought, 'Ey up, I must be doing more than just intro-ing Jonathan.' I were watching the other acts on before me and I fought, 'Shit, I'm gonna have to do a turn. A proper turn! I'm not a stand-up!' So Jonathan Ross comes out and I said, 'I fought I were just introducing ya, I'm not a stand-up. I've got no material'.

He said, 'Just go out there and talk, you'll be alwight.'

So I fought, 'Fuck Keith! Just go out there and talk. I can talk!' Yeah, I can talk me! So I went out there and talked. I even got to cop a feel of a ladies boob. Said to her that me mate works at NASA at t' weekend and he's been doing an experiment to see what's more common – the left tit or the right to be the biggest? Said I believe it were the left and it hangs lower. So I copped a feel. I say give it try: if ya own a pair have a go and if you're a man just ask politely. It dint work with Holly Willoughbooby when I tried it with 'er at V, but if at first ya don't succeed try, try, try again...

Filming me film

It were the first day on set with t' lady of dreams, Miss Kelly Brook. In the scene that I were doing, I were gonna be vigorously snogging her mouth then pushing her to the ground to smash her back doors in. Romantic like! I were a bit nervous to be honest, but how hard were it gonna be? Not hard at all hopefully! If I'd have got a hard on, I fink I would've got a bit embarrassed, but this were Kelly Brook. So, I practised the scene with the director first, then just put him in me mind when I were doing it with Kelly.

I always fink honesty is the best policy, so I just had it out with her. I said 'Kelly, has anyone ever got a straight on when they've been doing a naughty scene with ya?'

She said, 'A straight on?'

I said 'Yeah, ya know – a stiffy, a lob on, a bonk on, a hard prick?'

She told me that they all do and she'd be offended if they dint. Well she were gonna be offended by me then cos I made it me mission not to get a rocket in me pocket. Just wanted to be professional like. So I kept the director in mind when I were Parrot Tonguing Kelly. That were the name I give me kissing method with Kelly – The Parrot Tongue.

I kissed Rosie in the film, which were odd, cos it were a real kiss but we were acting. Of course, I'd kissed 'er nuff times in real life but this were in front of t' cameras and t'were proper odd. It just felt like we were opening and closing our mouths right close. I got a bit of a stiffy then, but I were allowed to with me bird. Still it were a little embarrassing in front of t' crew.

The next scene I were doing with Kelly were a right naughty scene. We were stripping off in front of each other and having a kind of flirt off. When she took her bra top fing off, it were pretty difficult to keep looking into her eyes even though she has lovely eyes. She's got equally lovely bangers! In scene it played in the film after the part where I've had a penis extension and I cudn't control me willy so a large amount of man milk squirts out when I get a bit excited. There were gallons of it. Of course it weren't real man milk. It were a mixture of water and egg white. Looked real enough though. Paul the Director were sat beneath me on t' floor pumping it up into me face from a big canister. We only had time to do it once so we cun't laff. And that were me first day shooting with Kelly. I just hoped she'd come back the next day. Luckily she did.

I fink that night were the night we all went out with t' crew. Rosie dint come out. I cudn't remember why, but we were getting on great and I were enjoying having a proper bird. Sex on tap – that's proper love I guess. I fink Rosie knew how well it were going between us so she dint mind me going out with Kelly, who, by the way, drinks like a fish and eats like Geoff Capes. Boy, can she put it away. Fair play to her. I hate women that fuss about their weight all t' time. Ya know the type that's constantly living off a salad and always down the gym. Apart from Rosie, of course.

Talking of Rosie, well some of the bits in the film are based on truth. Rosie says that she likes me cos I meke her smile. And I like meking 'er smile, mekes me feel right big in me heart. By that's soft as fuck, I know. Sexually she's me equivalent. She gives a great blow job and lets me seagull her bangers. Although she don't let me go in t' back doors. I'm always saying I'd smash those back doors in. The fact is I've only ever gone in a few people's back doors but I'm not gonna name any names.

I can remember when I asked Rosie if she'd ever got on t' tube and gone in an entrance where it says 'no entrance'. She dint really get me analogy and as she'd not really been on t' tube, she dint know what I were talking about. So I had to spell it out. I just said to her 'Would ya ever do it up t' arse'? This is where Rosie is clever. She said, 'Why? D'ya wanna do it up t' arse'?

I said not really. She's too sweet for that. Like I said it's naughty. When she asked me if I'd ever done it up t' arse, I just told her that I cudn't remember.

Changing the subject, there's one scene in t' film where I get mugged. This is the turning point in t' film where it switches to fantasy. I wanted this scene to be really dark and shocking. I spent two days on t' floor of a dirty, cold subway getting beaten up. When we got into t' edit with it though, it were just a bit too dark. We weren't meking *Kidulthood*, we were were meking a comedy about me origins.

Anywhere, I've got the best guy ever in t' film. Me dad, Billie Ocean! I know ya fink I'm joking but me mam says she had a fun time with him years ago at a gig and I never knew if she were joking. I like the idea of him being me dad. When I met him, we got on like an 'ouse on fire! He were a lovely, lovely man. He performed 'When the Going Gets Tough' on set and the atmosphere were ace! Everyone loved him. Avid Merrion were there from *Bo' Selecta*. He described Billy as a black Santa Claus. In't that a great idea! A black Santa Claus. I love the idea that Santa is a black rasta! Wun't that do great fings for equality? Same with James Bond. Wun't it be good if Will Smith were James Bond?! Or me! I'm part black if me mam's telling t' truth.

It were great to have Holly and Fearne in t' film too. It were lovely of them to come over to Belfast. I'd missed them both. I fink when Rosie saw me with Fearne though she fought maybe there were somet going on. The fact is we're good mates, that's all. I give her loads of abuse, pecifically about her massive nostrils, but we like each other really. I fink Rosie is a wee bit worried that we like each other a bit *too* much.

Lots of people featured in the film in the end – lots of me mates and it were a bit like *Juice*: Rizzle Kicks, Tinchy, Jedward, the Hoff (oh my god! Knight Rider! Can't believe I've done a film with him!), Denise Van Outen, me mate Bunton and Mel C and Gary Barlow. He's definitely one of me heros. He texted me while I were out there and asked me if I wanted to come to his gig he were doing. I said I were busy meking me own film, but asked him if he'd like to meke a little appearance in it. He said he would if he were around. Now people sometimes say that when they actually mean 'no', so I were right chuffed when the day came and we had him on set. He's a lovely fella. If I were hormone sexual I'd wank him defo.

Chris Moyles also did a bit for us, and Peter Andre, Jason Donovan, me mate Gino and me old pal Paddy McGuinness. I say 'old' but he's not really old, same age

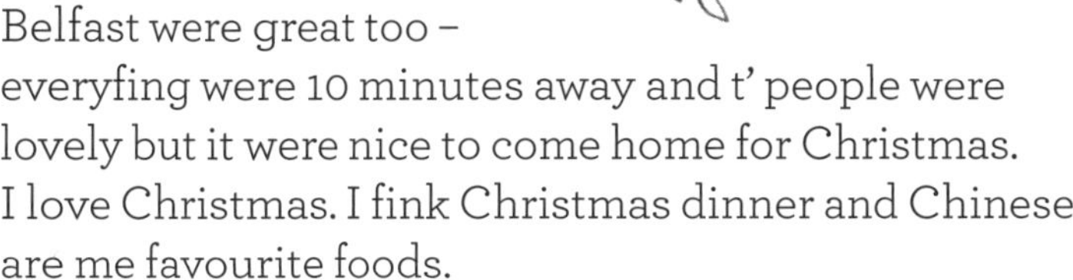

as me I fink. Paddy played 'Gary Apple', me cousin.

There were a lot of pissing about with Paddy being in t' film, but if we'd had more time he'd have been in it more. It were all to do with schedules. He's so busy. Next time if we do a sequel, *Keith Lemon: The Film 2, The Sequel,* he'll be in it more.

Belfast were great too – everyfing were 10 minutes away and t' people were lovely but it were nice to come home for Christmas. I love Christmas. I fink Christmas dinner and Chinese are me favourite foods.

Fink round about then I were doing more promotion stuff. I met Stella McCartney. She designed the Olympic uniform. She were nice. I would've banged her. She were sexy for a ginger! Everyone were walking on egg shells around her but at the end of the day we all take a shit, don't we? Just approach people with a friendly smile and good manners and that's all ya need. And that's all I did. Talked about finger blasting with her a little bit too and she loved it. She had a dirty twinkle in her eye!

Anywhere, after spending lots of quality time with Rosie doing the film and over Christmas, I fought it would be nice to take her on t' red carpet with me – kind of meking me and her official. So we went to NTAs together. A few people said that I were punching above me weight a bit with Rosie. I told them to 'Fuck off!'

Hey I'm good looking me, ya know! And I'm great at sex! She always sticks up for me does Rosie, tells people I'm not 'ginger' but strawberry blond and that I'm not punching above me weight cos scientifically I'm better looking than her. Proportionally me eyes are more centrific than hers. They're more equal apart than hers. And one of hers is a bit lazy. And she's got a large forehead. But it all works together as a unit, meking her the fittest girl at the NTAs that night. Fitter even than anyone from *Hollyoaks* or even Michelle Keegan. I were proud to have her on me arm. And the dress that I bought her that cost £45 in t' sale looked like it cost £145!

It were a really busy time of year and I were asked to present *The BRITs Red Carpet* show and the after party show on ITV2 with Laura Whitmore. I had the time of me life and just got drunk and had a good crack with Laura. She's right nice.

But the highlight of the night had to be meeting Kylie. I were overwhelmed. Cudn't believe she actually knew who I were. She came over and said 'Give me a cuddle. I'm freezing!' I'd have given 'er more than a cuddle. I din't want pull away when I pulled away from the cuddle because I'd thought they'd have to blur it out what were going on downstairs. She looked fit as chuff. Right small she is. A proper little spinner. I met Jessie J, too, who I'd recently developed a fancy for after having a mucky dream about 'er. Funny in't it, when ya have a mucky dream about someone and then ya fancy them t' next day. But to have a mucky dream and then actually *meet* them t' next day. Madness! It were good to see Noel Gallagher. Met him in a toilet years ago. Cool bastard he is. His brother Liam is cool too. Fink they should get back together like Spice Girls did or East 17. Dint go so well for East 17 though. Did they get back together?

Maybe they dint. Steps did though, dint they? Lovely Claire. She's still really pretty. Especially when she does that little rabbit nose fing that Bunton use to do as well. Right cute. Yeah it were a great night.

Dream meKer

In between all this madness, I started to film me new show *Lemonaid*. The idea of the show were to help all those people who were vexed by demolishing their problems and meking their dreams come true. I loved doing *Lemonaid*. It were a nice team and Sarah the producer were brilliant. Top lass. Fink she's pregnant now. Probably had it by now. I hope it's not strawberry blond. The first VT (that's short for videotape) we did, which were for the pilot, were in Bolton with a little kid called Liam, who wanted to be me for t' day. The show were like a mix of *Jim'll Fix it* and *Surprise Surprise*. The people on it were kinda nominated or put forward by a friend or family member. Should've seen t' look on t' little lad's face when he saw me standing there. I fought he'd shit a brick. If ya'd watched it then ya saw it. Ya wun't have seen his mam there eyein me up. I'm sure she wanted a piece of me Lemon, she did!

I felt a bit bad though cos I must've stunk of drink. I went around Paddy McGuinness' gaff with Dan, the executive producer, t' night before. Well we were shooting in Bolton and it felt only right that we pop round and see Paddy as he lives there. Between the three of us, we polished off three or four bottles of vodka. I can remember sitting there, watching MTV while Dan and Paddy were wrestling on the floor. All I could hear were glasses being broke. Cudn't remember getting back to the hotel. But the next day Paddy said we'd left his house smelling like Yates's winebar. He said he had us on CCTV footage trying to get into our cab. We cudn't walk; we were totally twatted... I can tell ya. I felt like I had two Jack Russells fighting in me belly.

I remember we were shooting with the DeLorean car from *Back t' Future*. I had to tell the man whose car it were (Steve) to pull over cos I fought I were gonna chuck up. Oooosh! I were rough that day. But I got through and it made for a good VT.

The Wedding VT were a good one, too. We stayed over night in a Premier Inn, I fink. No sign of Lenny Henry though. Use to love him when he use to say 'Ooooo oooooooooooooKaaaaaaaaaaaaay!'. The good fing about the Premier Inn (or Holiday Inn or Travel Lodge, can't remember which one it were) were the fantastic interiors. The toilet is positioned so that if ya sit with the door open, ya can see the telly perfectly. Ya can watch shite, while meking shite. I watched the whole of *Jeremy Kyle* on t' toilet before me surprise attendance at that wedding.

What happened were, the best man had got in touch with the researchers (I called them The Dream Team) and asked if I'd come. He were told I cudn't meke it and then... I made it! We hid in a backroom for ages being really quiet. I remember taking a picture of our lunch all laid on a blanket finking, 'While they're all enjoyed wedding cake and such, we're gonna be eating sandwiches and Scotch eggs.' I like Scotch eggs mind. So just as the best man is about to hand the rings over I jumped out. Weren't sure what kind of reception I were gonna get. Maybe, 'Get out of our effing wedding ya dingbat, can't ya see you're spoiling our day'. But t'were total opposite! Were a great response and even tears. I'd flown over their friends from Australia, paid for t' flight and everyfing. They were over t' moon. It were all about meking dreams come true after all. We got outta there before everyone started to get pissed. Otherwise all women start fingering me arse. But it wasn't all big gestures, it were the simple things in life too. One woman's glasses kept falling off her head so I sellotaped them on and sorted her right out. Rachel who were part of the team were a lovely lass, she did a great job of finding all t' people I'd be Lemonaiding. I would've had a go on her as she were fit. Looked like Jennifer Aniston, from behind. In fact she were Jennifer Aniston's body double in a film! Dint 'arf look like her from t' back.

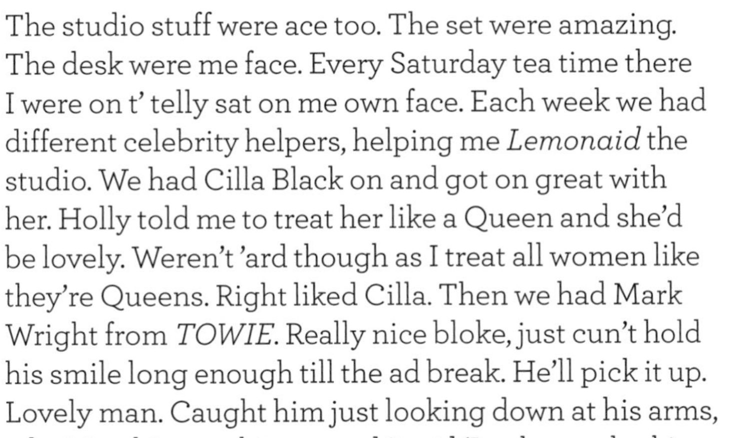

The studio stuff were ace too. The set were amazing. The desk were me face. Every Saturday tea time there I were on t' telly sat on me own face. Each week we had different celebrity helpers, helping me *Lemonaid* the studio. We had Cilla Black on and got on great with her. Holly told me to treat her like a Queen and she'd be lovely. Weren't 'ard though as I treat all women like they're Queens. Right liked Cilla. Then we had Mark Wright from *TOWIE*. Really nice bloke, just cun't hold his smile long enough till the ad break. He'll pick it up. Lovely man. Caught him just looking down at his arms, admiring his own biceps and I said 'Look at ya looking at ya arms. D'ya want a look at mine? Ya can count me freckles.' Nice fella, got good hair, but his clothes look too small for him. Guess that's his style.

We also had on the beautiful Michelle Keegan. She's got the best skin in telly, flawless her skin. Not sure what she uses.

We also had Peter Andre. The loveliest dingbat on telly. No matter what ya fink of Peter, he is a top bloke. Shite at telling jokes but he's a lovely man and a great sport. Would go for a pint with him any day. In fact we keep talking about it, but never arrange owt. For years I fought his hair were made out of tar. But it's actually real!

Me good mate Bunton did the pilot for *Lemonaid*. Love doing stuff with Emma. It's just like being at work with ya mate. I'm very lucky. When ya working on telly with ya mates ya can go that little bit further cos they know it's all just a joke. I remember putting me knob in Emma's mouth and I got away with it cos I said I were joking! I dint mean to put it in and it were just a joke. By the way, I dint really! But I did lick her tongue. Might as well tell you I'd put me knob in and all. Might have ruined our friendship though if I'd done that, I guess.

And finally we had Louis Walsh. By he's good crack. He's a great sport too. First fing he'll say is 'Say whatever ya want to me, take the piss I don't care'. He always says I should come over to Ireland. Louis, if ya reading this, let me know when? I'd love to meet Bono or Nadine from Girls Aloud. Actually I've met her. Stunning, she is. Could do with putting a bit of timber on though, but Bang Tidy! We had The Saturdays on t' last episode and all. All F.A.F. I wonder if they all sexually experiment with each other when they're on tour. Nice fought in't it? Lovely girls. Cudn't tell ya which one is me favourite though. I'd smash all t' back doors in. Balls deep!

It were a great show and we gave some amazing prizes away, iPads, cars, holidays. Sometimes I were a bit jealous.

But it were dead nice giving stuff away, I felt right good, like I were meking a difference to people's lives. Sometimes though I were a bit scared that me heart were gonna get too big for me chest. I remember a bit that weren't in t' show with this young lad who were about 21, so not much youngerer than me and he'd just graduated from 'uni', whatever that is, and he cudn't tie a tie. Who knows what he'd been doing all his life. Anywhere, I said to him that Michelle Keegan use to work at *Tie Rack* and she were gonna teach him how to tie a tie in t' ad break. If he learnt how to do that when we came back I'd give him a tie-related prize! He did it and guess what we gave him? A trip to the place where ties were invented, that's right Thailand! The lucky bastard! And we dint even use that bit in t' show. We could've just took the prize back off him. But it weren't about that. It were about fixing people's problems and meking dreams come true. To show just how nice I am. Cos I am ya know I'm nice, on a par with Cheryl Cole when she went to see t' troops.

I have to admit it's great meking telly and films. Sometimes I wake up and I fink 'How the eff...?' Then I'll go have a shit and wank in t' shower and I'll go have fun all day, whether its doing *Juice* with Holly and Fearne or rolling around with Kelly Brook for t' film. It were insane going to Cannes to promote the film with 'er. I remember being interviewed, glass of wine in me hand, which, by the way, were never empty. Soon as it started to go down they'd fill it up. I'm looking out over Cannes, where all 't boats are and I fought, 'Jesus on a bike. If me Leeds massive could see me now.'

In fact, I nearly dint meke it there, I picked up the wrong passport. Had Rosie's instead of me own. They all look t' same. I missed Rosie a bit while I were out there though. By now me and her were a proper 'un, an official item! We'd even started filming a reality show called *Lemon La Vida Loca*. At first it were a bit strange with t' cameras in ya face all t' time. Cudn't even take a shite without a cameraman stood in t' corner, but if it's hard for me, I fink it's all probably harder for Rosie. And as serious as we are, I still have a wandering eye.

We were filming the reality show fing other night and we had Jenny Powell over. Her from competition VTs on *This morning* or *Day Break*. She asks fings such as: 'Which children's TV presenter has a puppet called Edd the Duck?

'Is the answer
A) Metal
B) Wood
or C) Andi Peters

Anywhere, I were having a little flirt with her and it may have led to a little kiss. Nowt serious. I wun't do owt to hurt Rosie, I'm just a bit emotionally immature sometimes, apparently. It's an adjustment period for me I guess. Me tally wacker in't just mine to get it out and do what I want with it anymore. It's somet I share with Rosie and I've gotta respect it and her more.

If I don't see you through week...

This whole past few years have been a crazy journey that hopefully is gonna continue. This reality show fing comes out soon and hopefully people will like that and we'll do more. Its probably been out and gone now. Hope ya liked it. The films gonna be out soon and that is just total madness. *Keith Lemon: The Film.* Total effing madness. Cun't believe I made a film. I'm a bit bamboozled by it all to be honest. I were in Nando's today with me stylist Heather talking about what I'm gonna wear for t' premiere. Somet white with feathers, flash as fuck, I fink! I don't dress that mad when I'm just popping down t' Costcos. But for telly and what have ya I like to jazz it up a bit. Cudn't wear some of t' stuff I wear on telly in t' street, I'd get bricked.

So yeah, I fink I'm up to date with where I am in me life now. Gotta hand this in soon. It's been very ferapeutic looking back. Maybe I'll write another in a few years when I've done more stuff, if I'm still on t' telly. I hope I am cos it's a great job. I have such a good time and I meet great people. Who can say that 89% of the people they work with they'd actually have it off with? I can say that cos most of the people I work with are Fit as Flip!

So, I've got another series of *Juice* in September, and me film and me reality show fing. Who knows what the future holds. I expect one day I'll be married with kids. Mini Me Keith. I have them in t' film but that's just a film. I'd like to do another *World Tour* as that were good fun and I'd definitely like to do more films.

I'll do *Celebrity Juice* as long as Holly and Fearne are there. Imagine if we're still doing it when we're old farts. Holly's tits will be round her knees! Fuck knows what Fearne will look like. I suppose I'll look good – as men just get better looking with age, don't they? Well most men. I wonder what Michael Jackson would've looked like as an old man? What would the Moonwalk have looked like performed with a zimmer? Strange how fings turn out. But it's been a great ride and as me friend's mam use to say, 'If I dint see ya through week, I'll see ya through t' winda.' Oooshhhhhhhhhhhhhhhhhhhhh!

All t' best. Lots of love, Keith xxx

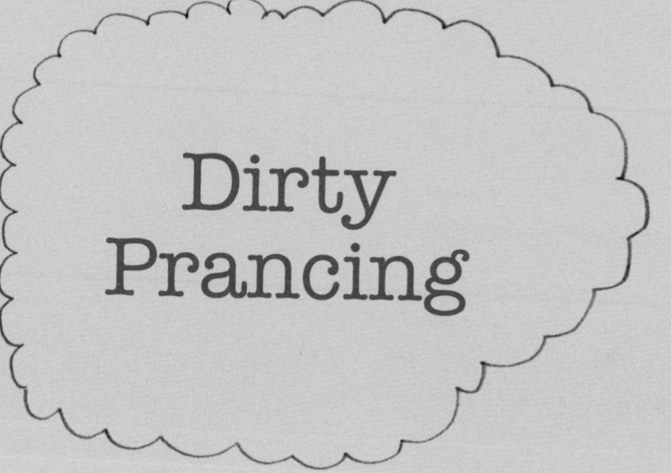

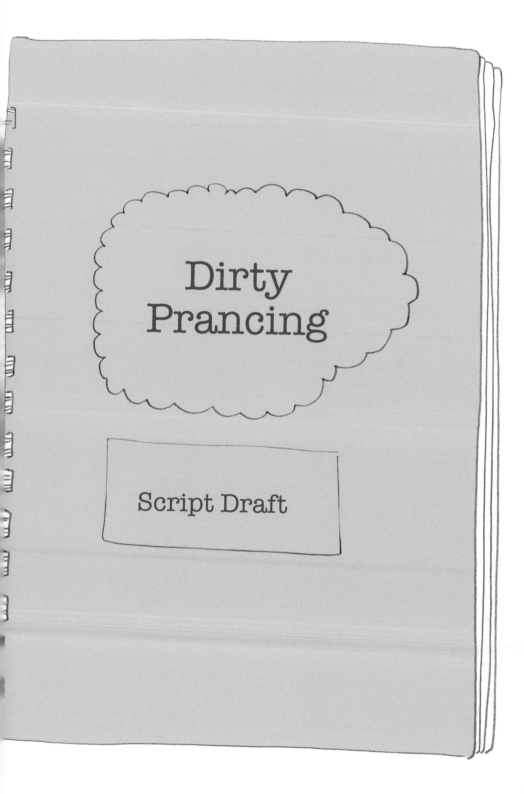

Script Draft

[Show starts with a black screen, we hear Keith and Paddy (V.O.) discussing the film they're going to spoof.]

KEITH [V.O.]

I always saw meself as a bit of a Patrick Swayze.

PADDY [V.O.]

What's my name?

KEITH [V.O.]

Paddy?

PADDY

Which is short for?

KEITH

Patrick.

PADDY

That's why I'm Swayze and you're gonna be 'Babby'.

KEITH

But I've got a tash...

PADDY
That's not all you've got, but we'll have to make do. So strap it up and press 'Record', flower!

[We cut to black-and-white footage of old people dancing in slow mo.]

[On screen graphics appear.]

'DIRTY PRANCING'

[Cut to Keith dressed as a young woman (Babby) in the back of a Ford Mondeo. It's towing a four-berth caravan. Music is playing in the background as we hear Keith's V.O.]

BABBY [V.O.]

It was the summer of 2007 and we where off on our jollydays. Everyone called me 'Babby' and it didn't occur to me to mind. although I did mind a bit, but not enough for it to occur to me. That was before Joe Swash won 'I'm a Celebrity Get Me Out of Here!', Fern Britton was slim and I couldn't wait to join the mounted police. I never thought I'd find a guy as great as my dad.

[Keith leans forward to wrap his arms around his dad, who is driving. His dad is sipping on a can of Tenants and smiling as he gives a wink back through the rear view mirror. Babby's sister, Lisa, is also sat in the car looking miserable combing her hair. We cut to a sign on the side of the road, 'Jellymans Mountain Retreat'.]

That was the summer we went to Jellymans.

[The car pulls into the resort, people mingling, lots of hustle and bustle, loads of rows of caravans and tents. A fat bloke is walking around shouting into a loud haler.]

FAT BLOKE

Welcome, welcome cockers. Hurry up and unpack folks, the first round of the knobbly forearms contest is about to commence in the Fred West suite!

[Babby and her family are getting out of the car and starting to unpack. Max Jellyman spots them.]

MAX

Doc, great to see you up here at long last.

BABBY [V.O.]

Everyone called me dad, 'Doc'. He wasn't a medical doctor, but in fact a travelling salesman for the shoe company Dr Martins, which where very popular with the skin heads of the 60s and 70s.

DAD

Max! How are those feet?

MAX [to Babby's family]

If it wasn't for this man I'd be in a wheelchair now. I was a slave to my bunions but the Doc here got me a pair of 18-hole lace-ups [He lifts up trouser leg to reveal bright red Dr Martins] and now life's good. I kept the best caravan for you and your girls.

LISA

Shit! I've left my trainers at home!

MUM

Language, Lisa!

LISA

That was English. I can say it in French if you like.

Merde, j'ai quitté mon formateurs à la maison.
[English subtitles].

DAD

This is not a tragedy. A tragedy is three men trapped in a mine or police dogs used in Birmingham.

LISA

What you on about?

BABBY

Or a dog with no legs that's had to have skateboard wheels grafted to its stumps to enable it to manoeuvre to and fro.

LISA

I don't know what you two have been smoking. But I's gotta get me some of that shi –

MUM

Lisa!

LISA

Merde!
['Shit' subtitled].

BABBY

I didn't know you could speak French.

LISA

I can't. I got a translator on my iPhone, in't it.

[Young ginger bloke approahes Babby.]

GINGER BLOKE

Hey! Later on there's a 'bring a watermelon' party up at the club house. Dirty dancing and everything! It's gonna be proper! But don't tell your parents!

[Cut ext. night shot of caravan.]

BABBY

Mum, Dad I'm just going out for a look around.

[Cut to int. of caravan.]

DAD

Babby, are those watermelons down your top?

BABBY

No they're my bangers!

LISA

Dad, man you're sick! Checking out Babby's bangers. Banger checker-outerer!

MUM

Were you just checking out Babby's bangers?

DAD

No, I thought they were watermelons. I heard there was a 'bring a watermelon' party at the club house. I don't want her up there. I know what goes on there. Dirty dancing and all sorts. Checking out her bangers? What do you take me for, some kind of pervert?

[Dad sits down sips on his tenants super and lifts up a dirty mag called 'Big Bangers'.]

[Cut to Babby running up to the clubhouse. Cut to her at the doorway as it opens to everyone dirty dancing. She walks in and spots Jonny (Paddy), who is dancing with a pregnant girl. He spots her. Their eyes lock. There's an instant attraction.]

JONNY [to girl]

Stay there.

GIRL [Maria]

Jonny!

JONNY

Button it!

[Jonny dances his way over to Babby.]

JONNY

How do?

BABBY

Ey-up! I brought some watermelons.

JONNY [disappointed]

Oh! For a minute there I thought they were your cheeky pippins. I were gonna say… Look, pop your melons down there with the rest of 'em, and why don't me and you have a dance?

[Babby puts the watermelons down on a pile of other watermelons and starts dancing with Jonny.]

BABBY

What about your bird?

JONNY

That in't me bird, it's me dance partner that I work with her on t' holiday camp.

BABBY

Is she up the duff?

JONNY

Aye. But we're getting rid. She puts it about a bit and we don't know who the father is. It in't mine, if that's what ya thinking. I fed her horse but that were it. I didn't give her me carrot, if you know what I mean.

BABBY

No, I don't know what ya mean.

JONNY

Like I said, she's just me dance partner.

BABBY

I din't think she'd be able to dance in her condition.

JONNY

Your right. It's like dancing with a whale. Fancy filling in for her? We do a big show at the end of the week for all t' holiday camp.

BABBY

Me? I can't even dance the Macarena.

JONNY

Don't worry. I once taught Steven Hawkins how to do the Moonwalk and he's never looked back!

BABBY

That's amazing. I think I'm falling in love with you.

JONNY

Slow down Babby! I've not even given you the plumbers wipe yet.

[He spits into his cupped hand while doing a miming motion.]

[Cut to next day.]

[Jonny is teaching Babby how to dance. Close up of their feet, Babby stands on Jonny's feet.]

JONNY

Oh god! Me in-grown toenail. Jesus tonight! Don't step on the two. You've gotta start on the two. Find the two, kapeesh?

BABBY

Well, actually no I don't. I don't understand the whole number thing. Ya see when I dance I go 'de-de-de, de-de-de'. I don't count.

JONNY

Is she tapped or what?

BABBY

Well I'm 47% dyslexic actually.

JONNY

Alright then Rain Man... Woman, let's go again. I'll go slow.

It's One, two, three. One, two, three. You don't start dancing till the two.

[Cut to montage of them both dancing. Babby is rubbish but progressively gets better.]

JONNY

The steps aren't enough. Feel the music.

[More dancing montage.]

JONNY

Let me try something.

[He takes Babby's hand and puts it on his chest.]

Ga-gun, ga-gun, ga-gun. Feel the music. And one, two, three. One two, three.

BABBY

De-de-de, de-de-de–

JONNY

FOUR, THREE, FOUR, THREE.

BABBY

I still don't understand. But, yeah, I can feel the music.

[Cut to ext shot of Jonny's caravan. Babby is running towards it. She enters, cut to int. shot. They're still practising dancing.]

JONNY

This is my dance space. This is your dance space. I don't go into your dance space, you don't go into mine. Friggin 'ell come on, Spaghetti arms.

BABBY

That's pretty harsh! If anyone's got spaghetti arms, its you. Your arms are longer than mine. Bleeding Mr Tickle! Your hands are all over the place trying to cop a feel of me boobs.

[They keep dancing.]

BABBY

I feel sick. Can we take a break?

JONNY

Your not preggers are ya?

BABBY

No, that's her, and I feel a bit weird with her here watching.

JONNY

Are you saying I'm the dad again?

BABBY

No! But you've fed her horse.

MARIA

Look Jonny, why don't I have a go with her?

[Both Babby and and Maria start dancing. Jonny sits down and watches.]

JONNY

Oooo, lez be friends!

[He grabs a box of Kleenex.]

MARIA

Right, I think she's got it. Why don't you practise the lift in t' paddling pool?

JONNY

Fair dos.

[Cut to Jonny and Babby outside practising the lift in a large paddling pool outside the caravan. After a few attempts they get it.]

BABBY

Yes, we've got it!

JONNY

Be better if you could get your arms out. [Under breath] And have a shave...

BABBY

Not happening!

JONNY

Bollocks.

BABBY

I love you, ya know.

JONNY

Behave, I told ya. I've not even shagged ya yet. Come on then let's go make love while ad breaks on.

BABBY

Oh Jonny!

JONNY

Lye darn, am bart fuck thee! [spits on hand].

END OF PART ONE

WELL, THAT'S JUST A TEASE! IF IT MADE YA MOIST FOR MORE AND YOU'D LIKE T' SEE IT ON TELLY, THEN START A PETITION FINGY TO THOSE LOVELY PEOPLE AT ITV...ADDRESS IT TO PETER FINNYGAN, ANGIE WAYNE OR CLAIRE ZOLTAN!

Just like to say a few fanks to:
Everyone on Twittor apart from t' rude people. They can go fuck themselves with a bag of nettles.

T' Facebook people for all t' support although I don' t go on it as much now cos its so depressing seeing girls from school that were once fit have now let themselves go.

All t' woman I've had that have made me the spectacular lover that I am today. Even to the ones that gave me STDs. It helped me develop me character.

All me friends and family for putting up with me and being there when I've needed ya the most. Like when I fell of a wall drunk having a piss and cut me knob and Paul took me to t' hospital. Fink that's what happened? Or did Paul cut his knob? Thanks anyway, Paul.

Phil and Shaun, me Leeds mates, for doing great music for the shows I've done. I got you a job so you owe me a drink!

Me mam for everyfing. I wun't be hear if it weren't for you. It were you that give me me beautiful strawberry blond locks. Ya must be so proud of me. But not as much as I am of you.

Julie who makes me hair strawberry blond. I fink it's a bit longerer on one side though.

Peter, Elaine, Angela and Claire at ITV for giving me a job in telly. Is there any chance I can have more holidays?

Or another show where I go on holiday and it's filmed for your channel?

The production companies I've worked with, cos its you guys that actually meck the shows and I just talk a lot. But without me you'd have no job. So like me mates Phil and Shaun, you owe me a drink too.

Big ups to Dan, Leon and Ed. Love you guys but not in a hormone sexual way. Even though you'd like it to be.

Spencer, Ben, James, Pete, Joe, Roy. Old times! One day we'll play silly buggers again hopefully.

George and Lara at James Grant Management and everyone else there, you've been brilliant! And honestly George and Lara if you ever want to have an orgy I'm up for it (if Rosie is ok with it).

All t' people that have been guests on whatever show it is I've been doing. I hope I've never offended ya in any way. Especially Craig David, I hope we can hang out one day and ya can buy me a beer.

Jane and everyone at Orion Books for letting me make a book. Next time can I have one of those ghostwriters? I'm slow as fuck at typing and that's why its taken so long.

All t' photographers I've worked with that have made me look Bang Tidy. Especially David, ya clumsy bastard.

The special lady in me life that keeps me in toe. Is that a real sentence? Not sure what being kept in toe actually means. But seriously I cun't have done it without you. They say behind every great man there is a great woman behind them. And I fank you for being great but mostly fank you for letting me behind you! I like it that way better so I can't smell ya morning breath. I've enjoyed sharing me with you and hope you've enjoyed me as much as I've enjoyed you. 'Ere's to us. Let's raise a glass and cheers and look into our eyes. Apparently if ya cheers and don't look into their eyes you have seven years bad sex. But that's hardly gonna happen if you're still shacked up with me. Cos 'sex' is me middle name. Well it in't actually, it's 'Ian', but ya know what I mean.

If I've missed anyone out, I am deeply sorry. But I honestly appreciate everyone I've come across. And all t' people I've met. You may not know it, but you've probably influenced me in some way. So in some way, you are responsible for some of the fings I may have said that I shun't of said. But I forgive you. It's not you, it's me. I'm very easily influenced. Fank you so much for everyfing, even if you just shouted 'sha-ting' or 'potato' at me in the street. It's a sign that you care. Without you I don't exist. Well I do, but it just means if you're not watching me on t' telly, there's no ratings and then I'll have to get a proper job, or go back to selling Securipoles.

Remember we are all Bang Tidy in our own special way. No matter what people tell ya. Words can't put you down. You are Bang Tidy in every single way! We are the voice of a new generation. Let's look at the man in the mirror and make that change. Free Melson Nandella. Much love. Peace Off!

Oooosh!

X

Me LooKeliKees

I love dressing up as you can see from me film nights with Rosie, so we ran a competition fingy through Twittor and asked you to send in your pics dressed as me! Fanks for all the entries. These were some of me favourites:

PAUL'S DOG

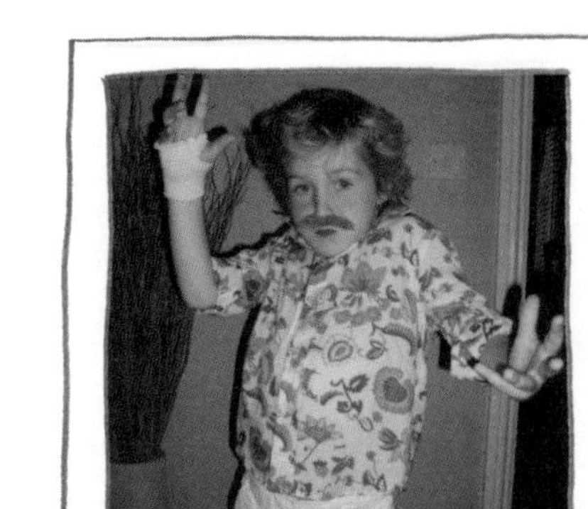

FREDDIE BAZ GRAY

KERRY PATERSON'S SON FINLEY

JOHN BLAKEY

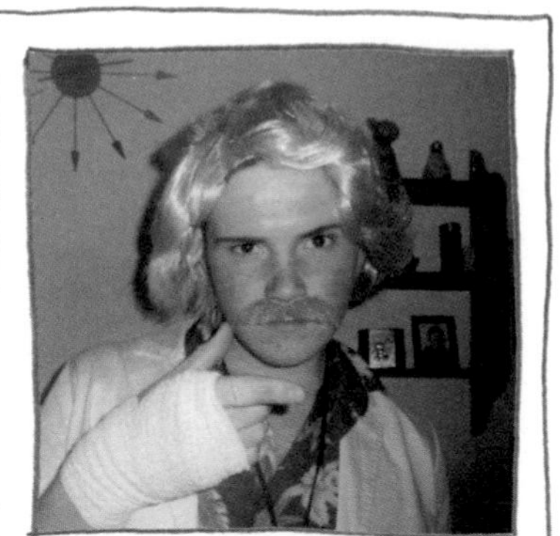

DECLAN MOORE

LUKE CONNOLLY'S MUM JULIE

FLORENCE HOWEY

BACK T' PRESENT: 2015!!!

Yeah boi! Recognise. So here we are in 2015. We're now in't future, no hover boards, no flying cars. Hopefully by t' time this book comes out we will now have those Nike mags with self-tying shoe laces like Marty McFly had in *Back t' Future 2*. So I'm still here! Still on't telly! I'm still Keith Lemon hear me Roar! Not like Katy Bang Tidy Perry, I mean hear me Roar like a fucking T-Rex from *Jurassic Park*. Always thought that T-Rex sounded like a bus stopping. Anyway, I'll start this chapter as I did with *Being Keith*.

Just back from the NTAs 2015!!!! *Juice* won!!!!!! Yeeeeesss! It had been two years since *Juice* won at the NTAs . . . we've still got it! Fuck knows what happen during the other years. Lots happened t' be persific. I was nominated again for best entertainment presenter for a second time, and I was again this year. Three times in a row loosing t' Ant and Dec. But ya know what, they're lovely blokes and they're fuckin good at their job. So it's cool.

I'm chuffed t' even be in that category with them. And Dermot! He's always in that category too. Another top bloke who is fuckin good at his job.

I'm still with me same fit agent. Big up yerself George! Fanks for all ya hard work. Still doing *Juice* with the girls, although Gino filled in for Holly as she was sprouting. Shout outs t' baby Chester! Obviously named after Holly's chester! Gino was in his words 'Fantastico'! Great having a mate on board just as it was when Kelly fit as fuck Brook was filling in for Fearne. Gino has a right old potty mouth, he's worse than me! Great at the Italian accent though. Sheffield born and bred that lad!

I'm not with me bird Rosie any more, that all dried out. It went as far as it could and then just ended. I was a brocken man for a while but I picked meself up and I got out there and started dating again. The reality show *Lemon La Vida Loca* went well enough for a second commission and everyfing that happened during the aftermath of that breck up was documented and came out on ITV2, then later on DVD. I guess it din't come out on Blu-ray cos people would've been too shocked at how good-looking I am in HD! Oooosh!

Speaking of HD, what does it mean when a telly has a sticker on it saying HD ready? Is that an HD telly or is it not ready? If it is ready why don't it just say HD? Don't understand HD ready?????

Anyway, I got out there and started dating again. Made a sex tape with Jenny Powell! That was a box ticked. She is silk! Doesn't age. Great at sex. It was crazy. She had props and everyfing! Very amazon like. Still friends I fink.

I had a show-mance with Kimberly Wyatt from t' Pussy Juice I mean Pussycat Dolls. She's married and had a kid since. Good luck to her, she's lovely. But I honestly thought that I were never gonna meet anyone. Then I met Nicol, which is French for Nicola. Yep, Keith Lemon is dating a French bird! She don't speak much English but I tell ya what it works! We have a connection, we don't ever argue simply cos we don't understand what each other are saying. It's perfect! Anyway I've learnt that it's probably best t' keep me intimate relationships with birds private. Apart from the fact that she gives wicked blozzers, and I've done the back doors a few more times but I'm still not sure about it. Mecks ya feel proper naughty.

Me brother our Gregory is all good in't hood! Still with his fella, even talking about getting married! He's proven t' be a great little actor too! He stars in me sketch show along with me mam, who's been great. Well, I say great. Great like *Snakes on a Plane*. So shit she's good! I mentioned her in me speech when *Juice* won best multichannel award. I don't even know what that means, multichannel. When I joked about it with other people they din't seem t' know what it means either. No matter, we fuckin won! *Juice* was up against *Game of Thrones*, not seen it but I know it's a big 'un! *Walking Bread*, I mean *Dead*, ain't seen that either, but again I know it's a big 'un, and that Geordie show. Now don't get me wrong. I've met a few *Geordie Shore* people. Charlotte Crosby is especially lovely, and people don't say it but she is fit as fuck also! Especially since she's lost a bit of timber. Hope she don't lose too much though and get one of those eating disorders. I remember when she was carrying a bit more beef she showed me her mono boob. That's what she calls it. She finks she's just got one long boob across her chest like a sausage dog. Looks like two t' me though. Nowt wrong with her boobs. Anyway, they're nice folk but I din't want t' loose t' *Geordie Shore*. We have a big team on *Juice* that work right hard and what I've seen on *Geordie Shore* is that they just get drunk and have sex. I do that when I'm not working but I don't expect an award for it!

So I really wanted to win an NTA just for the team. Even though if we won I was gonna keep t' award! So we won and, fuck me, I was stunned and overjoyed. Kissed Nicol, and high-fived Dan Baldwin (the executive producer) and hugged Leon (t' other exec). We were so happy! A few of the team were there and a few that din't actually work on *Juice*, but I din't ask Chappers, why were you there? Chappers directs the VTs for *Keyhole* ... ah shit, that's why he was there. *Through t' Keyhole* was up for best entertainment show so Chappers and Meriel who meck that were there. Lovely people. Meriel is so nice and Chappers is a great bloke. Filming an advert with him next week in Japan. In't that mad as fuck? D'ya know what my life is mad!

So we all went up on stage. Who was presenting the award? Only Kris Jenner! Yes Kim Kardashian's mam! She was fit but all I could see was me mam. We'd been filming a sketch in which we'd done a sketch called 'The Big Fat Gypsy Kardashians' and me mam played Kris Jenner. So as soon as I saw her I said 'All I can see is me mam.' She looked a bit offended. Don't know why as she don't know what me mam looks like. So to smooth it out I said 'Me mam in't as beautiful as you though.' When I got off stage I thought fuck! What's me mam gonna fink? 'Not as beautiful as me mam?' Me mam is like a beautiful angel and means t' world t' me. I don't care about Kris Jenner. Sure she was nice to me until I later heard she'd said I was the most annoying man in't world (sure she was joking cos I'm not annoying!) Anyway fank god me mam has got a sense of humour and knows that I mean well. Me mam is lovely, but Kris Jenner has wicked tits for an older lass, and well, I'd let her fart in me gob!

So looking back it's been an incredible couple of years. This year I'm about t' film me third series of *Through t' Keyhole*. Love doing that show. I was asked about doing it years ago. It were gonna be called 'Through the Keith Hole'. On the title alone I said yes. Then it went away then it came back. Apparently David Frost and Lloyd Grossman who own t' rights t' format of the show thought that I was the right person to bring enough anarchy t' show t' bring it up to date (very kind). So we did t' pilot. Grossman was sat in the green room watching. That felt a bit uneasy if I was honest. But when I came off stage he said he loved it. He was pissing himself. I was glad cos I wasn't sure he'd like me approach. I said c*nt three times in't first half.

Obviously that were just for t' studio audience cos they expect me to be a bit naughty and hadn't seen me do *Keyhole* so I thought I'd bring them in with somefing they know. I don't really use that sort of language now cos people have seen it and fankfully its been well received. But I thought it may teck time for people to adjust t' me doing let's say 'safer telly', compared to *Juice*. So t' first episode went out on a Saturday night at 9 p.m. and got just over 6 million viewers! The highest I've ever had. I was over the moon! Then I read that poor David Frost had died. So sad. Had such great news about the show doing well then I heard that. It was a strange morning. I new what people on Twitter and in the press would say that Frost died cos he was horrified by what I'd done to his programme. The fact was he'd obviously seen it before it went out and loved it!

So there I was hosting *Through t' Keyhole*, a primetime Saturday night show. I loved it and still do. When I was a kid I spoofed t' show using me video camera doing a shit impression of Lloyd Grossman. I can do voices but not really impressions. And now here I was hosting it for real. I remember in't pilot we did Kerry Katona's house. Lovely big house it was. People always ask me in interviews when I'm doing press, 'What's the weirdest fing you've ever found?' I always refer t' Kerry's house. People lock the door of a room they don't want ya to go in, or where they obviously hide their weird shit. But in Kerry's house, I found a dildo and a Dracula mask in a brown paper bag. Separately: cool. I've got lots of masks. But together in a brown paper bag? A Dracula mask and a dildo? What does that say? I don't know. Kinky! Each to there own. It's very interesting doing *Keyhole* though, but it takes a lot longer than ya fink. A full day t' do one house. We do all the houses then it's a week in't studio with the panel. I fink it all worked cos we had a great mix of guests and great panels, nice one Show Biz Liz! Liz is the lady that books the guests. If ya follow me on Twitter you'll know that I often tweet 'I don't book the guests.' I tweet that about three times a day. Liz books them. In fact I rarely know who's going to be on *Juice*. I just turn up and do my thang! That's jive talk for 'thing'.

It was a busy old time doing *Keyhole* as I was doing *Celebrity Juice* at t' same time. Me first movie, *Keith Lemon: The Film,* had come out and got the arse ripped out of it by critics, but made a profit at the box office then smashed it on DVD and ended up being one of the highest grossing British films of the year. It's a great achievement for a British film to even meck its money back and I'm very proud of it, and since its been on telly it feels like there's been a new-found love for it. It was made for a percific market and it worked. Of course there are fings I'd do differently now, but I din't know owt about mecking films back then. If anyone says me film's shit, I just say 'Have you made a film? No? Get back to me when ya do and if it does better than mine ya can give me some advice on how t' make a better film.' Everyone is a critic but when I look back at me life I know I'll be happier knowing I made stuff rather than just slag stuff off, na sayn!

So cos the film did well there were meetings about doing a second. So for the following year I was doing *Juice, Keyhole,* and writing a second film with me main

men Dan Johnston and Jammie Deeks, who worked on *Lemon La Vida Loca* with me. It was a busy old year. But when I'm busy it keeps me outta trouble. Hold on there's someone at t' door.

Ace! Me Versace Belt print jacket has just arrived! Looks proper. Gonna look ruthless in this, recognise! Will be wearing that on Friday night!

Anyway, so it was now the second series of *Keyhole, Juice* is still bubbling along nicely. We went to LA to film a few houses. Went t' Jane Seymour's in Malibu! It was immense! One of me favourite houses. Beautiful view of the ocean. It was as fit as Jane herself. Remember her in *Battlestar Galactica* and James Bond? I don't know what she drinks to stay so young looking. Proper MILF! Also went t' Gene Simmons' house from the rock band Kiss. His crib was proper off the hook. The slide in't garden that went in't pool was like a water theme park! I smashed me balls to bits on it. He was quite intimidating at first. But I just looked at his barnet that looked like black wool or burnt grass and it kept me cool. Nice man actually, but played it all alpha male at first. What did he say again? 'If you fuck with me, I'll fuck with you, I'll make sure you won't work again!' Well, those weren't his exact words but I got the message. Unless he knows someone high up at ITV I don't fink that's true. He was a great guest in the studio.

I can't remember what episode it was when we were in't studio when I was told we weren't doing the film we'd spent all year writing. But just as I went on stage I was told the bonding people, whoever they are, weren't gonna bond it, whatever that means, cos they din't believe we could deliver on time. So I turned to Claire Zolkwer and asked if she wanted to do a sketch show. She said 'Aye!' She's Scottish! I love Claire, she's been so kind to me. It's amazing that I was at a point where I could approach ITV in that way. 'You wanna do new show?' 'Aye!' Of course I cun't do any old shit. They're not mad. But ITV2 has been good to me. It all feels right. Unless I get sacked by t' time this book comes out for bumming a dog and snorting dog shit. Which ain't gonna happen. So straight after *Keyhole* we started writing a pilot for a sketch show whilst I was also finishing writing *Little Keith* and *The Beaver and the Elephant*, a kids book. That's right, me, Keith Lemon writing a kids book! I wrote it for all me mates who have got kids – nice aren't I?! If I'm honest, I got a bit sick of people saying 'Is it really a kids book?' Of course it is! I'm not gonna do a book with loads of shit, fuck and piss in it and pictures of tits and dicks for kids. This was a proper kids book about a beaver and an elephant that rented a house from a sweaty fox. Some of the characters in the book where based on famous people. The Beaver was Alan Carr in my mind, and the Fox was Russell Brand. Use to go skiing with Russell. Probably mentioned that already. Haven't seen him

for time. Hope his revolution fing has revolutionised! I'm not sure what he's trying to do, I don't have many GCECESEs. He's a nice bloke though!

So we shot the pilot. We got a rude boy fox, inspired by the wanker fox that comes in me garden and does a shit and looks at me as if to say 'Call the council then you prick.' True story. I have this fox in me garden and when its having it off with its bird it sounds like it is being killed. We had the big fat gypsy Kardashians starring me mam. I'm a big fan of the Kardashians, there're all fit! Even Bruce is fit now! I mean Caitlyn. We had a spoof of *Downton Abbey*. That were Dan and Jamie's idea, they must watch a lot of mam telly. For mams that kind of programme in't it. It all went well, but there were some fings I just weren't happy about. In the meeting with the lovely Claire Zolkwer and equally lovely Angela Jain (who is actually an amazing singer) I almost talked my way out of getting a commission. I just wanted the show to be right. But since the commission, I fink we have got it right. Fuck me! It starts next week. I'm really happy with it and I fink I've finally found me X-Men of Comedy. Got

Dickinson's
Any Old Shit
MICK

a wicked team of actors! One of them is me mate Zoe, she's ace, me bruv and me mam, George this funny bald guy who can do lots of accents, Mad Paul (had t' get him involved otherwise he may have murdered someone. He's a funny lad though), Big Tom who is brilliant, Black Tom (who doesn't like being called that. He wants to be called Tommy Nice), and me mate Ross who has put a bit of timber on and looks well for it. Oh and cameos by Fearne Cotton chops, Schofield, Carrie Fisher (yes, Carrie Fisher as in Princess Leia!), Sarah Harding (fit), Martine McCutcheon (fit since time), Ruth Langsford (MILF) Eamonn (telly Jedi), Jonathan Ross (legend) and Arnold fucking Schwarzenegger! There's loadsa people in it! John Thomson from *Cold Feet* and t' *Fast Show*! Me good old mate Paddy. By we laughed filming Keith and Paddy's film bits. When we did the *Jurassic Park* sketch, I smashed me teeth in with a torch. Had to go t' dentist and get it sorted. Bloody dentist put a picture of me on Twitter. Crank! It's strange sometimes. I remember when we were filming t' Jabba the Hutt spoof. I had to go t' opticians dressed as the top half of Jabba as I were glued into t' costume. But I got fewer looks from people in't street dressed as Jabba than meself. Crazy times. But yeah, I'm very excited about

The Keith Lemon Sketch Show. Fink its gonna be really good. But ya never know how fings are gonna be received. Just gotta be happy that ya enjoying yerself and normally when ya enjoying yerself people enjoy you. Next week I'm going t' Japan to film an ad, and will hopefully bump into Glen from *Keith Lemon's Very Brilliant World Tour*. Still talk to him from back in't day via email. Calls me the king of minges. I like that title. Then after Japan, it's a flight to LA to film houses for t' third series of *Keyhole*! And an hour special about me favourite film *Back t' Future*! Wonder if I'm gonna meet Michael J. Fox. If I do I'll tell ya all about it. Ey up just had a delivery from ASOS. Gotta go. If I don't see ya through t' week, I'll see ya through t' winda!

All t' best!
Keith

AN ORION PAPERBACK

Little Keith Lemon first published in Great Britain in 2014
by Orion Books
Being Keith first published in Great Britain in 2012
by Orion Books
This paperback edition published in 2015
by Orion Books, an imprint of the Orion Publishing Group Ltd,
Carmelite House, 50 Victoria Embankment,
London EC4Y 0DZ

An Hachette UK company

1 3 5 7 9 10 8 6 4 2

A CIP catalogue record for this book
is available from the British Library.

ISBN 978-1-4091-5983-4

Designer: Smith & Gilmour
Illustrations: Leigh Francis

PICTURE CREDITS
Andrew Hayes-Watkins: 2, 9, 15, 46, 85, 144, 166, 180-1, 228, 238, 240, 250-1, 269, 274, 276, 280 (left), 299, 404, 453, 456, 480; Getty: 10 (left), 13, 35 (left and far right), 40, 52, 55, 56, 113, 115, 122, 136, 212, 227, 243, 252, 253, 254, 259, 265, 267, 280 (right); 289, 296, 325, 340, 346, 370, 380, 407, 423, 428-9, 432, 438, 481; Rex: 53, 63, 88, 93 (bottom), 95, 99, 121, 169, 266, 277, 356, 424, 488; Richard Chambury/RichFoto.com: 389, 393, 394, 406; Shutterstock: 91, 98, 102, 130, 157, 161, 220; 241, 486; Talkback/*Keith Lemon's Back to the Future Tribute*: 494; All other photographs the author's own.

Printed in China

The Orion Publishing Group's policy is to use papers
that are natural, renewable and recyclable and made
from wood grown in sustainable forests. The logging and
manufacturing processes are expected to conform to the
environmental regulations of the country of origin.

www.orionbooks.co.uk

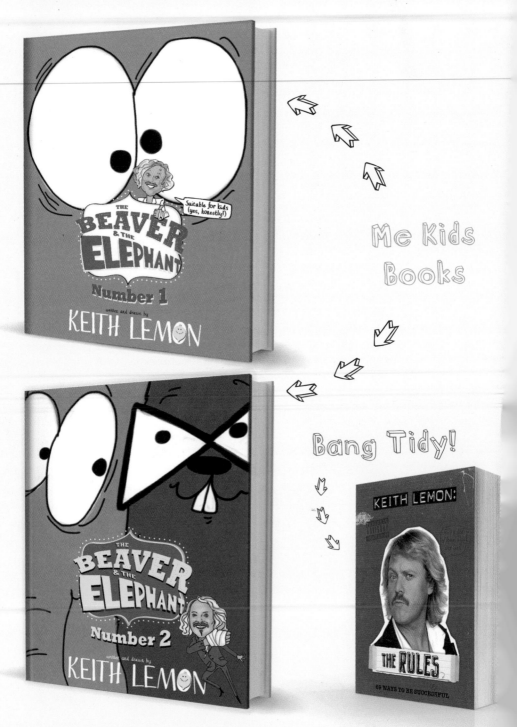